D0993469

ECONOMIC DEVELOPMENTS AND REFORMS IN COOPERATION PARTNER COUNTRIES: EXTERNAL ECONOMIC RELATIONS WITH PARTICULAR FOCUS ON REGIONAL COOPERATION

Colloquium
25-27 June, 1997
Brussels

L'EVOLUTION ET LES REFORMES ECONOMIQUES DANS LES PAYS PARTENAIRES DE LA COOPERATION: RELATIONS ECONOMIQUES EXTERIEURES ET PLUS PARTICULIEREMENT COOPERATION REGIONALE

Colloque
25-27 juin 1997
Bruxelles

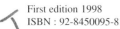
First edition 1998
ISBN : 92-8450095-8

1002745208

Contents

SUMMARY BY THE ECONOMICS DIRECTORATE   11

WELCOMING REMARKS
by the Secretary General of NATO
Javier Solana   19

KEYNOTE SPEECH
THE ECONOMIC DEVELOPMENT, REFORM AND REGIONAL
COOPERATION OF CENTRAL EUROPEAN COUNTRIES IN
TRANSITION, WITH EMPHASIS ON SLOVENIA
Marijan Senjur
Minister of Economic Relations and Development, Government of Slovenia   21

PANEL I: External Economic
             Relations of Partner Countries -
             Overall Developments and Their
             Place Within Economic Reforms.

AN OVERVIEW OF THE INTEGRATION TENDENCIES
OF THE TRANSITION ECONOMIES
Joe Smolik
Senior Economist, United Nations Economic Commission for
Europe, Geneva   37

RUSSIAN EXTERNAL ECONOMIC RELATIONS:
PROBLEMS AND PROSPECTS
Valery Oknyansky
Counsellor, Economic Cooperation Department, Ministry of Foreign Affairs,
Moscow   51

CURRENT STATUS OF EAST-WEST TRADE WITHIN
INTERNATIONAL TRADE
Ferry de Kerckhove
Director General, Planning Secretariat,
DFAIT, Ottawa   57

EVALUATION OF STRUCTURAL CHANGES IN POLISH INDUSTRY AND
IN FOREIGN CAPITAL FLOW TO POLAND IN THE PERIOD OF
SYSTEMIC TRANSFORMATION
Zofia Wysokinska
Advisor to the Minister of the Economy
and Institute of Economics, University of Lodz, Poland   61

FOREIGN CAPITAL AS A FACTOR OF STRUCTURAL CHANGES IN THE
POLISH ECONOMY
Janina Witkowska
Institute of Economics, University of Lodz, Poland   71

PANEL II: Regional Cooperation
         Among Partner Countries -
         The Institutional Settings

POLISH TRADE WITH CEFTA COUNTRIES:
IN SEARCH OF PROMISING SECTORS
Katarzyna Zukrowska
Institute of Development and Strategic Studies, Warsaw, Poland   91

BLACK SEA ECONOMIC COOPERATION
A TEST CASE
Ercan Özer
Directorate General for Multilateral Economic Relations,
Ministry of Foreign Affairs, Ankara, Turkey   105

ECONOMIC COOPERATION WITHIN THE CIS:
PROBLEMS AND OUTLOOK
Yuri V. Shishkov
Institute of World Economy and International Relations
Russian Academy of Sciences, Moscow   117

ECONOMIC COOPERATION AMONG
THE CBSS COUNTRIES
Martins Lacis
Secretariat of the Council of Baltic Sea States,
Ministry of Foreign Affairs of the Republic of Latvia   125

ECONOMIC COOPERATION IN THE EASTERN BALTIC SEA REGION: A
FINNISH VIEW
Pekka Sutela
Department of Economics, University of Helsinki
Advisor to the Board, Bank of Finland   131

**PANEL III: Regional Cooperation Among
Partner Countries -
A Sectoral Approach**

REGIONAL COOPERATION AMONG
CENTRAL ASIAN ECONOMIES
Michael Kaser
Institute for German Studies, University of Birmingham   149

COOPERATION IN THE FIELD OF ENERGY
Friedemann Müller
Senior Research Associate, Stiftung Wissenschaft und Politik,
Ebenhausen, Germany   157

THE ROLE OF RUSSIA ON THE EUROPEAN
ENERGY MARKET
Alexander A. Arbatov
Chairman, Committee for Productive Forces and Natural Resources, Russian
Academy of Sciences, Moscow.   165

ENERGY PERSPECTIVE: SOME PERSONAL
OBSERVATIONS OF THE 1990's IN RUSSIA AND THE UKRAINE
Tony Scanlan
Independent Consultant and Member of
Council, British Institute of Energy Economics   175

**PANEL IV: Economic Integration of
Partner Countries into
Pan-European Structures**

ECONOMIC INTEGRATION OF PARTNER COUNTRIES
INTO PAN-EUROPEAN STRUCTURES
Andras Inotai
Director General, Institute for World Economics of
the Hungarian Academy of Sciences, Budapest. 187

ECONOMIC TRANSITION, DEMOCRATIC
CONSOLIDATION AND THE INTEGRATION OF
CENTRAL-EASTERN EUROPEAN COUNTRIES
INTO EUROPEAN STRUCTURES
Thomas Nowotny
Political Adviser to the Chief Economist,
European Bank for Reconstruction and Development, London 195

THE INTEGRATION OF NATO PARTNER COUNTRIES INTO
PAN-EUROPEAN ECONOMIC STRUCTURES
Jean-Pierre Tuveri
Acting Director, OECD Centre for Co-operation with the Economies in
Transition 207

WORLD BANK PRIORITY SECTORIAL ACTIVITIES
Spiros Voyadzis
Manager of the Brussels Office, World Bank 213

THE EUROPEAN UNION, ENLARGEMENT AND
REGIONAL CO-OPERATION
Fraser Cameron
Foreign Policy Advisor,
DG1A, European Commission 219

FOREIGN DIRECT INVESTMENT IN SLOVENIA:
TRENDS, EXPERIENCES AND POLICY
Matija Rojec and Janez Potocnik
Slovenian Institute of Macroeconomic Analysis and Development 227

ECONOMIC REFORMS IN THE FORMER YUGOSLAV REPUBLIC
OF MACEDONIA*
Olgica Vasilevska
Ministry of Foreign Affairs, Skopje   243

Overview
ECONOMIC DEVELOPMENTS AND REFORMS IN COOPERATION
PARTNER COUNTRIES: EXTERNAL ECONOMIC RELATIONS WITH
PARTICULAR FOCUS ON REGIONAL COOPERATION
John P. Hardt
Senior Specialist in Post-Soviet Economics
Congressional Research Service
Library of Congress
Washington, D.C.   247

* Turkey recognizes the Republic of Macedonia with its constitutional name

Table des matières

RESUME ETABLI PAR LA DIRECTION ECONOMIQUE   11

MESSAGE DE BIENVENUE
du Secrétaire général de l'OTAN
Javier SOLANA   19

DISCOURS INTRODUCTIF
LE DEVELOPPEMENT, LA REFORME ET LA COOPERATION
REGIONALE ECONOMIQUES DES PAYS D'EUROPE CENTRALE
EN TRANSITION, AVEC UN ACCENT PARTICULIER
SUR LE CAS DE LA SLOVENIE   21
Marijan SENJUR

PANEL I: Relations économiques extérieures
           des pays partenaires -
           Evolution générale et place
           dans les réformes économiques

VUE D'ENSEMBLE DES TENDANCES A L'INTEGRATION
DES ECONOMIES EN TRANSITION
Joe SMOLIK   37

LES RELATIONS ECONOMIQUES EXTERIEURES DE LA RUSSIE:
PROBLEMES ET PERSPECTIVES
Valeri OKNIANSKI   51

ETAT PRESENT DES ECHANGES ENTRE L'EST ET L'OUEST
DANS LE COMMERCE INTERNATIONAL
Ferry de KERCKHOVE   57

EVALUATION DES CHANGEMENTS STRUCTURELS
DANS L'INDUSTRIE POLONAISE ET DANS
LES ENTREES DE CAPITAUX ETRANGERS
PENDANT LA PERIODE DE TRANSFORMATION SYSTEMATIQUE
Zofia WYSOKINSKA 61

LES CAPITAUX ETRANGERS COMME FACTEUR
DE CHANGEMENTS STRUCTURELS
DANS L'ECONOMIE POLONAISE
Janina WITKOWSKA 71

**PANEL II: Coopération régionale
entre pays partenaires -
Cadres institutionnels**

LES ECHANGES COMMERCIAUX DE LA POLOGNE
AVEC LES PAYS DE LA ZONE DE LIBRE-ECHANGE
DE L'EUROPE CENTRALE (CEFTA):
A LA RECHERCHE DE SECTEURS PROMETTEURS
Katarzyna ZUKROWSKA 91

COOPERATION ECONOMIQUE DE LA MER NOIRE (BSEC):
UNE INITIATIVE-TEST
Ercan ÖZER 105

LA COOPERATION ECONOMIQUE AU SEIN DE LA CEI:
PROBLEMES ET PERSPECTIVES
Iouri V. CHICHKOV 117

LA COOPERATION ECONOMIQUE ENTRE LES PAYS DU CONSEIL
DES ETATS DE LA MER BALTIQUE (CEB)
Martins LACIS 125

LA COOPERATION ECONOMIQUE
DANS LA REGION ORIENTALE DE LA MER BALTIQUE:
LE POINT DE VUE DE LA FINLANDE
Pekka SUTELA 127

**PANEL III: Coopération régionale
entre pays partenaires -
Approche sectorielle**

LA COOPERATION REGIONALE ENTRE
LES ECONOMIES D'ASIE CENTRALE
Michael KASER   149

LA COOPERATION DANS LE DOMAINE DE L'ENERGIE
Friedemann MÜLLER   157

LE ROLE DE LA RUSSIE
SUR LE MARCHE EUROPEEN DE L'ENERGIE
Alexander A. ARBATOV   165

LA PERSPECTIVE ENERGETIQUE: QUELQUES OBSERVATIONS
PERSONNELLES SUR LES ANNÉES 90 EN RUSSIE ET EN UKRAINE
Tony SCANLAN   175

**PANEL IV: Intégration économique
des pays partenaires
dans des structures pan-européennes**

INTEGRATION ECONOMIQUE DES PAYS PARTENAIRES
DANS DES STRUCTURES PAN-EUROPEENNES
Andras INOTAI   187

TRANSITION ECONOMIQUE,
CONSOLIDATION DEMOCRATIQUE ET
INTEGRATION DES PAYS D'EUROPE CENTRALE ET
ORIENTALE DANS LES STRUCTURES EUROPEENNES
Thomas NOWOTNY   195

L'INTEGRATION DES PAYS PARTENAIRES DE L'OTAN
DANS LES STRUCTURES ECONOMIQUES PAN-EUROPEENNES
Jean-Pierre TUVERI   207

ACTIVITES SECTORIELLES PRIORITAIRES
DE LA BANQUE MONDIALE
Spiros VOYADZIS   213

L'UNION EUROPEENNE, L'ELARGISSEMENT ET
LA COOPERATION REGIONALE
Fraser CAMERON   219

LES INVESTISSEMENTS ETRANGERS DIRECTS EN SLOVENIE:
TENDANCES, EXPERIENCES ET GRANDES ORIENTATIONS
Matija ROJEC and Janez POTOCNIK   227

LES REFORMES ECONOMIQUES
DANS L'EX-REPUBLIQUE YOUGOSLAVE DE MACEDOINE*
Olgica VASILEVSKA   243

Vue d'ensemble
L'EVOLUTION ET LES REFORMES ECONOMIQUES
DANS LES PAYS PARTENAIRES DE LA COOPERATION:
LES RELATIONS ECONOMIQUES EXTERIEURES ET
PLUS PARTICULIEREMENT LA COOPERATION REGIONALE
John P. HARDT   247

* La Turquie reconnaît la République de Macédoine sous son nom constitutionnel.

SUMMARY BY THE ECONOMICS DIRECTORATE

During this 26th annual NATO Economics Colloquium, over 100 participants examined economic developments and reforms in partner countries with an emphasis on external economic relations and regional cooperation. In his **Welcoming Address, NATO's Secretary General, Javier Solana,** noted that NATO has been in the forefront of creating a new cooperative approach to security across the whole of the Euro-Atlantic area. He stressed that NATO is helping to create the strategic confidence which is essential for sustained economic growth and the prospect of joining NATO is providing a strong incentive for reform in Central and Eastern Europe.

The **Keynote Speaker, Marijan Senjur,** Minister of Economic Relations and Development of Slovenia, referred to the comments by Lester Thurow that "tectonic" change in Central and Eastern Europe since 1989 would inevitably impact on the West. Dr. Senjur's speech provided a broad framework for the subsequent exchanges, highlighting critical yardsticks of economic transition in partner countries illustrated by practical (and successful) experience in his own country

PANEL I undertook a short overview of reform in transition economies, concluding that progress with reform is broadly (and positively) reflected in economic performance. Progress with **financial stabilisation** and **privatisation** were cause for particular optimism, although the latter has not led everywhere, especially in Russia, to the kind of industrial restructuring and associated investment expected. The Panel then examined trade and capital flow developments including foreign direct investment (FDI), foreign trade patterns, the link to reforms at large, and methodological questions. In part through **globalisation**, the World economy has become multipolar. It is marked by an information revolution and a worldwide market for investment, production, and distribution.

A global value system (McWorld) is spreading rapidly. Whether the economies in transition can integrate into this World economic system is still an open question. Preferential security treatment does not mean preferential economic treatment and free trade within Europe remains an elusive goal. Many rich countries fear that globalisation threatens their "social contracts", forgetting that both rich and poor countries stand to gain enormously from increased trade. On this basis, transition economies might perhaps look for further synergies beyond Europe. In particular, they should not pay too much attention to West European concerns over differences in social norms for that would run the risk of perpetuating them.

PANEL II discussed the status and perspectives/potentials of regional economic cooperation schemes. The **Central European Free Trade Area** (CEFTA) is seen as a "waiting room" for the EU in that no institutional structures or coordinated economic policies exist or are planned. Nevertheless, comparative advantages are becoming apparent and CEFTA has helped to increase trade within the group and promote economic liberalisation. The **Council of Baltic Sea States** (CBSS) has seen trade within the region increase by 20% per annum in recent years but it is unlikely that much of this growth can be attributed to the CBSS. The eleven states that comprise the CBSS are of diverse size and wealth, indeed,

---

NOTE

This collection of Colloquium papers has been prepared and edited by the NATO Economics Directorate. The articles contained in this volume represent the views of authors and do not necessarily reflect the official opinion or policy of member governments of NATO. For further information, please contact Mr. Reiner Weichhardt, Deputy Director, NATO Economics Directorate, 1110 Brussels, Belgium.

one of the longer-term goals of the group is to reduce income differentials between states such as Estonia and Finland. Cooperation is on a small scale yet important projects such as nuclear safety, environmental protection and improving transportation infrastructures have been organised. The focus of the **Black Sea Economic Cooperation** (BSEC) group is on social and practical issues such as transport, communications, energy, environment, tourism, culture and agriculture. Its membership is not in any way homogenous (Greece and Azerbaijan are both members; Austria and Egypt have observer status) yet the group does promote market and democratic values and brings a degree of social and political stability to an historically volatile and fractious region. The **Commonwealth of Independent States** (CIS) has proved to be ineffectual as an instrument of re-integration. The share of inter-regional exports as a percentage of GDP fell from 14.9% in 1990 to 4.8% in 1995. Notwithstanding the 6% growth in Russian trade with CIS countries in 1996, without faster growth in the near future, Russia risks losing its status as a "gravitation centre" for CIS members.

Overall, the lessons from this Panel were that regional cooperation groups need to be homogenous if any kind of economic integration is envisaged. Diverse groupings can however succeed on a limited scale (by concentrating on specific and micro-level projects) although economic and political goals must be shared for any higher level of cooperation to work. The global impetus is towards democracy and economic liberalisation - any regional group that bucks this trend is not likely to succeed or survive.

PANEL III was primarily devoted to an analysis of the **energy sector** in C&EE which is in the process of radical change. This involves privatisation (with significant Western participation everywhere except Russia where legal, fiscal and transportation uncertainties have restricted the development of joint-ventures, relative to progress in Kazakhstan and Azerbaijan), consumption decline, dramatic new resource developments in the Caspian Sea region, a greater emphasis on natural gas and oil at the expense of coal, and a reduction in energy dependence on Russia. The reorganization of the **Russian energy sector** will concentrate on maintaining Western markets while attracting Western capital necessary to modernise. Over the next 15 years, Russian energy exports to Europe are expected to increase, especially natural gas, but the rate of growth will depend on external demand, investment in production and transportation sectors, and the economic situation in Russia. Higher internal prices would help investment and reduce consumption but would also add to non-payment problems. Caspian projects are adding to competitive pressures but control over the pipeline network is a key asset for some Russian firms. This is an important sector for Russia's integration into the World economy, indeed, the **growing interdependence between buyers and suppliers is in itself a kind of security guarantee which drives Europe towards greater stability**.

Ukraine has the most serious energy deficits in Europe. Despite the recession which has seen a 50% reduction in energy consumption since 1988, Ukraine still imports 80% of its oil and gas requirements, over 90% from Russia. Gas production has fallen by 50% and coal production has fallen by two-thirds. A fuels revolution is needed if the energy import bill is not to crush the new currency. Over time, Ukraine could play a major role in oil and gas supplies from CIS and Middle East sources to Central and Western Europe, similar to that of Turkey.

Integration prospects in **Central Asia** will depend upon the development of economic complimentarities, meaning that economies that at present compete against one another as raw materials suppliers (of oil, natural gas, minerals and cotton) will need to become more diverse (thus boosting trade between them) by adding value to this existing and rich resource base.

PANEL IV examined the **integration** or planned integration of partner countries into transnational economic organisations and institutions such as the EU, NATO, the EBRD, the WTO and the OECD. Many countries have cleared the first hurdle of transition (macro-economic stabilisation) but the second stage of structural reform, institution-building and financial sector reform will be much more difficult. **Institution building is of key importance.** The quality and probity of public administrations, the legal system and the financial sector need to be further developed. Many transition economies now reveal themselves as being much poorer than historically thought, but this is because they are mis-developed, not under-developed. Significant human capital exists which has been mis-directed. The role of international institutions is to point people in the right direction.

A **summing-up** of the proceedings was provided by the **Rapporteur, John Hardt** of the US Congressional Research Service. Dr. Hardt suggested that transition countries take on faith that in following the democratic market model, a process leading to economic success will inevitably follow (after a short period of painful adjustment). The core reform requirements (stabilisation, liberalisation, privatisation) are necessary but not sufficient pre-conditions to reach the threshold of sustainable growth needed to be accepted as a normal participant in the global market place. This would require the creation of a truly plural society and the disempowerment of those resisting change, both within the surviving old political elites and within the new economic elites whose wealth is often more the result of arbitrary good fortune than of enterprise or thrift. Nevertheless, some transition countries have achieved the core conditions and are beginning to make the grade.

In conclusion it can be stated that the successes in transition economies are well known. But the transition record is uneven and that is what concerns us the most. The costs in terms of human suffering have been high, as noted in the 1996 Colloquium. As a result, in some countries, there has been backtracking on reform. Indeed, some of the security challenges Alliance members have faced recently had financial and economic roots.

Credible economic policies and security are two sides of the same coin: without effective economic policies, security will suffer; without a sound security environment, investment and economic growth will suffer. The external sector is a key element in the transition toward a market-based economy. Foreign trade, investment, technology and know-how can make strong contributions to higher living standards. Regional economic relationships have proven to be an important impetus to the external sector of many economies, in Central Europe and in the Black Sea region for example. They also promote good neighbourly relations, thereby strengthening peace and security.

Daniel George
Director, NATO Economics Directorate
Colloquium Chairman

diverse (thus boosting trade between them) by adding value to this existing and rich resource base.

PANEL IV examined the **integration** or planned integration of partner countries into transnational economic organisations and institutions such as the EU, NATO, the EBRD, the WTO and the OECD. Many countries have cleared the first hurdle of transition (macro-economic stabilisation) but the second stage of structural reform, institution-building and financial sector reform will be much more difficult. **Institution building is of key importance.** The quality and probity of public administrations, the legal system and the financial sector need to be further developed. Many transition economies now reveal themselves as being much poorer than historically thought, but this is because they are mis-developed, not under-developed. Significant human capital exists which has been mis-directed. The role of international institutions is to point people in the right direction.

A **summing-up** of the proceedings was provided by the **Rapporteur, John Hardt** of the US Congressional Research Service. Dr. Hardt suggested that transition countries take on faith that in following the democratic market model, a process leading to economic success will inevitably follow (after a short period of painful adjustment). The core reform requirements (stabilisation, liberalisation, privatisation) are necessary but not sufficient pre-conditions to reach the threshold of sustainable growth needed to be accepted as a normal participant in the global market place. This would require the creation of a truly plural society and the disempowerment of those resisting change, both within the surviving old political elites and within the new economic elites whose wealth is often more the result of arbitrary good fortune than of enterprise or thrift. Nevertheless, some transition countries have achieved the core conditions and are beginning to make the grade.

In conclusion it can be stated that the successes in transition economies are well known. But the transition record is uneven and that is what concerns us the most. The costs in terms of human suffering have been high, as noted in the 1996 Colloquium. As a result, in some countries, there has been backtracking on reform. Indeed, some of the security challenges Alliance members have faced recently had financial and economic roots.

Credible economic policies and security are two sides of the same coin: without effective economic policies, security will suffer; without a sound security environment, investment and economic growth will suffer. The external sector is a key element in the transition toward a market-based economy. Foreign trade, investment, technology and know-how can make strong contributions to higher living standards. Regional economic relationships have proven to be an important impetus to the external sector of many economies, in Central Europe and in the Black Sea region for example. They also promote good neighbourly relations, thereby strengthening peace and security.

Daniel George
Director, NATO Economics Directorate
Colloquium Chairman

RESUME ETABLI PAR LA DIRECTION ECONOMIQUE

Au cours de ce 26ème colloque économique annuel de l'OTAN, plus de 100 spécialistes ont examiné l'évolution et les réformes économiques relevées dans les pays partenaires, en se penchant plus particulièrement sur les relations économiques extérieures et la coopération régionale. Dans son **message de bienvenue, le Secrétaire général de l'OTAN, M. Javier Solana**, a fait observer que l'OTAN a été à la pointe de l'instauration d'une nouvelle approche coopérative de la sécurité dans l'ensemble de la zone euro-atlantique. Il a souligné que l'OTAN contribue à créer le climat de confiance stratégique qui est essentiel pour une croissance économique durable, et que la perspective d'adhérer à l'OTAN constitue un stimulant vigoureux pour les réformes en Europe centrale et orientale.

Dans son **discours introductif, M. Marijan Senjur**, Ministre des relations et du développement économiques de la Slovénie, a évoqué les observations faites par Lester Thurow selon lesquelles la transformation "tectonique" intervenue en Europe centrale et orientale depuis 1989 aurait inévitablement des incidences à l'Ouest. Le discours de M. Senjur a défini un cadre général pour les échanges de vues ultérieurs, en mettant en évidence les jalons essentiels de la transition économique dans les pays partenaires, illustrée par l'expérience pratique (et réussie) de son pays.

Le PANEL I a procédé à un bref tour d'horizon des réformes dans les économies en transition, arrivant à la conclusion que l'avancement des réformes se reflète largement (et favorablement) dans les résultats économiques. Les progrès accomplis en matière de **stabilisation financière** et de **privatisation** ont suscité un optimisme particulier, même si la privatisation n'a pas conduit dans tous les pays, en Russie notamment, au type prévu de restructuration industrielle et d'investissement correspondant. Le panel a ensuite examiné l'évolution des échanges commerciaux et des apports de capitaux, dont les investissements étrangers directs, les structures du commerce extérieur, le lien avec les réformes en général, ainsi que des questions de méthodologie. En partie du fait de la **mondialisation**, l'économie internationale est devenue multipolaire. Elle est caractérisée par une révolution de l'information et par un marché mondial des investissements, de la production et de la distribution.

Un système mondial d'analyse de la valeur (McWorld) se répand rapidement. La question de savoir si les économies en transition peuvent s'intégrer dans ce système économique mondial reste controversée. Un traitement préférentiel sur le plan de la sécurité ne signifie pas, en effet, un traitement préférentiel dans le domaine économique, et le libre-échange en Europe demeure un objectif hors de portée. Bon nombre de pays riches craignent que la mondialisation ne menace leur "contrat social", oubliant ainsi que les pays riches comme les pays pauvres pourraient bien avoir énormément à gagner de l'intensification des échanges. Dans ces conditions, les pays dont l'économie est en transition pourraient peut-être rechercher d'autres synergies à l'extérieur de l'Europe. En particulier, ils ne devraient pas accorder trop d'attention aux préoccupations de l'Europe occidentale relatives aux différences entre les normes sociales, car cela risquerait de perpétuer celles-ci.

Le PANEL II s'est penché sur l'état présent ainsi que sur les perspectives et les potentialités des mécanismes de coopération économique régionale. La **Zone de libre-échange de l'Europe centrale** (CEFTA) est considérée comme "l'antichambre" de l'adhésion à l'Union européenne, en ce sens que n'existe ou que n'est prévue aucune structure institutionnelle ou politique économique coordonnée. Des avantages relatifs commencent néanmoins à se manifester et la CEFTA a contribué à intensifier les échanges au sein du groupe de pays et à promouvoir la libéralisation économique. Le **Conseil des Etats de la mer Baltique** (CEB) a vu les échanges commerciaux dans la région progresser de 20% par an ces dernières années, mais une grande partie de cette croissance n'est probablement pas attribuable au CEB lui-même. Les onze Etats qui le composent sont de taille et de richesse diverses et, en fait, l'un des objectifs à long terme de ce groupe est de réduire les écarts de revenu entre des Etats tels que l'Estonie et la Finlande. La coopération se pratique sur une petite échelle, quoiqu'il existe des projets importants concernant la sûreté nucléaire, la protection de l'environnement et l'amélioration des infrastructures de transport. Le groupe de **Coopération économique de la mer Noire** (BSEC) centre ses activités sur des questions sociales et pratiques telles que le transport, les télécommunications, l'énergie, l'environnement, le tourisme, la culture et l'agriculture. Sa composition n'a rien d'homogène (la Grèce et l'Azerbaïdjan en sont membres, et l'Autriche et l'Egypte ont le statut d'observateur), mais ce groupe promeut effectivement les valeurs de l'économie de marché et les valeurs démocratiques et il apporte une certaine stabilité sociale et politique dans une région historiquement instable et turbulente. La **Communauté des Etats indépendants** (CEI) s'est révélée être un instrument inefficace de réintégration. La part des exportations interrégionales dans le PIB est tombée de 14,9% en 1990 à 4,8% en 1995. En dépit de la croissance de 6% enregistrée dans les échanges de la Russie avec les autres pays de la CEI en 1996, la Russie risque, faute d'une croissance plus rapide dans un proche avenir, de perdre son statut de "centre de gravité" des pays membres de la CEI.

D'une façon générale, il ressort des travaux de ce panel que les groupes de coopération régionale doivent être homogènes s'ils envisagent une forme quelconque d'intégration économique. Des groupements divers peuvent toutefois remporter des succès sur une échelle limitée (en concentrant leurs efforts sur des projets spécifiques au niveau micro-économique), mais il faut avoir des objectifs économiques et politiques en commun pour qu'une coopération à un niveau plus élevé puisse fonctionner. Dans le monde entier, l'impulsion générale va dans le sens de la démocratie et de la libéralisation économique; tout groupe régional qui va à l'encontre de cette tendance a peu de chances de réussir, voire de survivre.

Le **PANEL III** s'est consacré principalement à une analyse du **secteur énergétique** de l'Europe centrale et orientale, lequel est en train de subir une transformation radicale. Celle-ci comporte la privatisation (avec une participation non négligeable des Occidentaux dans tous les pays sauf en Russie, où les incertitudes d'ordre juridique et budgétaire et en matière de transport ont restreint la mise sur pied d'entreprises conjointes, comparativement au Kazakhstan et à l'Azerbaïdjan), une baisse de la consommation, la mise en valeur de nouvelles ressources considérables dans la région de la mer Caspienne, la place plus large faite au gaz naturel et au pétrole au détriment du charbon, et enfin l'amoindrissement de la dépendance énergétique à l'égard de la Russie. La réorganisation du **secteur énergétique de la Russie** consistera essentiellement à conserver les marchés occidentaux tout en attirant les capitaux occidentaux nécessaires à sa modernisation. On s'attend à ce que les exportations d'énergie de la Russie vers l'Europe augmentent au cours des 15 prochaines années, en particulier celles de gaz naturel, mais le rythme de la croissance dépendra de la demande extérieure, des investissements effectués dans les secteurs de la production et du transport, ainsi que de la situation économique de la Russie. Une hausse des prix intérieurs favoriserait les investissements et ferait diminuer la consommation, mais elle ajouterait aussi aux problèmes de non-paiement. Les projets de la mer Caspienne accentuent les pressions concurrentielles, mais le contrôle exercé sur le réseau de pipelines est un atout essentiel pour certaines sociétés russes. Il s'agit d'un secteur important pour l'intégration de la Russie dans l'économie mondiale et, en fait, **l'interdépendance croissante entre acheteurs et fournisseurs est, en soi, une forme de garantie de sécurité qui conduit l'Europe vers une plus grande stabilité.**

C'est l'**Ukraine** qui connaît le plus grave déficit énergétique en Europe. Malgré la récession, qui a entraîné une baisse de 50% de la consommation d'énergie depuis 1988, l'Ukraine importe encore 80% du pétrole et du gaz dont elle a besoin (de la Russie pour plus de 90%). La production gazière a diminué de 50% et la production de charbon a chuté de deux tiers. Une révolution des combustibles est indispensable pour éviter que la facture des importations d'énergie ne ruine la nouvelle monnaie. Avec le temps, l'Ukraine pourrait jouer un rôle majeur dans l'approvisionnement de l'Europe centrale et occidentale en pétrole et en gaz provenant de la CEI et du Proche-Orient, un rôle analogue à celui de la Turquie.

Les perspectives d'intégration en **Asie centrale** dépendent du développement de complémentarités économiques, ce qui signifie que les pays qui sont actuellement en concurrence les uns avec les autres comme fournisseurs de matières premières (pétrole, gaz naturel, autres ressources minérales et coton) devront diversifier leur économie (et stimuler ainsi les échanges entre eux) en ajoutant de la valeur à cette base de ressources existante et productrice de richesse.

Le PANEL IV a examiné l'**intégration** ou les projets d'intégration des pays partenaires dans des organisations économiques et des institutions transnationales telles que l'Union Européenne, l'OTAN, la BERD, l'OMC et l'OCDE. Bon nombre de pays ont déjà franchi le premier obstacle de la transition (stabilisation macroéconomique), mais la deuxième phase de la réforme structurelle, à savoir le renforcement des institutions et la réforme du secteur financier, sera beaucoup plus difficile. **Le renforcement des institutions est d'une importance primordiale.** La qualité et la probité des administrations publiques, du système juridique et du secteur financier doivent être encore accrues. De nombreux pays dont l'économie est en transition se révèlent aujourd'hui être beaucoup plus pauvres qu'on ne l'avait pensé à une certaine époque, mais cela est dû au fait qu'ils sont mal développés et non sous-développés. Il existe un important capital humain, qui a été mal orienté. Le rôle des institutions internationales est d'indiquer aux gens la bonne direction.

La **récapitulation des travaux** a été faite par le **rapporteur, M. John Hardt**, du Service de recherche du Congrès des Etats-Unis. M. Hardt a émis l'opinion que les pays en transition ont la conviction que, s'ils adoptent le modèle démocratique de l'économie de marché, un processus conduisant au succès économique s'en suivra inévitablement (après une brève période de douloureux ajustement). Les impératifs essentiels de la réforme (stabilisation, libéralisation, privatisation) sont des conditions préalables nécessaires mais non suffisantes pour atteindre le seuil d'une croissance durable, indispensable pour qu'un pays soit admis comme participant normal au marché mondial. Cela exigerait l'instauration d'une société véritablement plurielle et la mise à l'écart de ceux qui s'opposent au changement, aussi bien parmi les anciennes élites politiques qui survivent que parmi les nouvelles élites économiques dont la richesse est souvent davantage le résultat d'un heureux coup du sort purement arbitraire que le fruit de l'esprit d'entreprise ou d'un travail acharné. Néanmoins, certains pays en transition ont satisfait aux conditions essentielles et commencent à se montrer à la hauteur.

En conclusion, on peut affirmer que les succès remportés par les pays dont l'économie est en transition sont bien connus. Toutefois, le bilan de la transition est inégal et c'est là ce qui nous préoccupe le plus. La transition a coûté bien des souffrances sur le plan humain, comme cela a été relevé au cours du colloque de 1996. C'est pourquoi certains pays ont fait marche arrière sur la voie de la réforme. En fait, certains des défis auxquels les membres de l'Alliance ont dû faire face récemment en matière de sécurité avaient leur origine dans des facteurs financiers et économiques.

Une politique économique et une sécurité crédibles vont de pair : la sécurité pâtira de l'absence d'une politique économique efficace, et sans un contexte de sécurité favorable, ce sont les investissements et la croissance économique qui pâtiront. Le secteur extérieur est un élément clé de la transition vers une économie de marché. Le commerce extérieur, les investissements, la technologie et le savoir-faire peuvent contribuer résolument à la hausse du niveau de vie. Il est apparu que les relations économiques régionales donnent une vigoureuse impulsion au secteur extérieur de nombreuses économies, en Europe centrale et dans la région de la Mer noire par exemple. Elles favorisent aussi les relations de bon voisinage, renforçant ainsi la paix et la sécurité.

Daniel George
Directeur, Direction économique de l'OTAN
Président du Colloque

WELCOMING REMARKS
BY THE SECRETARY GENERAL OF NATO

Mesdames et Messieurs,

C'est pour moi un très grand plaisir de vous accueillir au 26ème colloque économique annuel de l'OTAN. Depuis sa création, en 1971, ce colloque a acquis une excellente réputation, celle d'un forum d'échanges où des experts discutent des liens entre économie et sécurité.

Pendant ses vingt premières années, le colloque a réuni d'éminents économistes d'Amérique du Nord et d'Europe occidentale pour débattre de la situation économique de ce que l'on appelait alors le "bloc de l'Est". La décennie en cours a vu le colloque se transformer progressivement afin de refléter les évolutions intervenues dans le contexte de la sécurité européenne. Aujourd'hui, nous réunissons des économistes des pays partenaires et des pays de l'Alliance. Le débat est plus large, plus riche et encore plus fructueux que dans le passé.

Le thème du colloque de cette année est l'avancement de la réforme économique dans les pays partenaires, l'accent étant mis sur la coopération régionale. Je suis tout particulièrement ravi que ce soit le ministre du développement et des relations économiques de la Slovénie, Marijan Senjur, qui prononce le discours introductif et contribue ainsi à engager le colloque sur la bonne voie.

Permettez-moi de vous présenter le contexte plus général de vos travaux et le rôle de la nouvelle OTAN dans une Europe transformée. Le point de départ de toute politique de sécurité harmonieuse repose aujourd'hui sur la constatation que le concept de sécurité s'est nettement élargi depuis la fin de la guerre froide. L'aspect militaire de la sécurité reste important, et demeure, de fait, l'élément fondamental de toute politique de sécurité équilibrée. Mais d'autres aspects ont acquis une importance de plus en plus grande. A ce volet militaire se sont en effet ajoutées des dimensions économiques, environnementales et politiques. Le principal défi stratégique auquel tous nos pays sont confrontés, qu'ils fassent partie ou non de l'OTAN, réside dans la question de savoir comment rendre l'Europe plus stable. Aujourd'hui, notre ennemi commun se nomme "Instabilité"!

Les rivalités d'origine ethnique ou nationaliste peuvent être des catalyseurs très puissants de l'instabilité. Au temps de la confrontation Est-Ouest, ces rivalités étaient masquées ou étouffées. Aujourd'hui, il leur arrive de se déchaîner, comme nous l'avons vu en Bosnie. Nous avons pu aussi y constater que des tensions plongeant leurs racines dans l'Histoire peuvent être aggravées par les disparités économiques.

$$* \quad * \quad * \quad *$$

Ladies and Gentlemen,

So what is NATO's role today in the face of these dramatic changes? What is the Alliance contributing to a more stable and secure Europe? I would make two points.

NATO has been in the forefront of creating a new cooperative approach to security across the whole of the Euro-Atlantic area. We have launched a number of initiatives to overcome the divisions of Europe and to introduce a new pattern of security relationships. Without going into detail, I would cite Partnership for Peace with its emphasis on developing close and practical cooperation on military and defence matters. We have established a Euro-Atlantic Partnership Council which brings Allied and Partner politicians, diplomats and military officers together regularly to consult, exchange information and coordinate our policies.

As you are aware, we have signed a "Founding Act" with Russia which has created the basis for working and consulting closely together in a new Joint Permanent NATO-Russia Council. We will have a distinctive relationship with Ukraine. And NATO has launched a Mediterranean dialogue, with the aim of developing friendly and productive relations to our South. Last but not least, next month we will announce the first countries which will be invited to join the Alliance by 1999. We will also make a commitment to keep the door of NATO open in future. The effect of all these initiatives has been to introduce a very positive dynamic into European security. To use an old phrase, there is a real sense of a single security space from Vancouver to Vladivostok.

The second major contribution that NATO is making is in the sphere of crisis management. Perhaps the major significance of NATO's intervention in Bosnia is that it has established a model for managing future crises by bringing Allies and Partners under a single chain of military command, united to achieve the same purpose: a lasting peace in Bosnia. This is a precedent which will have a powerful deterrent effect in the area and which provides many lessons for NATO's future involvement in crises.

The Madrid Summit will consolidate and reinforce the direction NATO has been taking in recent years as a dynamic organization providing stability and a forum for security cooperation to the whole Euro-Atlantic area. We will be setting the basis of a new NATO adapted to a new Europe. A NATO that will carry us forward into the XXI century. So what, then, is the connection between what NATO is doing in stimulating security-related cooperation, and the issues you will be addressing today and tomorrow?

The experience of Western Europe after 1945 shows that economic progress and security integration are closely linked. The effective security framework provided by NATO contributed to put past divisions behind us and allowed Europeans and North Americans together to look ahead to a better and more secure future. A modernized NATO is having the same effect to the East of this continent that it had throughout many decades in the West. We are helping to create the strategic confidence which is essential for sustained future economic growth. The prospect of joining NATO is providing a powerful incentive to the reform processes in Central and Eastern Europe. In addition, many long-standing bilateral problems have been resolved as countries prepare for joining NATO and the European Union.

NATO of course, cannot achieve or sustain transformation of Europe on its own. Other institutions have their part to play too. The OSCE has to develop its role in preventive diplomacy. The Council of Europe has to extend the habits and process of democracy. And of course, in the long run, the European Union will have the most significant effect in the economic sphere. But in terms of creating the initial impetus towards change, NATO's policies are already providing a very powerful stimulus today.

So, on that point, let me end these brief remarks. I look forward to hearing the results of your discussions. And I welcome you and wish you well for the 1997 Economics Colloquium.

KEYNOTE SPEECH

THE ECONOMIC DEVELOPMENT, REFORM AND REGIONAL COOPERATION OF CENTRAL EUROPEAN COUNTRIES IN TRANSITION, WITH EMPHASIS ON SLOVENIA

Marijan Senjur

Minister of Economic Relations and Development, Government of Slovenia

Transition

Transition in former socialist countries is principally characterised by three concurrent processes: **democratisation**, **privatisation** and **marketisation**.

The process of political **democratisation** in Slovenia has been relatively successful, as in other post-socialist countries. The plurality of political parties and voting patterns has led to the formation of coalition governments which have faced difficulties in making decisions and securing legislative support for transition programmes.

Slovenia is encountering problems with **privatisation** similar to those of other countries in transition. After a slow start, privatisation is now progressing well. The Law of Ownership Transformation of Companies has been almost entirely implemented. To date, ownership transformation programmes for more than 96% of the former social capital of companies have been approved. Of these programmes, more than two-thirds have been completed whilst the rest are underway. Privatisation has created a large number of small shareholders in individual commercial companies and authorised investment funds. In the coming years, ownership will gradually be concentrated in the hands of a few private and institutional investors. The number of individual shareholders is expected to consolidate at about 25-30% of the population. In the meantime, the transition process will be significantly dependant upon individual plant managers. New proprietors are owners only on paper and their will does not greatly influence the transition process, although they are expected to play a greater role in the future.

The goal of privatisation is to increase the efficiency of privatised enterprises thereby ensuring the greater efficiency of the national economy. Slovenia has started to monitor enterprise performance with regard to various ownership categories. The analysis involved around 2,000 enterprises accounting for 84% of the equity, 78% of the assets and 79% of the employees of the entire non-financial corporate sector. Results are shown in **Table 1** below, which reveals that enterprises with different ownership structures also differ greatly with regard to the various indicators. In short, it is possible to draw three general conclusions from Slovenia's experience:

* although internal ownership is the most frequent type of privatisation, these enterprises are of less importance than those with external ownership (except in the number of employees and value-added);
* state enterprises retain an important position in the Slovenian economy;
* the best results are achieved in private enterprises and enterprises with foreign capital, the worst in non-privatised firms and in enterprises with internal ownership.

Table 1
Selected Indicators of Enterprise Performance

Performance Indicators	AE-All Enterprises	Private AE=100	Foreign Owned AE=100	Internal AE=100	External AE=100	Non-private AE=100	State AE=100
Net sales per assets (%)	76.7	174	210	146	108	91	36
Assets per equity (%)	173	186	112	99	94	142	85
Value added per employee SIT'000	1,834	106	131	92	107	74	118
Assets per enterprise SIT'000	2,258	23	74	56	141	119	676
Sales per enterprise SIT'000	1,731	41	156	82	153	108	244
Number of employees per enterprise	188	30	72	108	146	125	261
Assets per employee SIT'000	12,009	77	103	52	97	95	259
Equipment in fixed assets (%)	23	120	203	96	99	84	93
Equipment per employee SIT'000	1,864	56	168	43	89	72	311
Labour costs in sales (%)	20	69	51	122	101	109	121
Labour costs per employee SIT'000	1,830	92	110	93	106	93	113
Share of exports in sales (%)	28	75	155	88	102	154	34
Liabilities/equity; % growth since 1994	65	315	133	97	81	208	65
Net return on equity	-0.5	5.7	4.6	-1.3	0.0	-8.8	0.3
Share of net profit/loss in sales	-0.4	1.3	1.5	-0.7	0.0	-5.1	0.8

Source : AP.

In addition to privatisation, **marketisation** (defined as the extension and development of the financial, labour and goods and services markets coupled with liberalisation of foreign economic relations) is also crucial to the success of transition.

Slovenia started with a relatively well-developed **goods and services market** as well as considerable price liberalisation. Despite this, the disparities between local prices and those in developed market economies were considerable. Prices of services and energy lagged behind while those of industrial goods were, as a rule, higher than in neighbouring market economies. This was a general characteristic of all countries in transition. The prices for services in Slovenia were on average 53% of the Austrian level in 1990, whereas rent was only 22% of the Austrian level. The price of energy for households also lagged behind by the same amount, although average prices for household appliances in Slovenia were as much as 68% more than for comparable Austrian products. These disparities have narrowed in the course of transition. The average disparity (Austria=100%) amounted in 1996 to 124% for household appliances, 66% for services, and 82% for household power.

Labour legislation in Slovenia attempts to find a halfway house between demands for greater flexibility in the **labour market** and demands to maintain the legal security of workers. Provisions regulating the hiring and dismissal of employees and the related costs greatly influence an employer's decision to hire new workers. Due to high dismissal costs (such as lengthy periods of notice and high redundancy payments), employers opt for flexible forms of employment and have become exceptionally careful about hiring new workers. The new labour bill retains a relatively complex process of dismissing workers very similar to the German model, yet reduces the costs of dismissing workers by cutting redundancy payments and reducing periods of notice. This has been compensated for by a secured preferential right to the payment of part of outstanding wages, compensation for loss of wages, compensation for industrial injury, and redundancy payments in case of compulsory settlement or bankruptcy proceedings. The Law on the Guarantee Fund of the Republic of Slovenia guarantees the payments of the stated employers' obligations even in the event of their insolvency.

The problems of transition in Slovenia are strongly tied to the development of **financial markets** and the high cost of resources for funding investments and production. After independence, Slovenia had to start almost from scratch with both the development of its capital market instruments and institutions and with the rehabilitation of a large part of its banking system that had been burdened by bad loans. The institutional regulation of the domestic banking system was explicitly transformation-oriented in Slovenia. Three of the largest banks were nationalised, their losses and bad assets being covered in the rehabilitation process with state bonds of various maturity periods (the longest up to the year 2010). Positive effects in the form of generated profits, capital adequacy and the employment of a conservative credit policy have emerged. The latter is based upon the safety of investments, taking into account the clients' credit status, insurance provision and investment plans. State banks in the rehabilitation process also now fulfil requirements on liquidity and investment limitations, these being (inter alia) on credit to a single borrower and ceilings on investment into building land, construction and office equipment. A resolution on the completion of the rehabilitation of these banks was passed signifying their readiness for gradual privatisation.

In addition to the two state banks, there are 26 private banks. The value of the largest three of these accounts for 72% of the balance sheet totals of all these banks, which gives an indication of the predominant role of large banks in conducting interest rate and tariff policies, in formulating new bank services, in domestic and foreign business affairs, and in the technical and personnel capability of banks. The profitability of the seven "large" banks was 1.22% of their balance sheet totals in 1996, whilst the profitability of 13 "medium-sized" banks was a little lower at 1.17% whilst that of the 9 "smallest" banks was only 0.26%. Slovenia is thus flooded with small banks that are no longer competitive.

The positive effects of the **securities market** on economic development (derived from the use of savings for financing investments into companies) is dependant upon the market's level of development and also on the relationship between trading on the secondary and primary markets. Market capitalisation of securities at the Ljubljana Stock Exchange amounted last year to only 5% of Slovenia's GDP. But in addition to this as yet modest level of business on the Stock Exchange, much trading goes on outside the organised markets. The motive for trading on non-transparent markets is the wish for a cheaper and swifter consolidation of ownership, but also one of pure speculation. The latter motive derives from the difference in the price of shares on the two markets. The potential positive influence of the capital market on economic development is also still restricted because companies do not yet issue securities as an alternative source of investment financing. Thus the Stock Exchange is to some extent restricted to privatisation and company take-over business. Further missing elements of the Slovene securities market are long-term households' savings funds. Financial savings, collected from pension funds and other forms of life insurance can assist with the development of the securities market. Trading in securities will also be positively influenced by changes to the taxation system: the current sales tax system for each transaction on the secondary market chokes trading; the introduction of a tax on capital profits on securities would also contribute to the stabilisation of trading.

Whilst Hungary, Poland, Bulgaria, Romania, and the Czech Republic are also encountering problems of transition, Slovenia, Slovakia and the Baltic States as well as most former Yugoslav and ex-Soviet Union countries are encountering additional problems associated with the **transition from a regional or local economy to an independent national economy**. In the case of Slovenia, this transition has been extremely difficult and characterised by the violent break-up of economic ties (the breakdown of the taxation system was followed by a breakdown of the monetary system and break-up of the single Yugoslav market) and war in the former Yugoslavia. The economic collapse of the country was followed by a political collapse and overnight Slovenia lost 70% of the former Yugoslav market, which together with the losses of Eastern European markets represented a disappearance of roughly half its former foreign market. Additional problems were the lack of both developed institutions and of qualified staff to manage the new state and the transition process. All this resulted in a slow and uncoordinated approach to economic reform which retarded economic revival. The new state did not have a developed legal system and could thus guarantee only limited legal security, a particular problem in the period of transition when moral and ethical norms are not yet clearly defined. The new state was left with no diplomatic network, no foreign exchange reserves, no economic identity, and in the vicinity of a war. In this respect, old countries like Hungary and the Czech Republic were at a great advantage since they all possesed state entities and institutions with a positive world image. Slovenia had to gain such recognition from scratch.

Unstable and stagnant transitional economies are additionally confronted with the question of **price stabilisation, restructuring of companies and the revival of economic growth**. Slovenia also faced high inflation and economic stagnation in the 1980s, which then mushroomed in the early 1990s into a real economic crisis of Latin American proportions. Other countries in transition did not have such an inauspicious start.

Restructuring of the economy

The transition towards a market economy has involved significant structural change. In particular, Slovenia's GDP structure has become more like that of other small European countries as charachterised by an increasing share of services and a decreasing share of manufacturing and, to a lesser extent, agriculture. **Table 2** below refers:

Table 2
Value-Added, Employment and GDP by Industry of Origin

			Agriculture, Forestry, Fishing (A+B)	Manufacturing, Construction (C+D+E+F)	Services (G to O)	TOTAL
Value-Added	(%)	1987	4.4	51.6	44.0	100
	(%)	1990	5.6	42.4	52.0	100
	(%)	1995	5.1	38.0	56.9	100
Employment	('000)	1987	80	505	385	970
	('000)	1990	75	456	387	918
	('000)	1995	58	353	411	822
GDP Structure	(%)	1987	8.3	52.0	39.7	100
	(%)	1990	8.2	49.7	42.1	100
	(%)	1995	7.1	42.9	50.0	100

Source : Statistical Office of the RS

Output from the Slovenian **manufacturing** sector grew marginally up until 1987, but fell thereafter and from 1989 went into a recession even more intensive than for other sectors of the economy. During this recession, output and employment in manufacturing has been reduced by around 30%. Industrial production started to grow again in the second half of 1993. The manufacturing revival continued with yearly output exceeding the previous year's level by 7.3% in 1994, by 2.5% in 1995 and by further 1.4% in 1996. The slowdown in growth reflects the problems connected with restructuring, reduced foreign demand and the appreciation of the *tolar* which hit profit margins in the manufacturing export sector.

Trends in manufacturing differ considerably between individual sectors, thus leading to structural change. In the first group of sectors are industries with intensive use of technology that have speedily and successfully adjusted to the market environment, redirecting their efforts to the more demanding Western market and intensively increasing production and exports. The most successful are the electrical machinery and chemical industries, which together create one-third of value-added in manufacturing. In the second group are those sectors where the government has helped companies facing bankruptcy, such as the paper industry, ferrous metals, and heavy machinery. In these sectors, there has been an increase in labour productivity and in sales to markets abroad. The third group would include sectors which have adjusted their production to the new market environment and whose business activity is stable, such as food-processing, but which have not increased either production or export activity. The fourth group includes labour intensive sectors (textiles, leather and footwear employing a mainly female workforce) which have been traditionally dependent upon former Yugoslav markets and which have had difficulties because of weak competitiveness in Western markets. As these sectors are traditionally large net exporters and are labour intensive, companies have additionally suffered both from unfavourable exchange rate trends and from too-high wage taxes.

Being more flexible than industry, **services** were relatively unaffected by the past recession and recovered more quickly. They have improved their share in value-added from 44% in 1987 to 56.9 % in 1995. In international trade, services are represented more modestly (20% of total exports), but enjoy a large surplus due mainly to tourism, thus contributing to a positive current account in the balance of payments. But Slovenia still lags behind in financial, property, business and other market services. Improvements within these sectors are occurring on the basis of bank rehabilitation, the adjustment of banks and insurance companies to higher standards with regard to capital adequacy and the structure of credits and investments, and, finally, through the reform of investment funds as initiators of privatisation.

Restructuring of economic policy

Stabilisation of prices, monetary policy and exchange rate policy

The priority objective of macro-economic policy since Slovenia's independence has been to achieve economic stabilisation within a context of trade and price liberalisation. This implies the creation of a stable and confidence-inspiring currency at a credible exchange rate, which in turn requires inflation to be under control, the build-up of sufficient international reserves, and the limitation of external and fiscal deficits to sustainable levels.

As a new country, Slovenia has had to create **new institutions** and a **new currency**. It succeeded in rapidly establishing the tolar as a strong currency and despite the absence of international reserves, a managed floating exchange rate has been introduced. **Monetary policy** and exchange rates have been pragmatic and have succeeded both in curbing inflation to a single-digit figure and in stabilising the exchange rate. The currency is freely convertible for current account operations whilst international reserves have been steadily accumulated to increase the Bank of Slovenia's room for manoeuver. A number of monetary policy instruments have been devised and used with success to control the evolution of monetary aggregates in a very open economy with a very narrow monetary market.

Monetary policy has been successfully supported by a consistent **fiscal policy**. The near balanced budget and the absence of monetary financing of the federal deficit since 1992 have been major contributions to stabilisation policy. However, the present level of inflation (between 8% and 9% per annum) will be difficult to reduce further unless economic policy instruments are widened and systemic changes realised. In 1995 and 1996, inflation was partly reduced at the cost of preserved price disparities in infrastructure and, especially, in the energy sector. In this period, one of the price policy priorities was the preservation of the position of Slovene exporters. Thus, policy has contributed to narrowing the gap between the appreciating tolar (which reduces export revenues) and growing domestic prices (which increasing costs).

Since one of the main reasons for current **inflation** is high costs, there is a need for a co-ordinated disindexation policy whereby all partners take their share of the burden. Despite its independent position, the Bank of Slovenia's consistent, quantified and transparent objectives should contribute to this agreement. A step-by-step approach should be used, because inflation will not be reduced immediately after disindexation is effected and there is a danger that household savings with banks will be discouraged. General disindexation (wages, pensions, interest rates, budget, contracts, etc.) should be undertaken by all economic policy decision-makers. Monetary policy instruments will not be enough to bring inflation down to European levels. They will also need to be supported by a more efficient incomes policy and a more stringent competition policy.

Lending and borrowing **interest rates** have decreased since 1991: both in nominal and real terms. The nominal decrease was caused by lower inflation. In real terms, the fall was due to the bank rehabilitation process. Although real interest rates have been decreasing since independence, they are still relatively high. The average nominal rate was 18.3% for short-term loans and 19.3% for long-term loans in December 1996. Growing investment demand over the last four years (the average real growth rate of investment is estimated to have exceeded 12% in the period from 1993 to 1996) was not spurred by the level of interest rates on the domestic capital market. On the contrary, relatively high domestic interest rates merely increased the borrowing of Slovene enterprises and households abroad.

In 1996, the central bank devised new instruments. A special liquidity loan was offered to good banks on condition that it be transferred to non-liquid enterprises under favourable terms. In addition, monetary policy has aimed at gradually matching the maturity of commercial banks' assets and liabilities. The compulsory 40% deposit for financial loans obtained abroad (the aim being that they would be converted into tolars) was extended to cover loans with a maturity of up to seven years. In addition, a 10% tolar deposit has been required for long-term financial loans obtained abroad whose maturity exceeds seven years. These measures were adopted as a means of reducing the excess supply of foreign currency which influences the tolar exchange rate. This inflow of foreign capital (by both households and firms) represents a problem in conducting the monetary and exchange rate policies in Slovenia. To sterilise the monetary effects of foreign exchange inflows, the Bank of Slovenia intervenes in the foreign exchange market by issuing foreign exchange bonds. The problem is that these operations are limited to the Bank of Slovenia's own resources. Slovene monetary authorities are aware that the country shall soon be facing full, as opposed to as at present partial, capital liberalisation. The Bank of Slovenia will carefully observe the possibilities of changing its exchange rate regime and will adopt a decision if and when appropriate.

Fiscal policy

The fiscal system is being progressively transformed with the double objective of maintaining a balanced budget consistent with the goals both of stabilisation and monetary policy, and of making it an efficient instrument of mobilisation and allocation of resources within the context of a market economy, i.e. without introducing distortions into price formation or incentives. The major policy directions are:

* a progressive reduction in the role of the state in the economy to reduce the share of total expenditures and revenues in GDP;
* structural reform within the social sectors and the adaptation of their financing sources to maintain the fiscal balance;
* the phasing out of subsidies and state interventions;
* revision of the taxation system and the introduction of new taxes, notably VAT in 1999.

These policies, which have all begun to be implemented, should also bring the structure of the government account more into line with those of other industrial countries by reducing high rates of taxation on wages, by relying more on indirect taxes and corporate taxes, and through a reduction in transfer and subsidies expenditure.

The reform of the pension system is a particularly important element of the reform of public finance given the pressure it puts on the consolidated fiscal account. It is also an essential reform in other aspects: the provision of social security services to the population, the impact on the competitiveness of enterprises, and regarding incentives in the labour market. For these reasons, this reform is being carefully prepared. The main directions (adoption of a three pillars system) have been set up and conform to the opinions of the international institutions consulted as well as the practice of certain EU member countries.

Slovenia has had balanced public finances for the past five years. This was one of the foundations of Slovenia's transition to a market economy and gave crucial support to the stabilisation efforts of monetary policy. In 1996, the overall government balance was in slight surplus (0.3% of GDP). The proportion of government revenues in GDP amounted to 46% and the proportion of government expenditure in GDP was 45.7%. Regarding revenue, 1996 was marked by a considerable reduction in social security contribution rates, by the introduction of a payroll tax and by reduced revenues from customs duties. Social security contribution rates were cut twice - from 44.7% of gross wages in 1995 to 42% at the beginning of 1996 and to 38% in July 1996. The government has reduced social security contribution rates and consequently cut labour costs (of which social contributions are an important component) in order to improve export competitiveness. Tax on payrolls has been introduced as a temporary measure in order to compensate for the loss of revenues due to the reduction in social security contributions. Besides, the tax on payroll re-distributes tax burden so as to decrease the burden on labour intensive sectors. In 1996, these various measures led to tax source restructuring in terms of a greater share of indirect taxes and a lower share of direct taxes.

Incomes Policy

Incomes policy is the weakest link of Slovenian economic policy. In 1996, the average gross wage per employee rose in real terms by 5%, including 4% growth in the market sector and 6.6% in the non-market sector. This increase was one percentage point higher than the estimated rise in total labour productivity - a particularly poor macroeconomic statistic, given the need to maintain competitiveness and in view of the high starting level for 1997.

In Slovenia, collective agreements are the main instrument determining employees' rights. The new Law on Employment Relationships and the Law on Collective Agreements will ensure that collective agreements are concluded on a voluntary basis instead of the previous compulsory basis, whereas the minimum rights and obligations will be set by the law. In 1997, as in previous years, the social partners, namely the government, employers and employees, will conclude the Social Agreement which also determines wage policy. This will be followed by the passing of the Law on Implementation of the Social Agreement in the area of wages. The 1997 Social Agreement will be concluded for a three-year period whereas previously it was always for one year only. Wages are expected to be adjusted by 85% of the growth in consumer prices once a year instead of three times yearly. In addition, certain security mechanisms should be built into the system to prevent a too-steep real drop in wages. The starting-level wages, which are determined by collective agreements, would be allowed to rise only on the basis of indexation with prices. This built-in mechanism will prevent further widening of already extensive wage ranges. Also, managerial salaries are to be further linked to enterprise performance. The government has been drawing up a special Law on Profit-Sharing among Employees aiming at reducing the pressures for wage increases. Special tax reliefs are to be introduced for employers and employees depending on the adopted profit-sharing scheme and in particular on the deadline up to which the use of these funds will be postponed.

Current economic trends and prospects

GDP levels of the early 1990s were reached again in 1996 whilst the production structure was substantially more favourable. The following achievements are assessed as particularly positive by both domestic and foreign analysts (OECD Country Report, 1997): fall in the rate of inflation in the period from 1992 to 1995; a relatively short period of recession; orientation to foreign markets; and the preservation of internal and external equilibrium. On the other hand, the pace of ownership transformation, tax reform, and reform of the pension and social security systems are regarded as having been less successful.

Economic growth, which began in 1993, continues in 1997. After growing 2.8% in 1993, 5.3% in 1994 and 4.1% in 1995, GDP rose 3.1% in 1996. 1996 was marked by modest growth in agriculture (1.7%) and manufacturing (1.4%), and more rapid growth in services (3.6%) and construction (11.1%). Economic growth was driven primarily by domestic demand, which grew by 3.4%. Nevertheless, growth in foreign demand of 2.5% should not be overlooked. Despite a balanced development in 1996, certain trends were reversed. There was a rapid growth in wages, an increase in social benefits and social transfers, a decrease in the share of savings in GDP, and investment grew at a slower rate. The development scenario for 1997 and 1998 projects strong economic growth, maintenance of external equilibrium, and a modest government deficit. Whether this scenario is realised will depend on whether Slovenia manages both to control the growth in budget expenditures (notably for wages in the public sector, social transfers and budget-financed investment) to ensure that the deficit does not exceed 1% of GDP, and to stabilise the rate of growth in wages in the economy as a whole. The government must also launch the reforms of pension and social security systems and complete the privatisation process. In addition, the tax system needs to be overhauled, the extent and mode of the privatisation of remaining state property (for instance, banks) must be decided upon, the service sector needs to be gradually liberalised, and the budget-financed part of services must be privatised or at least liberalised at an accelerated pace. The realisation of a balanced development in the period from 1999 to 2001 largely depends upon the effectiveness and co-ordination of these policies.

Provided the abovementioned preconditions are fulfilled, economic growth could reach 4% in 1997 and 4.5% in 1998. Attainment of such levels of economic growth is premised on favourable economic developments in the EU, improved export competitiveness and persistent moderate growth in domestic demand. Economic growth in the EU is estimated to accelerate in the years to come from 1.6% in 1996 to 2.4% in 1997 and 2.8% in 1998. Improved export competitiveness of domestic industry in 1996, which is expected to continue over the next few years, should boost Slovenian exports. Indeed, foreign demand is anticipated to grow at around 4% in 1997 and by 4%+ in 1998. In both years, domestic demand (especially for investment) is also predicted to grow (by 4.3% and 4.4%, respectively). Investment demand was up as much as 17% in 1995 and rose by a further 9% in 1996. Similar rates of growth (8-10%) are expected both in 1997 and 1998. Investment in infrastructure (often backed directly or indirectly by the state) represented an important part of total investment of around 20%. This share is expected to remain unchanged in the future.

Trade and current account deficits tend to grow in most transition economies, but Slovenia has managed to maintain external equilibrium. According to balance of payments statistics, the trade deficit amounted to US$852.8m in 1996, down US$100.7m from 1996. The current account recorded a small surplus of US$46.5m. In 1997, as in 1996, exports of goods and services grew by 2.8% in real terms whilst imports were up 1.3%. In 1998, both are expected to grow at higher rates. Although the trade deficit might increase slightly over the coming years, the surplus in services is expected to be high enough to preserve the external equilibrium as witnessed by a current account deficit of around 0.2% of GDP.

After a sharp decline in export competitiveness (measured in terms of unit labour costs within a currency basket) in 1995 of 11.2%, a considerable increase of 7.3% was recorded in 1996. This was primarily due to growth in productivity, the decrease in wage-related taxes and the real depreciation of the tolar. Better competitiveness is still impeded by the high rate of growth of wages and other remuneration. In 1997, export competitiveness is expected to improve slightly. This is, however, primarily dependant upon exchange rate developments and the ability of incomes policy to halt further wage rises.

In 1996, the average **gross wage** per employee was up 5.1% in real terms (deflated by the growth in retail prices) from 1995. In real terms, wages in the market sector were up 4% and in the non-market sector by 6.7%. Wages in the non-market sector grew most in the pre-election period. Wages in the market sector grew mostly as a consequence of individual agreements. Social partners will, however, need to agree on new incomes policy mechanisms if wage ratios are to be improved and the one percentage point lag in the growth of wages behind that of productivity is to be reversed. Government endeavours are mostly focused on extending the period in which wages are indexed to retail prices and on setting up a mechanism to more closely link the growth in wages (set by individual agreements) to enterprise performance.

Employment decreased slightly (down 0.5%) in 1996. In particular, the number employed in industry was down 6.5%, whilst it rose in some services and public administration. Despite a lower level of employment, the average annual level of registered unemployed (13.9%) remained the same as in 1995. The unemployment rate based on ILO criteria (7.3%) also remained unchanged. In view of high structural and regional labour market disparities, there is little likelihood of a substantial decrease in the number of unemployed in the near future.

In 1996, end of year **inflation** (annualised rate of growth of retail prices) was 8.8%, similar to the 8.6% inflation at the end of 1995. In 1996, the average annual rate of inflation was a single digit - 9.7% - for the first time, representing a reduction from 12.6% in 1995. As certain price disparities still need to be abolished (notably energy prices), there is little prospect that inflation will be reduced substantially either in 1997 or in 1998. A prudent price policy will be required in order to reduce inflation further and to remove price disparities. Such a policy must also be supported by neutral monetary and effective income policies.

The **federal budget** recorded a surplus of 0.3% of GDP in 1996. But a significant and growing deficit appeared in the **Pension Fund** which amounted to 2.7% of GDP and in 1997 is expected to reach around 4%of GDP. This is a consequence both of the reduction in the social security contribution rate, and of a rise in the Pension Fund's expenditure. A balanced government budget will also be difficult to maintain in 1997 due to a higher level of other expenditure. The share of wage-related expenditure has soared as wages in the non-market sector rose due to strikes whilst employment in public administration increased in 1996. In addition, expenditure for social transfers has increased as the number of child supplement beneficiaries increased. VAT will not be introduced before 1999. Although a tax on new motor vehicles was introduced and the tax on payroll was maintained, it is unlikely that a budget deficit will be avoided this year. Since the share of government revenue in GDP has fallen by a percentage point (from 46% of GDP in 1996 to 45% in 1997), a viable budget deficit of 1% of GDP will only be attained if the share of state expenditure remains at 46% of GDP. This would be only marginally above the 1996 level of 45.7% of GDP. Provided that all necessary measures aimed at holding back government spending are taken, in particular concerning federal expenditure on wages, investment and social transfers, the deficit could possibly even drop to 0.5% of GDP in 1998. However, this figure is premised on government revenue amounting to 44.9% and expenditure to 45.4% of GDP in 1998. On the revenue side, this projection also presumes that the payroll tax is kept and excise duties are introduced. On the expenditure side, the real increase is presumed not to exceed 3.1%.

If economic policy manages to improve investment and implements key reforms, hitherto delayed, **Slovenia can expect relatively high economic growth** in the period 1999-2001. The introduction of VAT, which would replace the current sales tax, and a halt in growth of government expenditure would make the abolition of the payroll tax and the re-establishment of fiscal equilibrium possible. The medium-term development scenario forecasts a matched reduction in the proportion of federal expenditure and revenue in GDP from 45.4% in 1998 to 45% in 1999 and then to 44.1% in 2001. Relatively high economic growth of between 4.5-5.0% combined with greater labour market flexibility may cause the current stagnation in levels of employment to ease a little in 1998.

Integration and cooperation

Slovenia's **international economic relations** are primarily oriented towards Europe, especially the EU which in 1996 provided the market for 64.6% of Slovenian exports and 67.6% of imports. The EU also accounts for almost three-quarters of Slovenia's trade in services and virtually all FDI. The second most important (and over-lapping) category of countries in Slovenia's international economic relations are the neighbouring countries of Italy, Croatia, Austria and Hungary. Proximity is one of the key factors for economic co-operation, especially since Slovenia has a large number of small size enterprises for which this is a particularly important factor. Close economic ties between Slovenia and Croatia have probably been because both were recently part of the same state, but proximity undoubtedly contributed greatly to the maintenance of economic relations after the break-up of Yugoslavia. In the case of Italy and Austria, the fact that they are neighbours is probably more important than their membership in the EU.

In 1996, neighbouring countries accounted for 31.5% of Slovenian exports and 34.5% of imports. Hungary lags considerably behind the other three countries. At the same time, Austria, Italy and Croatia (due to its share in the nuclear power plant at Krsko) are also among the five most important investors in Slovenia. The importance of these countries for Slovenia's international economic relations increased after the break-up of Yugoslavia, not only because of the collapse of the Yugoslav market, but also because Slovenia has maintained the largest volume of trade of all former-Yugoslav republics with neighbouring Croatia.

Throughout the 1990s, Slovenia's trade balance for goods has been negative and growing. The deficit has been concentrated within a small number of countries, mostly Italy, Austria and Hungary. In 1995 and 1996, the deficit with these three countries accounted for 79.5% and 82.8% of the total deficit respectively. Apart from these three, Slovenia generated a deficit only with France (US$326m in 1996) and the Czech Republic (US$90m in 1996). In trade with Austria, the deficit is structural in that Austria is an intermediary for imports of third countries' products. In the case of Italy, the deficit was primarily a result of the high depreciation of the Italian lira since 1993. Negative trade balances with Hungary and the Czech Republic were because these countries partly compensated for the loss of suppliers from former-Yugoslavia regarding primary and semi-finished products. **Table 3** below summarises recent Slovenian trade patterns with CEFTA and former Yugoslavia.

Table 3
Slovenian Trade with CEFTA and Former Yugoslavia (FY) (US$million)

	Exports 1994	Exports 1995	Exports 1996	Imports 1994	Imports 1995	Imports 1996
Czech Republic	82.5	132.0	145.8	177.8	246.9	236.0
Hungary	98.7	114.6	105.2	192.6	266.8	236.9
Poland	96.3	104.8	141.4	22.5	37.7	48.4
Slovakia	30.3	51.7	57.2	58.1	82.3	91.9
TOTAL CEFTA	**307.8**	**403.1**	**449.6**	**451.0**	**633.7**	**613.2**
Bosnia	-	118.9	263.1	-	8.1	15.2
Croatia	-	891.1	858.7	-	575.6	581.2
FRYugoslavia	-	9.5	95.6	-	1.6	31.9
Macedonia	-	189.3	169.9	-	85.7	70.1
TOTAL FY	**-**	**1,208.8**	**1,387.3**	**-**	**671.0**	**698.4**

Source : Statistical Office of the RS, 25.7.1996&13.2.1997. (data for 1996 are preliminary)

Slovenia's most important existing trade partners will remain so in the future. Irrespective of a likely slower growth in imports, EU countries will as a group retain their dominant position in Slovenia's international economic relations. Alternatives to EU markets (both quantitatively or qualitatively) do not realistically exist. Neighbouring countries will remain the second most important group and their importance is expected to increase for the following reasons:

* the existence of solid institutional foundations for cooperation (EU in the case of Italy and Austria, CEFTA in the case of Hungary);
* a forecast of faster import growth in Italy and Austria than elsewhere in the EU;
* the end of the war and the beginning of reconstruction in Croatia;
* the inclination of small and medium sized Slovenian enterprises to operate in nearby, known and trusted markets, particularly in service sectors such as tourism and transport.

The basic goals of Slovenia's international economic relations policy are to strengthen the position of the economy in the EU, recapture a share of the markets of former Yugoslavia, substantially increase performance in USA and CEFTA markets, and to penetrate (with selected products) the markets of Japan and the more successful NICs. Since Slovenia is a European country, countries from Europe, in particular EU members, are and will remain its most important trading partners. In cooperation with neighbouring countries, Slovenia must expand its trade beyond Friuli-Julian Province in Italy and beyond Steyria and Carinthia in Austria.

As two neighbouring countries, Austria and Italy, are members of the EU and Hungary is an Associate Member, the institutional framework of cooperation with the EU will be of key importance to developing economic relations with neighbouring countries as well. Among these, cooperation with Croatia (because of previous close ties) and Hungary (which has been the least important Slovenian partner so far) have the greatest potential. To intensify ties with Croatia, the two countries must first resolve their political disputes and in the shortest time possible conclude agreements on free trade, protection of investment and property rights. Inter-regional cooperation presents another opportunity for the intensification of economic relations with neighbouring countries, in particular since the EU favours cross-border regional cooperation.

To enhance economic cooperation with neighbouring countries, economic policy must support the export of services. This will greatly depend on activities in the transport sector. With the lifting of sanctions against FR Yugoslavia, the bottleneck on the Hungarian border will ease although another may develop on the border with Croatia. As road truck transport is restricted in Austria, Slovenia will need to improve rail freight transport. The construction of road and railway networks with Hungary must be accelerated and exports through the Port of Koper increased. The Port of Rijeka may also take over a substantial portion of trade for certain kinds of goods. In border regions (and important road inter-sections), the Italian example should be followed and large discount department stores built selling goods at more competitive prices and of better quality than in neighbouring countries. The development of casino tourism as an important source of foreign currency should be encouraged. Slovenia should not oppose the establishment of an "off-shore" centre in Trieste, but instead consider how to cooperate with this venture whilst developing complementary activities in the Port of Koper. Slovenian enterprises should also take advantage of enterprises owned by Slovenian minorities abroad when accessing neighbouring markets. This would also support the objective of assisting these minorities to strengthen their economic base.

PANEL I

External Economic Relations of Partner Countries - Overall Developments and Their Place Within Economic Reforms

Panelists and contributors:
Joe SMOLIK
Valery OKNYANSKY
Ferry DE KERCKHOVE
Zofia WYSOKINSKA
Janina WITKOWSKA
Marie-Hélène BÉRARD *

* Did not contribute a paper

AN OVERVIEW OF THE INTEGRATION TENDENCIES OF THE TRANSITION ECONOMIES[1]

Joe Smolik

Senior Economist, United Nations Economic Commission for Europe, Geneva

Since the turn of the decade, the former centrally planned economies have undertaken dramatic economic reforms which have resulted in various degrees of reintegration into the World economy. This paper reviews some recent key developments and the issues they raise. It should be borne in mind that the transition countries have not reformed at the same pace and that this is broadly reflected in their economic performance. This diversity of policies and results makes generalisation difficult. Hence, the text below focuses mainly on eastern Europe (defined in table 1) although the tables are more comprehensive. External trade is discussed first and then financial relations.

The development of trade and current account balances

Following the steep decline in trade in the early 1990's - precipitated by the dissolution of the CMEA and the collapse of domestic output - the trade of eastern Europe has expanded for several years (see **Table 1**), recently achieving historically high levels. As a result, the area's share of World trade has partially recovered although it still falls short of the roughly 2% recorded in 1990. This recovery has involved a reorientation of eastern Europe's trade from the former CMEA market toward the industrial West (particularly the European Union)[2], more or less restoring the pattern of trade prevailing in Europe prior to World War II and before the adoption of central planning[3].

Intra-east European trade started to recover only in 1994. Early in the decade, the rejuvenation of this segment of trade was not considered very important by the eastern authorities, even though there were benefits to be gained from the reemergence of trade based on market principles (unlike the organization of CMEA exchanges). The liberalisation of trade within the framework of CEFTA and other local trade agreements appear to have contributed to the recent upturn.

The external factors which have contributed to the reorientation of eastern Europe's exports have included (initially) the collapse of intra-CMEA exchanges (prompting exporters to seek new markets), the expansion of western import demand, and increased access to western markets[4]. In particular, countries which have signed European Agreements have benefited from free trade in most manufactured goods[5]. However, eastern policy makers complain about the persistence of contingent protection, especially anti-dumping measures, although their countries ran large structural trade deficits with the West. The role of the West in east European imports has also risen sharply, reflecting a pervasive appetite for Western consumer goods and automobiles. Eastern industry has imported more sophisticated Western intermediate goods for production and, increasingly, capital goods for modernisation.

In general, the merchandise **imports** of the transition economies have been more buoyant than exports which has resulted in chronic current account deficits. In 1996 the trade deficits of many transition economies deteriorated. This raised the combined **current**

account deficit of eastern Europe to US$14bn (see **Table 2**), up from US$1.4bn in 1995 (Russia continued to post a large current account surplus).

The proximate reasons for the deterioration in trade balances in 1996 were a sharp deceleration in the growth of **export** values - in eastern Europe they declined from 25% in 1995 to only 1% in 1996 - and a continuing strong growth of imports, although these increases were also smaller than in 1995. Although the volume of exports of several east European countries continued to expand (e.g. Hungary and Poland) those of several others stagnated or actually declined. The growth of service exports (9% in 1996) has been a bright spot and many countries have earned a growing surplus on this item.

The slowdown in export growth appears to be due to a number of external and domestic factors. Slower economic growth in western Europe was an obvious factor with the increase of import demand falling by nearly two thirds between 1995 and 1996. On average, the volume growth of import demand facing the individual transition economies declined from over 7% in 1995 to just under 3% in 1996. However, not all countries' exports were as adversely affected (e.g. Hungary, Poland, and the Baltic states). Other factors were the strong growth of domestic demand (absorbing part of tradeables produced), a decline in the overall competitiveness of goods, in some cases a strong appreciation of the exchange rate, and generally slow restructuring.

One of the issues raised by the deceleration of eastern Europe's export growth is its high, perhaps excessive, dependence on the EU market. Needless to say, such concentration is an advantage during periods of rapid EU import expansion (e.g. as in 1991 and 1994-1995) and has been used as an argument to advance several countries' candidature for EU membership. On the other hand, this dependence adversely affects eastern exports when the growth of the EU market is slow as in 1996 and, according to some forecasts, in 1997 as well. Although there has been some diversification of exports toward other transition economies in 1995-1996, the share of the rapidly expanding developing countries in eastern Europe's exports has declined, in some cases to as little as 5%.

In addition to diversification, the east European countries could reduce their dependence on the Western business cycle by steadily increasing their market shares. Given that these are still very small, gains should not be difficult to achieve. However, it would require improvements in competitiveness and faster structural change. In the first years of reform, rapid export growth was achieved in part by the draw-down of stocks and the use of existing production capacity. Increasingly, however, incremental export growth will depend on the reorganisation of enterprises and new investment. Although some countries have made more progress than others, in general, restructuring and modernisation have been slow. This has been reflected in domestic investment which has generally been weak, although that of the Czech Republic, Poland, Slovakia, and Slovenia has recently become increasingly buoyant.

Imports of capital goods, including by FDI enterprises, are counted on to help increase export capacity and competitiveness. However, only a few countries have reported a significant growth of such imports, and of those some (e.g. Czech Republic) have none the less seen their export growth falter. This suggests that other factors (macroeconomic and exchange rate policies, slow restructuring, etc.) have been the dominant determinants of export performance. Foreign machinery and equipment are most likely to foster the expansion of exports if they are absorbed into companies with export potential. However, from the debate in some countries it is not clear whether their capital goods imports are actually destined for exportable production. Even if they are, the timing and strength of the supply response are uncertain.

The developments in 1996 and outlook for 1997 raise the question whether the current account deficits of many transition economies are sustainable. In 1996 more than half of these countries posted large deficits, often of 5% or more of GDP. According to the conventional wisdom, persistent deficits of this magnitude are a warning signal of a potential balance of payments crisis, particularly if they are financed by short-term or other volatile funds, or by depleting foreign currency reserves. In such circumstances, governments are generally recommended to make adjustments to avoid a "hard landing", which could be precipitated by a loss of confidence by foreign investors.

In reality, the relationship between current account deficits and crises is not so straightforward. Deficits are considered acceptable, indeed desirable, if they are accompanied by higher domestic investment, particularly in export industries. In this way, a country has a better chance of achieving higher growth and remaining solvent (i.e. retaining the ability to pay). In addition, a recent study suggests that the actual occurrence of a crisis also depends on the country's willingness to service its debt and on the willingness of foreign investors to continue to lend on current terms[6]. The current account imbalance also needs to be considered in conjunction with exchange rate policy, the external financial position and various structural factors, including the degree of openness of the economy, the levels of domestic savings and investment, and the health of the financial system.

A related issue is to what extent the balance of payments is likely to be a constraint on economic growth. In the extreme case of a lack of external finance (e.g. Bulgaria in 1996), imports fall and the current account moves into balance (or even surplus), with adverse implications for output. The more common situation among the transition economies has been large current account deficits matched by the availability of adequate financing for at least a year or so (i.e. in the form of inflows of private capital, high foreign currency reserves, and access to external finance). But even in these cases, the deficits have evoked official concern, leading to the implementation, or at least the consideration, of restrictive policy measures.

Curbing the growth of current account imbalances in 1997 is likely to require cuts in the growth of domestic demand below the rates officially forecast at the beginning of the year. Indeed, various independent forecasts show growth rates of output which are lower than the official forecasts or below those of 1996. It should be borne in mind that even recent rates of GDP growth in eastern Europe - 3.9% on average in 1996 - are not particularly high, especially if compared with the performance of the more dynamic Asian economies. Current account considerations might therefore limit the region to relatively modest growth rates which are below the expectations of the population and short of what is required to substantially narrow the income gap between them and their Western trade partners[7].

External financing

The initial transformation leaders - the Czech Republic, Hungary, Poland and Slovakia - have made great strides gaining access to foreign private capital. Recently, this group has grown to include the Baltic states, certain countries of southeast Europe and some members of the CIS. However, several transition economies remain dependent on official and short-term finance. The ability to attract private capital is, of course, important because the additional resources can boost economic growth and welfare beyond the possibilities offered solely by domestic means (although growth prospects are largely determined by internally generated resources). For creditworthy borrowers, foreign markets offer funds at better terms than those available domestically (if they are available at all), the opportunity to issue securities beyond the absorptive capacity of local markets and a chance to diversify their financial sources.

The conditions which have increased the attractiveness of many transition economies for foreign capital include political stability, successful stabilisation policies, various structural reforms and improved growth prospects. In general, these countries have also strengthened their external financial positions by boosting foreign exchange reserves and, in the case of some of the most indebted ones, by substantially reducing debt burdens (e.g. Hungary and Poland). Finally, those countries (or their successor states) which at one time defaulted on their external debt have made various degrees of progress in normalizing relations with London and Paris Club creditors[8].

Perhaps the most widely recognised indicator of financial market integration is an **international credit rating** from the major rating services (see **Table 3**). By the end of May 1997, thirteen transition economies had been rated[9]. Seven of them have received investment grade ratings, opening the door to the huge resources commanded by institutional investors. By comparison, only Hungary was rated at the beginning of the decade, and currently only nine non-European developing countries are considered investment grade risks. Sovereign ratings have paved the way for the international rating of creditworthy municipal and corporate/financial borrowers.

In 1996 the transition economies raised record funds in the **international markets**, including US$9.7bn in medium-and long-term debt (see **Table 4**) and US$1.4bn in equity (IPOs). This rapid pace carried over into 1997 when Russia emerged as the major borrower. However, most creditworthy countries had little need of new funds, enjoying sizeable inflows of other types of capital. The combination of favourable credit ratings, the relative scarcity of transition economy issues and intense competition in the international markets have led to better borrowing terms, some on par with certain Western market economies[10]. However, yields on sub-investment debt have remained high (e.g. Romania and Russia have paid over 300 basis points), although this has contributed to the large oversubscription of their new offerings. There has been a further diversification of the financial instruments used and in the investor base. Banks and corporations have surpassed sovereign entities as borrowers, prompted by the availability of cheaper and longer-term funds than are available on domestic markets.

In general, the debt segment of the **internal securities markets** of the transition economies has made the most progress. Most governments now regularly issue T-bills, often relying on foreigners to help finance public deficits. Equity markets have become operational in an increasing number of countries, but their liquidity and capacity to absorb new issues generally remains limited. The influence of foreign investors can be considerable, as in 1996 and early 1997 when they contributed to the record stock market performance in several countries. Portfolio investment in local currency denominated securities amounted to over US$1bn in the Czech Republic and Poland in 1995 and to at least US$7bn in Russia's GKO market in 1996.

Following the heavy outflows at the turn of the decade, eastern Europe has attracted significant foreign funds. **Total net inflows** surged in 1993, peaked in 1995 at US$24bn, and then fell in 1996 (see **Table 5**). The recent decline occurred primarily because two major capital importers took measures to curtail net inflows: the Czech Republic widened the fluctuation band for the koruna while Hungary made sizeable repayments of official debt. This and greater inflows helped Poland emerge as the largest recipient of foreign capital in eastern Europe. There is considerable diversity in the composition of flows into the transition economies. However, FDI has generally been the most important (though not in

Russia) and the role of potentially volatile short-term flows (including unrecorded capital) has increased.

Foreign direct investment in the European transition economies has developed irregularly (see **Table 6**). In 1995 net FDI flows rebounded reaching a record US$11.6bn thanks largely to the exceptional privatisation activity in Hungary and the Czech Republic. Flows into both countries and the region as a whole declined in 1996, but Poland and Russia received markedly more investment, the former emerging as the chief destination for FDI in the whole region. Barely half of these countries attracted larger inflows in 1996, despite some further improvement in the investment climate in the region.

FDI inflows have been concentrated in the leading reforming countries. As a result of its privatisation strategy - early sales of key assets to foreign strategic investors - Hungary has received over one-third of cumulated flows in the region while the Czech Republic has accounted for about 15%. Only recently have their shares tended to diminish, due to FDI surges into Poland and Russia. Some further diversification of flows would occur if the new economic programmes of Bulgaria, Romania and (possibly) Ukraine accelerate foreign investment. So far these countries have attracted small amounts of FDI. Only in Hungary, the Czech Republic, Estonia and Latvia has FDI amounted to around 5% of GDP, and in all except Latvia the ratio declined in 1996. Those countries which were slow in attracting FDI early in the transition have shown little sign of catching up.

In 1996 FDI flows into Hungary and Poland were associated chiefly with greenfield investments and additions to the existing capital base. Previously, by contrast, they were linked closely to the privatisation of state assets[11]. This suggests that recent FDI has been attracted by expectations of economic growth and profitability and the other usual arguments in the investment function rather than by governments' timetables for privatisation. This development also improves the outlook for sustained inflows of FDI, especially into countries such as Hungary which have already disposed of most of their stock of saleable state enterprises.

In general, FDI flows have fallen short of expectations and perceived needs. However, the initial hopes appear to have been unrealistic. A common view at the beginning of transition was that FDI would flow in quickly and jump start these economies. FDI was expected to provide resources to these economies (lacking adequate systems for savings and intermediation), introduce management skills and new technology and promote restructuring. However, experience from other countries has indicated that while foreign investors are willing to participate in privatisations in the early stages of economic reform, they commit sizeable resources to greenfield projects only after sufficient progress has been made in the areas of political and economic stabilisation, the creation of legal and institutional frameworks, and with improving business infrastructures. In fact, the absence of a positive investment climate appears to explain the small investments received by certain countries.

To date, no statistical relationship between FDI and economic growth has been discernible among the transition economies. For example, Poland, which until recently had received relatively little FDI, has led the region in economic growth while Hungary, by far the largest recipient of FDI, has managed only low rates of growth. Other factors have been more influential. However, in some countries (e.g. Hungary) FDI enterprises account for a large share of national exports, or of the exports of specific sectors (e.g. automobiles). Even in these cases, it appears that such enterprises or sectors have not yet developed strong linkages to the rest of the economy, which also makes them heavily import intensive.

Irrespective of FDI's contribution to economic growth to date, it has often helped to positively transform these countries' external financial positions, boosting reserves, raising credit ratings and allowing current account deficits to be financed without an excessive build-up of debt.

Footnotes

1. This paper draws on material presented in recent volumes of the secretariat's *Economic Survey of Europe* and the *Economic Bulletin for Europe*. Other members of the team working on the external sector include V. Gaucaite, P. Rayment, C. Wittich and J. Hirvonen (statistical assistance). Any errors are mine.

2. On average, in 1995 the EU accounted for around 60 per cent of the exports and imports of eastern Europe, the shares ranging from some 37 per cent in Bulgaria to nearly 80 per cent in Albania.

3. See "The Changing Intensity of East-West Trade, 1955-1984", *Economic Bulletin for Europe*, Vol. 37, No. 4, 1985.

4. As part of G-24 support for the transition, most reforming economies were accorded GSP privileges at the turn of the decade and, from the USA, MFN treatment. Restraints on trade were also removed or reduced within the framework of various trade agreements (e.g. with EFTA).

5. The restrictions on "sensitive" goods (e.g. textiles and clothing) are subject to special protocols and have been reduced at a slower pace, and agricultural goods are largely excluded.

6. G. M. Milesi-Ferretti and A. Razin, *Current Account Sustainability*, Princeton Studies in International Finance, No. 81, October 1996. In a study of seven countries, five were able to sustain large current account deficits for several years, but two were unable to do so and suffered severe external crises.

7. This was already the case in Hungary in 1994-1996 and Bulgaria in 1996 (among others).

8. Albania, Bulgaria, Poland, Croatia, Slovenia and The Former Yugoslav Republic of Macedonia (the latter three being successors of the former SFR of Yugoslavia) have completed this process. Russia, which has assumed the responsibility for the debt of the Soviet Union, is reportedly near finalization of an agreement with the London Club.

9. This includes the B3 rating given to Bulgaria by Moody's, which precludes access to new funds.

10. For example, within the past year, margins obtained by Hungary have fallen from 185 to around 50 basis points. Czech and Slovene borrowers have paid only 22-25 basis points. OECD membership has contributed to better terms.

11. See *Economic Survey of Europe in 1996-1997*, table 3.6.17.

TABLE 1
Foreign trade of the European transition countries by direction, 1993-1996
(Value in billion dollars, growth rates in per cent)[a]

	Exports					Imports			
	Value	Growth rates				Value	Growth rates		
Country or country group[b]	1995	1993	1994	1995	1996	1995	1993	1994	1995
Eastern Europe, *to and from:*									
World	92.4	-0.1	16.4	25.0	1.1	112.3	10.4	9.9	31.3
Transition economies	24.5	-7.3	5.2	24.2	6.5	28.4	4.0	-1.6	30.3
Soviet Union/successor states	6.6	-14.2	8.5	27.5	9.5	12.2	7.9	-6.2	26.9
Eastern Europe	11.7	-9.7	6.9	27.0	5.2	10.6	-2.3	3.3	34.1
Developed market economies	60.2	1.2	24.5	25.3	-0.9	75.3	12.9	16.6	31.3
Developing countries	7.8	5.6	2.6	24.9	-0.1	8.5	8.6	0.1	33.3
Baltic states, *to and from:*									
World	5.9	44.3	12.9	35.5	16.1	8.0	75.0	27.1	41.7
Transition economies	2.9	43.6	-2.9	18.5	22.2	3.4	73.2	0.7	22.9
CIS	2.1	34.6	-6.4	19.1	19.5	2.5	75.6	-9.1	16.1
Baltic states	0.6	111.6	35.2	22.9	41.5	0.5	76.3	24.4	58.1
Developed market economies	2.8	39.7	47.8	59.9	8.4	4.4	76.9	75.4	64.2
Developing countries	0.1	114.9	-2.8	20.4	52.7	0.2	81.2	-6.5	-21.7
Russian Federation, *to and from:*									
World	63.7	4.5	8.4	29.5	8.0	33.2	-27.5	5.2	17.0
Transition economies	14.8	-10.6	-14.9	36.3	21.9	6.3	-32.3	-15.8	38.1
Eastern Europe	8.0	-5.1	-19.5	42.4	15.7	3.5	-51.1	-16.6	55.5
Baltic states	2.3	-16.5	26.4	31.5	16.3	1.1	-48.3	-17.4	57.4
Developed market economies	38.6	7.6	21.7	19.5	3.2	23.1	-29.6	20.2	15.9
Developing countries	10.3	11.2	0.4	20.1	5.8	3.8	-10.3	-4.5	-12.2
Other CIS countries, *to and from:*									
World	13.7	-14.8	13.1	43.8	17.1	11.3	15.5	17.0	34.3

Source: United Nations Economic Commission for Europe, *Economic Survey of Europe in 1996-1997,* table 3.5.1. This source includes more detailed notes to this table.

[a] Growth rates are calculated on values expressed in dollars. Values for 1995 and growth rates for 1994 and 1995 include the "new" foreign trade (trade among successor states of former Czechoslovakia and SFR of Yugoslavia).

[b] "Eastern Europe" refers to Albania, Bulgaria, Croatia, the Czech Republic, Hungary, Poland, Romania, Slovakia and Slovenia.

TABLE 2
Current account balances of eastern Europe, the Baltic countries and European members of the CIS, 1994-1997
(Million dollars and per cent)

			Jan.-Sept.			Per cent of GDP		QI-QIII		
	1994	1995	1996	1996	1997ᵃ	1994	1995	1996	1996	1997ᵃ
*Eastern Europe*ᵇ	..	-1 389	-7 387	-13 802	..	..	-0.4	-3.1	-4.1	..
Former presentationᶜ	-4 203	-9 143	-8 521	-20 942	..	-1.6	-2.8	-5.4	..	..
Albania	-43	-15	-85	-100*	61	-2.4	-0.6	-4.3	-3.8	2.3
Bosnia and Herzegovina	-189	-134	..	..	..	..	..	..	..	..
Bulgaria	-25	-26	-34	-22	..	-0.3	-0.2	-0.5	-0.2	..
Croatia	103	-1 711	-745	-1 452	-1 239	0.7	-9.5	-5.3	-7.8	-6.6
Czech Republic	-50	-1 362	-3 083	-4 476	-6 500 – -7 500ᵈ	-0.1	-2.9	-8.0	-8.7	-11.1 – -12.8ᵈ
Hungary	-3 911	-2 480	-1 104	-1 678	-1 500 – -2 500ᵈ	-9.4	-5.7	-3.3	-3.8	-1.8 – -3.0ᵈ
Polandᶜ	..	5 455	-311	-1 352	-3 900 – -7 800ᵈ	..	4.6	-0.3	-1.0	-2.6 – -5.5ᵈ
Former presentation	-944	-2 299	-5 828	-8 505	..	-1.0	-1.9	-6.1	..	..
Romania	-428	-1 639	-713	-2 336	-1 375	-1.4	-4.6	-2.7	-6.6	-4.5
Slovakia	712	646	-1 032	-1 941	-2 000ᵈ	5.2	3.7	-7.2	-10.1	-10.5ᵈ
Slovenia	540	-36	68	46	-35	3.8	-0.2	0.5	0.3	-0.2
The FYR of Macedonia	-158	-222	-348	-491	..	-5.7	-6.2	-13.2	-14.0	..
Baltic states	-67	-827	-908	..	..	-0.7	-5.9	-7.2	..	..
Estonia	-178	-185	-223	..	..	-7.7	-5.1	-7.0	..	..
Latvia	201	-27	-273	-454	..	5.5	-0.6	-7.1	-8.9	..
Lithuania	-90	-614	-412	-642	-481	-2.1	-10.3	-7.4	-8.7	-5.5
CIS										
Belarus	-506	-567	-752	..	..	-10.3	-5.5	-7.6	..	..
Republic of Moldova	-82	-115	-134	-245	-180	-5.8	-6.8	-11.2	-15.4	-11.3
Russian Federation	11 378	9 801	5 571	9 342	..	4.1	2.6	1.6	2.1	..
Ukraine	-1 161	-1 152	-657	-1 185	..	-3.1	-3.2	-2.0	-2.7	..

Source: National balance of payments statistics; press reports; UN/ECE secretariat estimates.

ᵃ Official forecasts.

ᵇ Includes revised data for Poland. Eastern Europe aggregate excludes Bosnia and Herzegovina.

ᶜ Revised data for Poland.

ᵈ Independent forecasts.

TABLE 3
International credit ratings of eastern Europe, the Baltic countries and the CIS

Standard and Poor's			Moody's		
Rating	Country	Date received	Rating	Country	Date received
Investment grades					
AAA			Aaa		
AA			Aa		
A	Czech Republic	November 1995	A2		
	Slovenia	May 1996			
A-			A3	Slovenia	May 1996
BBB+			Baa1	Czech Republic	September 1995
BBB	Latvia	January 1997	Baa2		
BBB-	Croatia	January 1997	Baa3	Croatia	January 1997
	Hungary	October 1996		Hungary	December 1996
	Poland	April 1996		Poland	June 1995
	Slovakia	April 1996		Slovakia	May 1995
Sub-investment (speculative) grades					
BB+			Ba1		
BB			Ba2	Republic of Moldova	January 1997
				Russian Federation	October 1996
				Lithuania	September 1996
BB-	Romania	March 1996	Ba3	Romania	March 1996
	Russian Federation	October 1996		Kazakstan	November 1996
	Kazakstan	November 1996			
B+			B1		
B			B2		
B-			B3	Bulgaria	September 1996

Source: Press reports.
Note: Foreign currency, long-term, sovereign debt ratings.

TABLE 4
Medium- and long-term funds raised on the international financial markets by eastern Europe, the Baltic countries and the CIS, 1992-1997

	1992	1993	1994	1995	1996 Jan.-Dec.	of which: Bonds	of which: Loans	1997 Jan.-Mar.[a]	of which: Bonds	of which: Loans
Eastern Europe	1 494	6 314	3 587	6 483	8 266	3 033	5 233	2 618	1 111	1 506
Bulgaria	–	–	–	–	–	–	–	–	–	–
Croatia	..	–	–	60	317	–	317	300	300	–
Czech Republic	..	903	638	1 000	2 191	546	1 645	150	–	150
Hungary	1 446	5 071	2 541	4 178	2 108	326	1 782	1 213	540	672
Poland	9	–	3	324	526	500	26	195	50	145
Romania	–	–	–	268	1 400	1 025	375	221	221	–
Slovakia	..	240	331	427	1 130	280	850	484	–	484
Slovenia	–	100	75	226	594	356	238	55	–	55
Former Czechoslovakia	40	..	..	..	..	..	..	..	..	..
Baltic states	–	–	–	101	189	89	100	153	93	60
Estonia	–	–	–	–	64	39	25	78	18	60
Latvia	–	–	–	41	–	–	–	–	–	–
Lithuania	–	–	–	60	125	50	75	75	75	–
CIS	–	28	75	1 345	1 315	1 230	85	3 845	1 230	2 615[b]
Georgia	–	20	–	–	–	–	–	50	50	–
Kazakstan	–	–	–	–	200	200	–	–	–	–
Kyrgyzstan	–	–	–	140	–	–	–	–	–	–
Republic of Moldova	–	–	–	–	30	30[c]	–	–	–	–
Russian Federation	–	8	75	1 205[d]	1 085	1 000	85	3 795	1 180	2 615[b]
Total above	1 494	6 341	3 662	7 929	9 770	4 352	5 418	6 616	2 434	4 181
of which:										
Bonds	1 250	5 751	2 445	4 120	4 352	4 352	..	2 434	2 424	..
Bank loans[e]	244	590	1 217	3 809	5 418	..	5 418	4 181	..	4 181
Memorandum item:										
Eastern Europe, Baltic and CIS countries' share of funds raised globally (*per cent*)[f]	0.33	1.01	0.55	0.94	0.92	0.61	1.57	..	..	..

Source: UN/ECE secretariat based on press reports; OECD, *Financial Statistics Monthly*, Part I (Paris), April 1997 and previous issues.

Note: Funds are recorded as of the date on which the deal was signed.

[a]   Preliminary.

[b]   Includes a $2,500 million loan to Gazprom and a $115 million loan to JSC Nizhnekamsbneftekhim of the Republic of Tatarstan.

[c]   Floating rate note, private placement.

[d]   Includes a $320 million convertible bond converted to equity in April 1996.

[e]   International bank loans in Eurocurrencies and in domestic currency of lending countries, excluding guaranteed loans and rescheduled debt.

[f]   As a share of bonds, syndicated loans and other debt facilities.

47

TABLE 5
Net capital flows into eastern Europe, the Baltic countries and the European members of the CIS, by type of capital, 1994-1996
(Billion dollars)

| | Eastern Europe | | | | | Baltic states | | | | European CIS[a] | | | |
| | | | Jan.-Sept. | | | | | Jan.-Sept. | | | | Jan.-Sept. | |
	1994	1995	1995	1996	1996[b]	1994	1995	1995	1996	1994	1995	1995	1996
Capital account	9.0[c]	21.5	13.7	7.5	13.1	0.9	1.5	1.0	0.7	2.1	2.2	1.2	1.1
Capital account[d]	8.7[c]	24.0	14.8	9.4	15.4	0.4	1.1.	0.6	1.1	2.4	2.4	1.9	1.6
of which:													
FDI	3.3	9.1	4.1	4.8	7.1	0.5	0.5	0.4	0.3	0.2	0.3	0.2	0.4
Portfolio	3.0	4.7	3.5	0.7	0.6	–	–	–	-0.1	–	–	–	0.1
Medium-, long-term funds	2.0	5.4	3.4	0.9	3.4	0.4[e]	0.5	0.3	0.4	1.2	–	-0.2	0.2
Short-term funds	0.9[c]	4.5	4.2	1.3	1.8	..	0.6	0.4	0.1	0.3	0.4	0.2	0.1
Errors and omissions	-0.2	2.4	1.1	1.9	2.3	-0.5	-0.4	-0.3	0.4	0.3	0.2	0.7	0.6

Source: UN/ECE secretariat estimates, based on national statistics.

[a]   Belarus, Republic of Moldova and Ukraine.

[b]   January-September for Albania and Bulgaria; January-November for Slovakia.

[c]   Excluding for Poland non-classified current account items estimated at $1.7 billion in 1994.

[d]   Including errors and omissions and excluding valuation effects for Poland.

[e]   Includes short-term funds.

TABLE 6
Foreign direct investment into eastern Europe, the Baltic countries and the CIS, 1994-1996

Reporting country	Net flows[a] (million dollars)			Net flows[a] per capita[b] (dollars)		Net flows[a] /GDP (per cent)		Cumulative FDI end-1996[c]	
	1994	1995	1996	1995	1996	1995	1996	Million dollars	Per capita[b]
Eastern Europe	3 403	9 073	7 253	84	67	2.9	2.2	30 459	282
Albania	53	70	76[d]	20	21	2.9	2.9	277	77
Bulgaria	105	98	134	12	16	0.8	1.4	452	54
Croatia	98	81	354	17	75	0.4	1.9	623	132
Czech Republic	842[e]	2 526	1 388	244	134	5.4	2.7	7 371	712
Hungary	1 097	4 410	1 986	431	194	10.1	4.5	13 377	1 307
Poland	542	1 134	2 741	29	71	1.0	2.1	5 492	142
Romania	341	417	210	18	9	1.2	0.6	1 184	52
Slovakia	170	157	178	29	33	0.9	0.9	858	160
Slovenia	131	170	180	85	90	0.9	1.0	786	393
The FYR of Macedonia	30	9	6	4	3	0.3	0.2	39	19
Baltic states	535	518	496	67	64	3.7	3.0	1 820	237
Estonia	225	202	58[d]	136	39	5.6	1.4	752	507
Latvia	279	245	285	98	114	5.5	5.6	770	308
Lithuania	31	72	152	19	41	1.2	2.1	298	80
European CIS	808	2 046	2 618	9	13	0.5	0.5	9 507	44
Belarus	9	15	16[d]	1	2	0.1	0.1	57	6
Republic of Moldova	12	64	36	15	8	3.8	2.3	112	25
Russian Federation	636	1 711	2 158	11	14	0.5	0.5	8 092	54
Ukraine	151	257	408[d]	5	8	0.7	0.9	1 245	24
Total above	4 746	11 637	10 366	35	31	1.6	1.2	41 786	125
Asian CIS	783	1 596	..	6	..	4.2	..	..	..
Armenia	3	19	..	5	..	1.5	..	22[f]	6[f]
Azerbaijan	22	155	..	22	..	6.4	..	176[f]	25[f]
Georgia	8	6	..	1	..	0.3	..	18[f]	3[f]
Kazakstan	519	859	884	50	54	5.1	5.0	2 591	150
Kyrgyzstan	45	191	..	41	..	12.8	..	245[f]	53[f]
Tajikistan	12	13	..	2	..	2.2	..	42[f]	7[f]
Turkmenistan	103	233	..	57	..	7.8	..	415[f]	101[f]
Uzbekistan	72	120	..	5	..	1.2	..	280[f]	13[f]

Source: UN/ECE secretariat Foreign Investment Database, based on national balance of payments statistics. For the Asian CIS (except Kazakstan), The World Bank, *Statistical Handbook 1996, States of the Former USSR* (Washington, D.C.), 1996.

[a] Cash basis; FDI in reporting country less its FDI abroad.

[b] Dollars per capita.

[c] Cumulative foreign direct investment in reporting countries from 1988, balance of payments cash basis, end of period.

[d] Annualized rate (January-September).

[e] Excluding flows between the Czech Republic and Slovakia.

[f] 1995.

RUSSIAN EXTERNAL ECONOMIC RELATIONS: PROBLEMS AND PROSPECTS

Valery Oknyansky

Counsellor, Economic Cooperation Department, Ministry of Foreign Affairs, Moscow

Foreign Trade

Looking at the Russian economic landscape today one can observe various contradictary trends. Among the most visible signs of progress is the recovery of the external sector. Notwithstanding the dramatic fall in production, the breakdown of past trade ties and the collapse of traditional trade arrangements over the last few years, foreign trade turnover has been steadily increasing mainly due to the implementation of economic reforms which have resulted in Russia's transition to an open market economy, the liberalisation of price and currency exchange systems, and the restoration of financial stability.

However, the growth rate of Russian foreign trade fell substantially in 1996, although total volume reported at US$150bn (including private trade) was 7% up against 1995. Exports accounted for US$85.5bn and imports amounted to US$64.5bn. As always, trade statistics must be viewed with some caution, but it is evident that Russia witnessed a strong growth in exports of 8.7% while imports declined by 2% following two years of increase. As a result, the 1996 trade surplus grew to a level much higher than that recorded in 1995. Paradoxically, this trend, which in general looks favorable, is connected with some negative features of the present economic situation in Russia. For example, the appreciation of the rouble made some goods uncompetitive on the World market, but their exports continued to increase mainly because of the depressed domestic market. Regarding energy, high World prices increased the dollar value of what in quantative terms were static exports. Low consumer demand, caused in part by wage arrears, has adversely affected imports despite the strengthening rouble. Indeed, exports represented some 20% of GDP in 1996 against only 4% in 1991, but this is more a reflection of the collapse in domestic production than of any real achievement in the external sector.

Regarding the qualitative aspect of Russian foreign trade, there have unfortunately been no essential changes in its commodity structure. Oil, oil products and gas made up the largest input in export value growth, and now account for 46% of Russian exports (1996). About half the oil and more than 30% of the gas produced in Russia in 1996 have been exported. Coal, iron ore and timber, in that order, are the next most prominent items of Russian exports. While the main part of Russian manufacturing industry continues to falter, the World market is encouraging the relatively rapid recovery of some export oriented sectors. This concerns not only mining industries but also non-ferrous metallurgy, the chemical industry and some others. About 70% of the output of the non-ferrous metallurgy industry was exported in 1996.

The only sign of real improvement in the structure of exports has been the intensification of Russian activities in the World **arms market**. In 1996, arms exports increased to US$3.3bn compared to US$2.3bn in 1992, whereas global arms exports declined from US$27bn to US$22bn during the same period. Correspondingly, Russia's share of the World arms trade rose from 8.5% to 15.7%. According to some estimates, it might reach some 25% in 1997 and draw closer to the USA whose share amounted to 36% in 1996.

This growth is likely to be stimulated by the fact that there are now 16 entities producing weapons and military equipment in Russia that have the right to operate independently in the foreign market, whereas before 1996, arms sales were the monopoly of just a single firm.

Imports, in spite of their fluctuation, accounted for more than 50% of domestic retail commodity circulation in 1996, about the same ratio as in 1995. Food imports are now estimated to be around 35-45% of total consumption. Such a high level of dependence creates some problems of national economic security. Machinery and equipment amounted to 30% of Russian imports in 1996 and rose to 37% in the first five months of 1997, a trend that will probably continue. After decades of isolation from World markets, many specialists now consider Russia to be a tremendous potential market for most goods and services. Demand is emerging in waves. First, in the early 1990s, came demand for food products. Relatively strong demand for consumer products followed. 1995 saw a surge in demand for construction materials, hotel and restaurant equipment, and furniture.

The hard currency-earning industries of oil and gas, mining and timber are the most promising sectors in Russia for the exporters of equipment and services. Significant opportunities also exist in long-term equipment sales to the coal industry. Although the quality of Russian building products is substantially lower than in the West, the price is just as high. As a result, Russian firms generally prefer to buy Western products. Demand is strong, driven by urban renovation. Commercial property (offices, banks, department stores, hotels and restaurants) are also a strong source of demand. Virtually all major Russian cities have embarked on urban construction projects to modernise and upgrade both residential and commercial property. These projects supplement private sector initiatives serving the same strong market demand. New large multi-story construction projects along with the renovation or demolition of old buildings are now commonplace in Moscow, St.Petersburg and other cities. Thus trade in self-erecting and mobile cranes, earth moving machinery, concrete trucks and pumping equipment will be much in deficit. In 1997, as Moscow geared up for its 850th anniversary, strong demand for construction equipment continued, although this demand could now shift to regional markets.

Over the last few years, the private sector has grown dramatically with a commensurate increase in car ownership. Liberalisation of foreign trade in the 1990s stimulated the flow of imported cars, 80% of which were used vehicles. To protect local automobile manufacturers, the Russian government has levied import duties of approximately 100%. It is likely, however, that these tariffs will be gradually reduced over the coming years, thereby stimulating demand for imported vehicles.

The Russian telecommunications market suffers from a lack of installed lines, outmoded switching equipment and inadequate revenues to finance investment. However, the cost of telecommunications equipment imported by Russia in 1995-1996 was over US$2bn. The Russian Ministry of Communications is dedicated to bringing the telecommunications infrastructure up to the international norm as quickly as possible, and many multinational firms are vying for the opportunity to participate in this undertaking.

The significant change in the geographic structure of Russian foreign trade which has been visible over the last two years has been the growth of the CIS countries' share to about 25%. Integration within the CIS is essential for Russia. In 1992-1994, Russian foreign trade with these countries nearly halved although it stabilised in 1995. In 1996, trade with the CIS grew by 6% reaching US$34.2bn, including US$16.5bn (+8%) exports from Russia and US$17.7bn (+4%) imports to Russia. This suggests a modest revival of economic ties between former Soviet states. In the past, Russia faced a serious problem of **trade imbalance** with CIS countries to the tune of about US$20-25bn each year. The resulting accumulated debt owed by CIS states to Russia had become a real obstacle to further trade development. But this imbalance was slightly reduced in 1996.

The European Union now dominates Russian foreign trade, amounting to 40% of total turnover. Russia's chief export market is Germany, which imports nearly twice as much as the next largest importer of Russian goods - China. Italy, the United Kingdom, Hungary, Japan and the United States, in descending order of importance, follow Germany and China as markets for Russian goods, predominately energy and raw materials. Official statistics for Q1 of 1997 confirm the above trends.

Balance of Payments Situation

Russia's consolidated current account in 1996 was in surplus for the fifth year in a row at US$9.3bn. The 1996 surplus reflected a US$21bn merchandise trade surplus, offset by a US$11.7bn deficit in non-merchandise trade.

The Russian Federation is a net importer of services - in 1996 imports more than doubled the value of exports. More than 80% of imported services into Russia were accounted for by three sectors: tourism (US$10bn against US$5.5bn exports), transportation and construction.

In 1996 Russia sustained a capital account deficit of US$5.2bn. Capital flight continues to plague the Russian economy although official data suggests that its rate has slowed significantly since the peak year of 1992. Assessments vary greatly, but a realistic figure for net capital outflows from Russia since the start of transition would be between US$60-80bn. It appears that little of this is related to criminal activity. Most represents a desire for safe havens abroad for foreign exchange earnings.

Foreign Trade Regulation Regime

Custom procedures are constantly being revised in Russia and need to be closely followed by trade partners. Most foreign trade is already regulated according to WTO rules and this has been confirmed by special treaties and agreements with some countries. For example, an agreement (on partnership and cooperation) was signed with the European Union in 1994 and ratified by Moscow in November 1996. But many Russian specialists feel that excessive haste in opening up the domestic market without any corresponding investment in Russian enterprises would create, indeed is creating, tremendous difficulties for the stimulation of economic growth and structural reform. This concerns many industries which are not yet ready for competition without state support because of their obsolete equipment and technology. The Russian authorities have also adopted an "import passport" system whereby an importer has 180 days either to document the entry of goods with the Russian Customs Service or return the hard currency issued in payment. This should help to stem the tide of illegal contracts for imports into Russia which results in capital flight.

Foreign Investment Environment

The enactment of foreign investment legislation is currently being completed in Russia. Its basic principles are oriented towards international norms and WTO procedures. Treaties relating to the encouragement and protection of investment as well as double taxation avoidance have been signed with more than 40 countries. With certain specific exceptions, the legal regime for foreign investors may not be less favorable than that for Russian legal entities and individuals. Foreign investments on the territory of the Russian Federation may be channeled into any business not prohibited by federal law. Certain types of activity are subject to licensing, such as insurance, banking and certain other services.

Government policy towards investment also covers foreign capital participation in the privatisation process and defense conversion, but with a few exemptions. Foreign investments in Russia are not subject to nationalisation, requisition or confiscation, except for cases which are specifically provided for under Russian legislation. After the payment of the appropriate taxes and duties, foreign investors are guaranteed by law unhindered transfer abroad of profits, dividends, interest, license fees and commissions.

Because of limited national financial resources, the volume of investments in Russia in 1996 fell by 18% compared with 1995 and amounted to only 30% of such investment in 1991. But the average age of fixed assets in Russia is now 35 years and the Russian economy needs approximately US$350bn just to finance the replacement of obsolete equipment. Russia's large domestic market, its vast supply of national resources, its skilled labour force and finally its proximity to CIS markets should enable it to attract considerable foreign investment. But while foreign direct investment in Russia has by far outpaced investment in other CIS States, the level is still low when compared with foreign direct investment in Eastern Europe. In 1996, per capita total foreign direct investment in Russia amounted to US$14 against about US$200 in neighbouring Poland.

Estimates of foreign direct investment in Russia vary widely due mainly to company confidentiality and the relative lack of definitive means to establish actual cash inflows. At the end of 1996, officials estimated total cumulative direct investment in Russia to be US$7bn, with US$2.1bn coming into the country during 1996 itself. About 50% of 1995-1996 foreign investment was accounted for by four sectors: trade, finance, the food industry and energy. In the previous two years, the energy sector held a much more dominant role in investment, accounting for 44% of total foreign investment in 1994. The ascendancy of investment in other industrial sectors can be interpreted as a positive sign that the economy is becoming more diversified and less reliant on the extraction of natural resources.

Since the break-up of the Soviet Union, the US is clearly the leading foreign investor in Russia accounting for about 30% of the total. The US is followed by Switzerland with 15% and Germany with 10%. Opinions differ as to which countries are the next most prominent investors, but generally include France, South Korea, Japan, the UK and Italy. Moscow, St.Petersburg and their respective hinterlands are the areas receiving the largest amounts of foreign money. There are more than 15,000 joint ventures in Russia, of which about 45% operate in trade, 22% in industry and 10% in construction.

Free Economic Zones

Russian customs legislation permits the creation of free customs zones and free warehouses within which foreign goods may be placed without customs duties and taxes being levied and from which goods may be exported to third countries. The territory of free zones and warehouses is considered as being outside the customs territory of the Russian Federation. Between 1990-1996, the federal authorities decided to establish some 20 zones with special regimes for doing business, including foreign trade privileges. However, these privileges granted by various regulations were not always subsequently confirmed by Russian tax, customs and currency legislation. The draft Law of the Russian Federation on Free Economic Zones is under consideration in the State Duma.

National debt

Russia maintains a substantial foreign debt which amounted to about US$135-140bn at the beginning of 1997. Approximately US$103bn of this debt has been inherited from the Soviet Union while the remainder has accumulated since 1991. Russia's chief creditor is Germany which holds roughly 40% of outstanding foreign debt. In April 1996, the Paris Club of official creditors agreed to reschedule Russia's outstanding stock of sovereign debt (more than US$40bn) over 25 years. This agreement is subject to periodic reviews which are tied to performance under the IMF program. In May 1996, the London Club of commercial bank creditors reached an agreement in principle with the Russian government to reschedule US$32.5bn in debt. The agreement calls for principal to be repaid over 25 years with a seven-year grace period. The corresponding agreements with Germany, the US, France and Switzerland were signed last year. These structural improvements have lightened the re-payment load of outstanding Russian debt and given Russian firms the ability to tap into international capital markets.

Some other countries (such as Cuba, Mongolia, Vietnam, India, Syria and Libya) are in debt to Russia. The total amount is estimated to be some US$150bn. Thus, on paper at least, Russia still retains its position as a net creditor and as such could participate in the activities of the Paris Club.

CURRENT STATUS OF EAST-WEST TRADE WITHIN INTERNATIONAL TRADE

Ferry de Kerckhove

Director General, Planning Secretariat, DFAIT, Ottawa

(The views expressed below are those of the author and should not be construed as representing the official view of the Government of Canada).

As a former member of NATOs Economics Committee in the early eighties, it is a pleasure for me to return to the fold. The title of this panel is wide ranging, so this paper will focus more on linkages than on the statistical dimension of the current state of East-West trade within the international trading World.

The first key question to address is what are the broad structures of international trade within which East-West trade occurs. In that respect, Economies in Transition (ETs) are clearly facing a rough ride. They are coming of age precisely at a time when economic capacity and knowledge are the defining elements of international standing. Trade continues to be the engine of global economic growth and competitiveness is the ultimate law for making it or not. Furthermore, the multilateral system as seen from the perspective of ETs is somewhat in a state of flux. In certain parts of the World there is a surfeit of institutions; in others there is a dearth. It so happens that ETs belong mostly to an area where the nexus of institutions is the most complex of all regions and where economic and security variables are deeply intertwined. Furthermore, new players with new weights are emerging and the key for ETs is to determine which model to follow and which group to belong to. Geography doesn't necessarily tell the tale.

Whether ETs like it or not, East-West economic relations, including reform efforts, take place within the broad international context of globalisation, the G word, and that World is also a multi-power centered one, marked by an information revolution. This is a lot to adjust to for ETs which are indeed facing, as we are, the emergence of worldwide markets for technology, investment, production, distribution and consumption, including global capital markets and the growing power of multinational enterprises and non-governmental organisations (remember that Greenpeace's budget is twice that of UNEP). ETs are not ready for it and the question is: can they catch up?

On the more intangible side, ETs are slowly moving away from the remnants of an imposed ideology only to face an emerging global information infrastructure and, relatedly, the global spread of a value system which takes little account of local differences, past histories, and national pride. "McWorld" is neither a fad nor a fiction but stark reality. For those new economies emerging from the economic dark ages of "Communist" Central and Eastern Europe, aspiring to both "renewal" and respect for their cultural traditions, it leaves a lot to be desired.

To reap the benefits of globalisation - for not trying to do so for autarchic/ideological reasons, as perhaps in Russia, is not an option unless ETs wish to be left out of the process of economic transformation - ETs need to open up to the World which leaves them extremely vulnerable to pressures from the outside.

A variable, often forgotten, is the human dimension. Citizen insecurity in ETs is one of the most pervasive results of the Brave New World they have entered. We have seen the dangers and risks of this process of cultural transition: ethnic and cultural nationalism, feelings of marginalisation, and a fertile ground for ethnic conflict and even persecution of minorities. The events in the former Yugoslavia have also much to do with the results of the economic and societal transformations affecting Central and Eastern Europe. The profound upheaval in these societies is also cause for the growing and devastating potential for crime, drugs and related ills which know no frontier but seem to prefer certain borders over others.

How much "wild capitalism" is too much? I must quote here - he will forgive me for my skepticism - the reassuring comment made to me one day by Alexander Maximovitch Yakovlev, a well known lawyer and one time go-between President Yetsin and the Russian Duma on legislative matters: "wild capitalism is a necessary evil in a transitory stage until such time as Russians discover that ownership requires law and order to defend property". There has been more wildness than true capitalism for quite a long while. And in the meantime, import substitution, capital export, or more precisely capital flight, transfer pricing and unbridled selling of natural resources seem to be the bedrock of Russia's trade surpluses while former Comecon countries are slowly moving from semi-manufactured to unsophisticated manufacturing. **How** competitive will they be over the long run in **what** markets remains to be seen.

So where are we today or how did we get here? For Central and Eastern European economies the answer is most likely slower than expected and worse than could be imagined.

My three years in Moscow have probably given me a Russian bias, both favourable and also probably more critical. The following analysis will therefore reflect more my perception of how things went in Russia than elsewhere although we all know how it started. The theory had it that shock therapy would stop hyper-inflation, cure budget deficits and initiate the start of structural reform. The result of the process would be first an induced recession which would eventually bottom out and lead to real transformation.

Five elements were involved in the key decision tree of the neophyte economists of ETs:
   * price liberalisation;
   * balanced budgets;
   * tight monetary policy;
   * tight wage policy;
   * foreign trade liberalisation.

The latter called for the ending of export and import licences, the freeing of enterprises who would then be allowed to engage in foreign trade, tariffs cuts or reductions to expose domestic production to competition abroad, limited convertibility to ease up foreign trade operations, and although this may sound a bit brutal, pegging the currency to black market rates, something which was much more effective as an instrument in Russia than the horse-riding militia trying to pick-up money changers on the streets. There was to be of course a strong correlation between price liberalisation and meeting the challenge of competition abroad. Domestic monopolies were no longer to be protected. World prices would be assumed to be able to correct the deficiencies of the previous import price structure and the new shape of exchange rates would deter imports. At least that was the theory.

Fundamentally at issue in Russia, during my time there, was the political credibility of shock therapy. Close seconds were the management of the correlation between privatisation and price liberalisation, inter-enterprise debt, and taxation - or more precisely, the size of the tax base. While it is gratifying to agree with Madame Bérard that privatisation is an irreversible process and to note that in Russia it has gone further than in any other economy in transition, the system has not entirely adjusted to the process, if at all. In three years in Moscow from 1992 to 1995, I don't recall having ever seen a major bankruptcy despite the debt overhang affecting so many and despite the shaking down which should have followed privatisation.

The results for all ETs, as World Bank statistics show, can be characterized as "the good, the bad and the ugly". My diplomatic status prevents me from drawing a list under each heading. Clearly I would not want to define a new "Nomenklatura".

What is interesting is that of all the macroeconomic stabilisation measures taken, external balancing appears to have been the most successful. Indeed, in the beginning, ETs exports to the West increased and a good chunk of exports formerly going to the CMEA region as a share of total exports were being redirected toward the West. Trade balances and current account balances improved. However, since 1993, some opposite trends have appeared quite extensively in ET countries. The reasons are complex. There was excessive devaluation in the beginning and the real value of currencies, even today, is still an issue as long as the rate of depreciation and the changes in the price levels are not stabilised. Furthermore, in Russia there was such a dollarisation of the economy that price levels were profoundly distorted. I recall that, at some stage, it was hard to find roubles in Russia. And the story has it that, at the time, there was some US$20bn in cash in the Russian economy.

The other reason for the worsening of trade balances is related to what Marie Lavigne, the well known specialist on Central and Eastern European economies, calls "Distress Exports" which could not be sustainable over the long run. Indeed, the future of the export capacity of ETs is very much in question particularly in sensitive sectors like textiles, agriculture and steel products. Finally, foreign debt constitutes a major overhang which is not helped by the reluctance of ETs to accept sovereign guaranties. It is amazing that some ETs have either not understood or not accepted the consequences of the fact that the most important variable for transition/transformation is **investment**, both foreign and domestic. Although privatisation is an irreversible process in ETs, it has not led everywhere, particularly in Russia, to the kind of investments expected, whether with or through foreign capital beefing-up existing production units or with foreign investment replacing existing structures.

So the issue of ETs being poised to reintegrate or, in the case of Russia, to integrate fully into the World economy is still very much out there. Or put differently, it is still more a theology than a fact despite recent remarkable progress in some countries like Poland. I think some of the ideological underpinnings of the great rush to the West by the ETs need some sober rethinking. There is an assumption out there that joining Western institutions is not only the ultimate panacea but that it is necessarily an accepted holistic proposition. I wish to unscore that **preferential security** treatment in the post Cold War world does not mean automatic **preferential economic** treatment.

I am aware that it sounds irritating for ETs to be told not to give up former trading linkages among themselves and with Russia entirely. Of course, at present, that trade is collapsing and the Central European reorientation of its trade toward the West appears irreversible. Yet the integration drive is very much a political process and ETs should be alert to the fact that the economic reality check will hit, notably in the sensitive areas I mentioned earlier.

During recent trilateral consultations with my counterparts in Poland and Ukraine I underlined the fact that the "merchants of Venice" would be guided by their economic interests which will not necessarily coincide with the political aspirations of countries from Central and Eastern Europe. The question of the relevancy of the CIS also needs to be answered. Trade is growing but the institutionalisation of the CIS seemed to be either faulty or scaring away potential partners. The existence of a rouble zone may not be readily accepted but it is a fact; and maybe it would help if that was appreciated for its economic virtues rather than for political implications drawn of the scarecrow variety. Now, in the West, we too need to get our act together. We are both critical of the CIS when we try to see in it some kind of reconstitution of the USSR as if that were possible, but at the same time we encourage the deepening of intra-CIS and Central and East European trade. It is high time that we recognize that economics are somewhat more relevant today than past anguish on security grounds. Russia's "strategic partnership" with China may have as a political goal "keeping Washington honest", but it is clearly driven much more by the economic imperative. Old bonds die hard. While Russia is more advanced in terms of privatising its former public sector compared to China's huge, bloated, and inefficient public enterprise system, China can help in terms of economic zones and reform.

There are also some very useful series of agreements with the European Union, including EU Association Agreements, Partnership Agreements, Trade Agreements and also EFTA Arrangements. There has been some very good relief in terms of quantitative restrictions and tariffs but it remains to be seen when the limit will be reached in the area of sensitive products such as agriculture, textiles, coal and steel products. The European Union is going through a major period of adjustment and implementation of its own remarkable commitments and one should ask honestly whether economics can catch up with politics. EU enlargement is not a panacea, neither is it a done deal and my fear is that while so much effort is focussed by ETs on the enlargement of the EU, there is the train of globalisation out there which may be leaving the station. When and where Central and East European ETs wish to board is to be decided soon. I am aware of, and admire, the commitment of West European leaders to making enlargement happen. I am also profoundly sensitive to the fact that the negotiations will be very long and arduous and that our East and Central European friends should not necessarily be wedded to a timetable because they might be sorely disappointed. They also need to look at the broader world and see if, beyond Europe, there are further synergies that might work.

EVALUATION OF STRUCTURAL CHANGES IN POLISH INDUSTRY AND IN FOREIGN CAPITAL FLOW TO POLAND IN THE PERIOD OF SYSTEMIC TRANSFORMATION

Zofia Wysokinska

Advisor to the Minister of the Economy and Institute of Economics, University of Lodz, Poland

Programme of industrial policy in Poland

The programme of industrial policy prepared by the Polish Ministry of Industry and Trade for the years 1995-1997 under the title of *International Competitiveness of Polish Industry* lays stress on three essential directions of action: **export promotion policy** aimed at accelerating the rate of economic growth, **technological policy** intended to raise the technological level in industry and finally a **policy of structural changes** both to boost the commercialisation and privatisation of enterprises, and to make changes in the structure of industry in regions with high industrial concentration and with regard to enterprises' internal restructuring[1]. The growth of international competitiveness of Polish industry is also the main strategic goal of Poland's industrial policy until the year 2010; this goal will be achieved thanks to gains in innovativeness, entrepreneurship and efficiency in the economic sphere with simultaneous respect for the principles of durable development[2].

Both of the above-mentioned programmes take into account the World Bank's approach which stresses the maintenance of economic growth and improving the international competitiveness of firms as the fundamental goals of structural policy[3]. Besides the macroeconomic aspects of economic stabilisation and liberalisation of the economy, the Bank's approach also stresses the need to limit structural policy to suprasectoral (horizontal) tools in such areas as technology, export promotion and the creation of favourable conditions for the development of small and medium-sized enterprises[4].

The approach taken by the World Bank and the European Commission differs from the industrial policy pursued in the countries of South East Asia in the 1970s and 1980s; the latter having the following main conditions necessary to achieve structural adjustment:
* the creation of investment funds to gain durable economic growth;
* the need to pursue a long-term industrial policy that promotes targeted industries;
* the creation of funds to promote infant industries;
* the need to allow for the specific national features of a reforming economy, in particular its stage of economic development[5].

The programme of industrial policy *International Competitiveness of Polish Industry* adopted by the government on 16 May 1995 is based on the horizontal approach of the World Bank, but adjusted to suit the present-day external determinants in the form of international commitments (WTO/UE/OECD). Nevertheless, it is hard to negate the efficacy of the methods of industrial policy applied chiefly in the 1970s in South-East Asia, especially in the context of the high rates of economic growth, of export growth, and of FDI inflows to target industries that contributed to the enhanced standing of these countries in the World economy.

Changes in the structure of industry by intensity of use of production factors in the period 1992-1995

Introduction

This paper presents the results of analysis carried out to examine the structural changes which took place in Polish industry, foreign trade and the structure of foreign capital flows from the viewpoint of whether these changes had a favourable impact on the growth of competitiveness of the economy and of industry in particular.

The analysis of the changes taking place in the structure of industry (regarding sales, employment and financial results) was conducted according to the European Classification of Activity (EKD) used in Poland since 1993. To get comparable statistics on industry in 1992 expressed according to the Classification of the National Economy, these statistics were converted into EKD in accordance with the binding "conversion key". Also, the EKD was used to analyse changes in the structure of foreign capital flowing into Poland in the form of foreign direct investment.

Structural changes in foreign trade were analysed in accordance with the Standard International Trade Classification (SITC) used by the UN. In accordance with the theory of international trade, the assumption was taken that a "shift" in the structure from resource-intensive products to labour- and next capital- intensive products to products with a higher technology input can constitute a trend favourable to the growth of competitive exports by a given country[6].

Changes in the structure of sales

The share of resource-intensive sectors decreased (by about 7%) in favour of an increase (by about 1.5%) in the share of sectors turning out standard products using basic technology and in favour of technology-intensive sectors based on supplies of components (by 1%) and on technologies at a higher innovation degree (by about 4%). Labour-intensive sectors kept their position in the structure of industry in the analysed period of time, increasing their share slightly (by 0.5%). Changes in the structure of the above-mentioned sectors of industry should be evaluated as positive especially owing to the drop in the share of resource-intensive sectors and growth in importance of sectors with a higher level of technology.

Changes in the structure of industrial employment

Resource-intensive sectors as well as technology-intensive sectors based on technologies at a higher level of innovation recorded drops in their shares of employment (by 2.0% and 1.7% respectively) in favour of an increase in the share of labour-intensive sectors (by 3.4%) and a minimal increase in technology-intensive based mainly on supplies of components (by 3%). Sectors producing standard products based on mature technology kept their share in the structure of employment at a steady level (16.6%) throughout the entire examined period. In general, the growth in the share of technology-intensive sectors in the structure of sales with a simultaneous decline in their share of employment can be regarded as a positive tendency because it may indicate an increase in labour productivity. The reverse, less favourable trend is observed in the case of labour-intensive sectors.

Changes in the structure of exports

In the years between 1992 and 1995, the following changes were recorded in the structure of total Polish exports of goods and in exports to major buyers, i.e. to the European

Union, Central and Eastern Europe and the former USSR, CEFTA, EFTA and developing countries including newly industrialised countries of South East Asia:

* Total exports recorded a fall of over 10% in the share of resource-intensive products and of 1% in the share of capital-intensive products in favour of an increase in the share of labour-intensive products (by over 12%);

* Exports to the EU and EFTA recorded structural change trends similar to those in total trade (see **Table 1**). Additionally - which should be noted as a positive development - the share of high-level technology-intensive products rose by over 2% in 1995 in comparison with 1994 (see **Table 2**).

* Exports to Central and Eastern Europe and to the CIS recorded trends similar to those in total exports. The fact that the share of high-level technology-intensive products lowered considerably in 1995 (by over 3% in comparison with 1993) should be recorded as a negative tendency, and simultaneously there was a considerable growth in the value of exports to that region.

* Exports to CEFTA had a greater drop in the share of resource-intensive products than the drop in Poland's total exports in favour of an increase in the share of labour-intensive goods and a small increase (of about 2%) in the share of capital-intensive products.

* Exports to developing countries recorded a reverse tendency in the case of resource-intensive products compared with total exports, for these products increased their share by about 1%. This increase was especially notable in exports to newly industrialised countries of South East Asia (by about 4%). In 1994-1995, both high- and low- level technology-intensive goods increased their share slightly in comparison with 1992-1993 (see **Table 2**). This growth was most conspicuous in Polish exports to Asian NICs in 1995 - up from the level of 8.15% in 1994 to 18.72% in 1995 (see **Table 2**).

Changes in the structure of exports by companies with foreign capital participation

Exports by companies with foreign capital participation reached the level of US$ 4,716.3m, or 20% of total Polish exports. As for the share of total imports, these firms exceeded 30%. Almost 80% of these exports and 70% of these imports were to the EU. The structure of exports by firms with foreign capital is dominated by labour-intensive products (over 46% and their share was steadily rising in the analysed years). Technology-intensive goods increased their share by over 3% in 1995 in comparison with 1994 - which should be noted as a positive development - while resource- and capital-intensive products recorded falls by over 2% and 3% respectively (see **Table 3**).

Changes in the structure of foreign direct investment flows

The structure of cumulative flows of FDI into Poland - which reached US$6,832.2m spread over 362 firms with capital exceeding US$1m - recorded the following trends in the years 1992-1995:

* Since 1991 there has been a tendency towards a steady increase in foreign direct investment in labour-intensive branches (from 13% at the beginning of 1992 up to 25% in 1995) which is in accordance with the attraction of foreign capital to areas in which Poland has a so-called relative comparative advantage in exports against industrialised market economies resulting mainly from lower labour costs;

* The share of foreign investment in sectors with advanced technology fell in the analysed period to a level of about 25%, but this was accompanied by a fivefold

increase in the volume of investment flow to these sectors (from the level of US$355m at the beginning of 1992 to US$1,643m by the end of 1994);

* In 1995, nearly half of all FDI was located in labour- and technology- intensive sectors, about 11% in capital intensive sectors characterised by a high share of standard, undifferentiated production, about 8% was concentrated in resource-intensive sectors, whilst the remaining 30% or so was placed in the service sector, mainly in finance (about 28%) and in trade and distribution of products (over 4%) - see **Table 4**.

Summing up

Changes which occurred in the structure of sales, exports and FDI flow between 1992 and 1995 can be evaluated as positive although slow, for they are characterised by a decrease in the share of resource-intensive sectors characteristic of less developed economies. By contrast, the almost 30% share attributable to labour intensive sectors remained constant whilst an increase of over 35% in total exports and of 44% in exports to the EU - now Poland's main trading partner - occurred. This is in line with Poland's comparative advantage resulting from its lower labour costs in comparison with those in developed market economies.

The fact that sectors turning out the so-called technology-intensive products increased their share in the structure of sales in 1995 should also be evaluated as positive. A similar increase in the share of these products was also revealed in the structure of Polish exports mainly to the EU, EFTA and CEFTA and to Asian NICs. The above structural changes do not ensure the competitiveness of Polish exports of technology-intensive goods to Western Europe, CEFTA and to Asian NICs, but if this trend were continued, they may become a factor conducive to achieving this goal in the future. An essential impact on the structural changes in exports was exerted by companies with foreign capital which almost doubled the value of their exports of technology-intensive goods in 1995 compared with 1994.

Foreign direct investment was located mainly in labour- and technology- intensive sectors. Firms with FDI accounted for over 20% of Polish exports and for 30% of total imports.

A relatively high share of foreign investment in technology-intensive branches may have a positive impact on the structure of industry in the future and may also lead towards growth in the share of technology intensive products in the structure of exports by firms with foreign capital participation. The growth in the share of products with higher advanced technology occurred also in exports to Western Europe, CEFTA and Asian NICs in 1995, a favourable trend should it continue.

Changes in the structure of production, exports and flow of foreign capital may be evaluated as favourable for the growth in competitiveness of industry, although these changes are still insufficient to ensure this goal in the near future. Such changes should be accompanied by a tendency towards the intensive growth of Poland's share in the international division of labour (mainly world trade) - this share was a mere 0.5% in 1995 compared with an even lower figure of 0.42% in 1992. These figures compare unfavourably with the late 1970s and early 1980s when Poland's share was about 1%, itself an unsatisfactory level given Poland's development capacity.

Table 1
Structural changes in industry in 1992-1995 by use intensity of production factors

Factor of production/Sectors	Year	Proceeds from sales (PLZ million)	Share %	Net financial result (PLZ million)	Gross financial result (PLZ million)	Employment (thousands of persons)	Share %
Labour-intensive food products, beverages, tobacco, fabrics, clothing, furs, leather, leather goods, footwear, jewellery, musical instruments, sports goods, games and toys, waste processing.	1992	27427.7	28.0	-616.0	167.9	990	29.4
	1993	33775.5	26.3	-664.4	223.7	1073	32.2
	1994	47286.0	28.2	236.9	1305.4	1039	32.2
	1995	66249.3	28.5	620.5	1743.9	1067	32.8
Resource-intensive coal mining, peat extraction, petroleum and natural gas, uranium and metal ore mining, other mining, wood and wood products, cellulose pulp, paper and paperboard, coal and coke products, oil refining, nuclear fuels, furniture, supply of electricity, gas and water	1992	35997.8	36.7	-279.5	1481.1	846	25.1
	1993	48408.3	37.7	230.5	2280.9	791	23.8
	1994	63008.7	37.6	2192.9	4279.0	762	23.6
	1995	69407.1	29.9	1575.0	3236.6	752	23.1
Standard products based on mature technology products from paper and paperboard, publishing, products from non-metallic materials, metals production, metal end-products	1992	13278.7	13.6	-737.7	-47.6	561	16.6
	1993	16597.3	12.9	-353.5	344.1	547	16.4
	1994	23784.2	14.3	262.5	1040.1	532	16.6
	1995	35065.9	15.1	1429.0	2571.2	539	16.6
Technology-intensive sectors based on component supplies artificial fibres, products from rubber and plastic, electrical machinery and equipment (except lighting), motor vehicles parts	1992	7012.8	7.1	-442.9	-140.5	263	7.8
	1993	10568.8	8.2	-232.3	78.2	255	7.7
	1994	12451.0	7.4	80.5	484.8	255	7.9
	1995	18778.4	8.1	438.6	843.0	262	8.1
Technology-intensive sectors based on innovative technology chemicals and chemical products, mechanical machinery and equipment, office machinery and computers, lighting equipment, radio, television and communications equipment, musical instruments, specialised and optical equipment, clocks and watches, motor vehicles, other transport equipment	1992	14365.5	14.6	-1061.3	-299.1	713	21.1
	1993	19118.1	14.9	-1202.2	-278.2	661	19.9
	1994	20940.1	12.5	420.8	1262.7	634	19.7
	1995	42620.9	18.4	942.5	2099.1	629	19.4

Source: Calculated on the basis of official data of the Central Statistical Office according to the EuropeanClassification of Activity. The classification of products used in the table was based on the international project sponsored by the Commission of the European Union under the ACE Programme 1993 "Foreign Direct Investment East-West".

Table 2
Commodity and geographical structure of Polish exports in 1992-1995 (%)

Commodity group	Year	World - total		Central and Eastern Europe and the former USSR				Developed countries								Developing countries			
				former USSR		CEFTA				European Union /12/		EFTA /7/		Non-European countries				NICs of the Far East	
		structure com.	geog.	structure com.	geog.	structure com.	geog.	structure com.	geog.	structure com.	geog.	structure com.	geog.	structure com.	geog.	structure com.	geog.	structure com.	geog.
Exports - total	1992	100	100	100	15.4	100	5.1	100	72.0	100	58.0	100	10.4	100	3.6	100	14.4	100	2.9
	1993	100	100	100	13.2	100	4.8	100	75.2	100	63.3	100	7.8	100	4.0	100	11.6	100	3.4
	1994	100	100	100	14.5	100	4.8	100	75.3	100	62.7	100	8.2	100	4.5	100	10.2	100	2.8
	1995	100	100	100	17.3	100	5.4	100	75.1	100	63.8	100	7.8	100	3.4	100	7.7	100	2.1
I. Resource-intensive	1992	32.7	100	43.8	20.6	41.1	6.4	31.6	69.7	31.1	55.3	38.0	12.0	21.7	2.4	22.0	9.7	5.1	0.4
	1993	25.2	100	30.8	16.1	37.5	7.2	25.2	75.2	23.7	59.6	40.6	12.6	18.2	2.9	18.7	8.6	3.1	0.4
	1994	24.1	100	34.1	20.5	34.5	6.8	22.9	71.5	21.4	55.7	35.4	12.0	20.8	3.9	19.0	8.0	5.1	0.6
	1995	22.5	100	35.9	27.6	30.0	7.2	19.4	64.7	18.3	51.8	27.7	9.6	22.0	3.3	22.9	7.8	9.1	0.8
II. Labour-intensive	1992	23.6	100	12.7	8.3	9.9	2.1	28.2	85.9	29.5	72.4	18.8	8.2	22.3	3.4	9.6	5.8	8.1	1.0
	1993	31.6	100	14.9	6.2	12.7	1.9	38.0	90.3	40.1	80.3	22.3	5.5	35.0	4.4	9.5	3.5	4.5	0.5
	1994	33.8	100	19.2	8.2	16.3	2.3	39.9	88.8	42.6	78.8	24.3	5.9	30.6	4.0	10.1	3.1	6.4	0.5
	1995	35.7	100	23.0	11.2	17.5	2.7	40.8	86.0	43.1	77.2	25.2	5.5	23.9	3.2	13.5	2.9	6.1	0.4
III. Capital-intensive	1992	20.4	100	14.8	11.2	25.4	6.3	19.6	69.2	20.5	58.1	16.2	8.2	17.0	3.0	28.0	19.7	59.8	8.3
	1993	21.4	100	19.5	12.0	25.8	5.8	18.8	66.1	18.8	55.8	22.1	8.1	11.9	2.2	40.2	21.9	72.0	11.3
	1994	21.1	100	19.9	13.6	24.0	5.4	19.6	69.9	19.5	58.1	21.0	8.2	17.3	3.7	34.1	16.5	72.5	9.5
	1995	19.6	100	17.9	15.8	27.9	7.7	19.1	73.3	19.2	62.6	21.1	8.2	13.2	2.3	28.0	10.9	53.5	5.7
IV. Technology-intensive (low-level)	1992	7.1	100	10.0	21.7	9.6	6.9	6.4	65.2	6.0	49.4	9.0	13.2	5.2	2.7	6.4	13.0	13.7	5.5
	1993	5.9	100	14.1	31.6	11.8	9.6	4.3	54.9	4.1	44.0	5.6	7.4	5.1	3.5	6.9	13.5	13.5	7.7
	1994	5.7	100	12.3	31.1	12.9	10.8	4.4	58.2	4.4	47.9	5.1	7.3	3.9	3.0	6.0	10.7	7.9	3.8
	1995	6.3	100	10.4	28.4	11.6	10.0	5.2	62.2	5.1	51.4	6.5	8.1	5.1	2.8	7.7	9.4	12.6	4.2
V. Technology-intensive (high-level)	1992	15.7	100	18.0	17.6	13.3	4.3	13.4	61.4	12.3	45.2	17.3	11.4	20.2	4.6	23.0	21.0	12.9	2.3
	1993	15.8	100	20.7	17.3	12.3	3.7	13.6	64.7	13.2	52.5	9.4	4.6	29.7	7.5	24.7	18.1	6.9	1.5
	1994	15.2	100	14.5	13.8	12.3	3.9	13.2	65.4	12.1	49.8	14.1	7.6	27.5	8.1	30.9	20.7	8.2	1.5
	1995	15.9	100	12.7	13.8	13.0	4.5	15.4	72.8	14.3	57.4	19.5	10.0	26.9	5.8	27.9	13.5	18.7	2.5

Note: Types of products: *(1) RESOURCE-INTENSIVE PRODUCTS*: food and live animals SITC 0, non-edible crude materials except textile materials SITC 2-26, fuels and lubricants excl. electricity SITC 3-35, edible oils and fats SITC 4, artificial fertilisers SITC 56; *(2) LABOUR-INTENSIVE PRODUCTS*: textile crude materials SITC 26, manufactured products at a lower processing level excl. rubber products, iron, steel and non-ferrous metals SITC 6-(62, 67, 68), other manufactured products excl. specialised equipment, lighting and optical equipment SITC (Rev.) 8-86, SITC (Rev. 2) 8-(87,88); *(3) CAPITAL-INTENSIVE PRODUCTS*: beverages and tobacco SITC 1, electricity SITC 35, dyes and tans SITC 53, essential oils and scent substances SITC 55, rubber products SITC 62, iron and steel SITC 67, non-ferrous metals SITC 68, road vehicles SITC. Rev. 732, 733, SITC (Rev. 2) 78, SITC (Rev. 3) 78; *(4) TECHNOLOGY-INTENSIVE PRODUCTS, LOW LEVEL*: organic chemicals SITC 51, inorganic chemicals SITC (Rev.) 51, SITC (Rev. 2) 52, SITC (Rev.3) 52, pharmaceutical and medicinal products SITC 54, resins, plastics SITC (Rev.) 58, SITC (Rev. 2) 58, SITC (Rev. 3) 57, 58, other chemical products SITC (Rev.) 59, SITC (Rev. 2) 59, SITC (Rev. 3) 59-593, office machines and computers SITC (Rev.) 714 ...

UCTS, **HIGH LEVEL**: explosives and pyrotechnic materials SITC (Rev. 2) 57, SITC (Rev. 3) 593, transport machinery and equipment excluding office machines and computers, telecommunications machines and equipment and road vehicles SITC (Rev.) 7-(714, 724, 732, 733), SITC (Rev. 2) 7-(75, 76, 78), SITC (Rev. 3) 7-(75, 76, 78), specialised equipment, optical equipment, clocks and watches SITC (Rev.) 86, SITC (Rev. 2) 87, 88, SITC (Rev. 3) 87, 88.
Source: Calculated on the basis of official data of the Central Statistical Office.

Table 3

Exports by companies with foreign capital participation in 1992-1995 (US$million)

Groups of products	Year	World - total	Central & Eastern Europe and former USSR	CEFTA	Developed countries				Developing countries	
						European Union /12/	EFTA /7/	Non-European countries		NICs of the Far East.
Exports - total	1994	2978.6	250.0	78.3	2650.7	2373.1	227.7	49.9	77.9	16.4
	1995	4716.4	466.7	130.7	4079.0	3665.8	338.5	74.7	170.7	26.3
I. Resource-intensive products	1994	496.3	73.1	23.0	393.6	331.9	39.1	22.6	29.6	9.1
	1995	685.2	153.0	37.4	487.6	420.7	40.0	26.9	44.6	2.6
II. Labour-intensive products	1994	1324.9	52.7	21.7	1257.1	1132.1	114.4	10.6	15.1	1.7
	1995	2198.2	129.1	33.7	2010.9	1834.0	154.8	22.1	58.2	4.6
III. Capital-intensive products	1994	716.5	74.5	16.3	634.5	591.1	42.1	1.3	7.5	0.8
	1995	992.1	94.7	28.4	885.0	809.9	73.9	1.2	12.4	0.8
IV. Technology-intensive products (low level)	1994	64.4	17.2	2.4	46.1	39.3	5.6	1.2	1.1	0.5
	1995	162.3	40.4	9.3	120.5	104.6	9.9	6.0	1.4	0.1
V. Technology-intensive products (high-level)	1994	376.5	32.5	14.9	319.4	278.7	26.5	14.2	24.6	4.3
	1995	678.6	49	21.9	575.0	496.6	59.9	18.5	54.1	18.2

Note: Classification of products as in Table 2.
Source: Calculated on the basis of official data of the Central Statistical Office.

Table 4

Structure of cumulated flow of foreign direct investment according to European Classification of Activities

Factor of production	End of 1991			End of 1992			End of 1993			End of 1994			End of 1995		
	Value in US$ million	Share in %	Number of firms	Value in US$ million	Share in %	Number of firms	Value in US$ million	Share in %	Number of firms	Value in US$ million	Share in %	Number of firms	Value in US$ million	Share in %	Number of firms
TOTAL	**1147.6**	**100**	**23**	**1705.6**	**100**	**78**	**2819.6**	**100**	**188**	**4320.8**	**100**	**267**	**6832.2**	**100**	**342**
1. Labour-intensive sectors	406.9	12	9	277.2	16	22	644.9	23	44	1058.1	25	72	1686.2	25	94
2. Resource-intensive sectors	122.7	14	2	169.7	10	8	288.3	10	17	371.8	9	18	565.3	8	2
3. Sectors of standard production based on mature technology	158.2	19	2	75.2	5	6	196.0	7	21	316.3	7	33	755.8	11	56
4. Technology-intensive sectors	354.7	42	7	576.8	34	17	836.2	29	36	1212.9	28	53	1642.9	24	66
4a. Technology-intensive sectors based on supplies of components	87.0	10	2	193.8	11	4	275.9	8	8	343.9	8	10	541.8	8	18
4b. Technology-intensive sectors based on innovative technology	267.7	32	5	383.0	23	13	560.3	21	13	869.0	20	28	1101.1	16	48
5. Services	105.1	12	3	602.6	36	21	774.8	28	47	1217.4	28	65	1886.2	28	89
5a. Financial services	1.5		1	342.7	20	13	374.1	13.5	17	812.1	19	23	1287.5	19	34
5b. Other services including construction	103.6	12	2	259.9	16	8	400.7	14.5	30	405.3	9	42	598.7	9	55
6. Investment in distribution, trade and real estate turnover				4.1		4	79.4	3	23	144.3	3	26	295.8	4	35

Note: Classification of sectors as in Table 1.

Source: Calculated on the basis of data of the Polish Agency for Foreign Investment

Footnotes

1. International Competitiveness of Polish Industry. The programme of Industrial Policy for the Year 1995-1997, Ministry of Industry and Trade, Warsaw, 1997.
2. Assumptions of the Strategy and Policy of Industry Development until the Year 2010, Ministry of Industry and Trade, Warsaw, October 1996.
3. World Development Report 1996, *From Plan to Market, The World Bank, Washington DC, 1996.*
4. As above.
5. T. Yanagihara, The Role of Structural Adjustment Policy and Remaining Tasks - In Search of a New Approach to Economic Development , the 6th Economic Co-operation Symposium Keynote Report , 23-24 Oct. 1995, pp. 13-18; T. Ozawa, Foreign Direct Investment and Economic Development, Transnational Corporations, 1992, vol. 1 no. 1.
6. Z. Wysokińska, Dynamic Interdependences of Foreign Trade in Central and eastern Europe in the Light of the Theory of Integration and International Trade, Lodz, 1995.

FOREIGN CAPITAL AS A FACTOR OF STRUCTURAL CHANGES IN THE POLISH ECONOMY

Janina Witkowska

Institute of Economics, University of Lodz, Poland

Introduction

Capital flows in the form of foreign direct investment (FDI) taking place between Central and Eastern Europe and the rest of the World are still insignificant in comparison with the flows between other regions of the World economy. The evaluation of the importance of FDI flowing into Central and Eastern Europe made through the prism of FDI influence on CEE economies may lead to divergent conclusions. One of the ways of examining the impact of FDI on the host country is to analyse the influence of FDI on such macroeconomic indices as endowment with factors of production (capital and know-how), productivity of factors of production, employment, GDP, proportions of income distribution, balance of trade and balance of payments. A thorough examination of the influence of FDI on the host economy goes beyond the scope of a short paper. For this reason my paper focuses on analysis of the relations between the flow of foreign capital in the form of FDI and structural changes in the Polish economy, and especially the structural changes in industry.

Evaluation of structural changes in the Polish economy : 1991-1996

At the threshold of the systemic changes, Poland recorded a dramatic fall in GDP. In spite of growth resuming in 1992, GDP in 1993 still did not reach its 1990 level. It was only in 1994 that GDP exceeded by 4.2% its 1990 level. In the following years growth continued. In 1995, GDP was 7% higher than in the preceding year and 11.5% higher than in 1990 (see **Table 1**). There arises the question as to whether the increase in GDP has been accompanied by desirable structural changes. It is difficult to evaluate the structural changes in Poland owing to the fact that the Polish Central Statistical Office introduced a new statistical classification, namely the European Classification of Activities, in 1994 which was part of the adjustment process to the requirements of the European Union. Only some of the data on the national economy in previous years were re-calculated according to the new classification. For this reason, the statistical data calculated according to the so-called National Economy Classification will be used for the early years of transformation whereas the following years (1992-1995) will be covered by the new classification (**Tables 2 and 3**). In spite of the limited comparability of the statistics, it is possible to evaluate the general trends occurring in the economy.

The analysis of the structure of GDP by branches of the national economy shows that certain changes occurred in 1990-1995. The share of industry in GDP went down in the analysed period from 43.6% in 1990 to 28.9% in 1995. The share of trade in GDP rose from about 13% in 1992 to 15% in 1993 but then fell to 13.1% in 1995. The share of construction in GDP, following a temporary increase at the beginning of the transformation process, decreased steadily in the years 1992-1995 (5.2% in 1995). The share of agriculture decreased slightly (6.6% in 1995 compared with 7.3% in 1990), as did the share of transport (2.9% in 1994 and 4.1% in 1990).

A more detailed analysis of the situation in industry in the surveyed period shows that the collapse of industrial production in the years 1989-1991 was particularly large (see **Table 4**). This downward trend was reversed in 1992 since when an increase in sales has been recorded. It should be noted that in the period of revival, the growth rate of sales registered by industry was higher than the GDP growth rate. On the assumption that the previous year equals 100, industry increased its sales in constant 1992 prices by 2.8% in 1992, by 6.4% in 1993, 12.1% in 1994, 9.7% in 1995 and by 8.5% in 1996 (see **Table 5**).

Between 1991-1995, industry recorded the following trends in the structure of its sales (see **Table 6**):

* after a clear fall which occurred at the beginning of transformation in the share of manufacturing activities in total sales by industry (from 84.2% in 1990 to 78.6% in 1991), this share was rising steadily (82.8% in 1995);

* after a temporary increase in the shares of such sectors as mining and extraction, and supply of electricity, gas and water in total sales by industry, a slow downfall can be observed in these shares; it should be underlined that these shares were still higher in 1995 than in 1990 (e.g. coal, lignite and peat had a share of 5.6% in 1995 compared with 4% in 1990, and supply of electricity, steam and hot water had shares of 8.8% and 7.3% in the respective years).

A more detailed analysis of the changes in manufacturing industry (see **Table 6**) points also to changes occurring in this area:

* the group of *labour-intensive, light industries* recorded a high and growing share of sales, with food products and beverages going up from 17.5% in 1990 to 20.2% in 1995. The shares of other labour-intensive industries such as fabrics, clothing and leather goods showed downward tendencies;

* the group of *resource-intensive industries* recorded slight increases in their shares in total sales by industry in the case of wood and wood products, whilst the share of coke and of oil products was going down;

* the group of *capital-intensive industries* turning out basic manufactures recorded a fall in the share of sales in the early period of transformation followed by a gradual increase in 1994-1995. The share of chemicals and chemical products, after a small decline, was at the same level in 1995 as in 1990;

* the group of *knowledge- (technology-) intensive industries* (among others machinery and equipment, office machines and computers, electrical machinery and equipment, radio, television and telecommunications machinery and equipment, medical, specialised and optical instruments, clocks and watches, motor vehicles, trailers and semitrailers) recorded decreases in their shares in total sales by industry in the initial period of transformation, followed by a very slow rise between 1993 and 1995.

This analysis justifies the conclusion that the structural changes started in Polish industry in the years 1990-1995 should be regarded as positive. However, a very slow decline in the shares of resource-intensive sectors points out that this process is very difficult. Favourable tendencies are also observed in manufacturing industries, assuming that the slow improvement in the position of knowledge-(technology-) intensive industries can be maintained. However, it is necessary to underline that labour- and resource-intensive activities continue to have a strong position in the structure of industry with about 59% of total sales.

Generally, the changes recorded in the structure of production in the years 1991-1995 support the thesis that the process of structural change has only just started. This is corroborated by changes to the structure of employment in industry in the analysed period (see **Table 7**) which have on the whole followed a parallel course to changes in the structure of sales. However, in the case of some industries, the fall in their share in total industrial sales was accompanied by an increase in their share of average employment (e.g. supply of electricity, gas and water recorded an increase in average employment from 7% in 1992 to 8% in 1995; a similar situation occurred in the clothing industry where these shares amounted to 6.2% and 7.9% in the two years). This points to the weakness of the restructuring processes taking place in the above sectors.

Other industries revealed a tendency towards a drop of their shares in total employment while increasing their shares in total industrial sales (e.g. machinery and equipment, radio, television and telecommunications equipment, motor vehicles, medical equipment). This fact suggests an intensification of the restructuring processes and a growth in productivity (see also **Table 8** showing labour productivity growth rates in industry). These phenomena should be evaluated as clearly positive on the macroeconomic scale, much more so as they occur in knowledge- (technology-) intensive industries. On the microeconomic scale, it is necessary to consider the social tensions which may be triggered by these processes.

Flow of foreign capital to the Polish economy - volume and branch structure

Similar to other countries in Central and Eastern Europe, Poland experiences a shortage of capital. The legacy of a highly inefficient economic structure requires huge investment outlays for its transformation.

According to the Polish Agency for Foreign Investment (PAFI) collecting data about investments of at least US$1m, foreign capital invested in Poland amounted to over US$12bn as of the end of 1996 (see **Table 9**). The PAFI estimates that its data covers about 80% of total foreign capital invested in Poland. The scale of foreign capital invested in Poland is also corroborated by UN data for the years 1989-1995 (again see **Table 9**). According to UN data, in 1995 Poland came second - after Hungary and before the Czech Republic - in terms of absolute value of stock capital (UN, World Investment Report 1996, p. 64). The annual streams of FDI flowing into these countries at the time (US$3.5bn to Hungary, US$2.5bn to the Czech Republic and US$2.5bn to Poland) were recognised as record highs (UN, World Investment Report 1996, p. 64). However, the initial data for Poland for 1996 show that the flow of FDI had already doubled and amounted to over US$5bn.

There is a close relation between growth of FDI in the world economy and processes of economic growth (D.A. Julius, 1990, pp. 28-29). The economic growth rate in developed economies - the main source of FDI - reached a level of around 2.5% in the years 1994-1995 (UN, 1996, p. 4). As a rule, there is a time lag of 1-2 years in investors' response to proceeding growth. For this reason, the record high FDI in 1995 of over US$300bn and the estimations for 1996 are not a surprising phenomenon. At this point it should be noted that the size of FDI flows is also positively influenced by other factors, inter alia, the integration processes in different parts of the world economy.

Increased FDI on a global scale mean that many more investors are looking for profitable employment for their capital. Poland was evaluated - it appears - more favourably as regards its location advantages than in previous years and hence the marked growth in the flow of FDI. The importance of foreign capital in the form of FDI for the Polish economy measured in the share of FDI stock in GDP and in the share of annual flows of FDI in investment outlays is not as high as could be expected (see **Tables 10 and 11**). In 1990-1995, the share of FDI stock capital in GDP rose steadily and amounted to 6.2% in

1995. The share of FDI annual flows in investment outlays - after a nearly three-fold increase in 1992-1993 - settled at a level of below 13% in the years 1994-1995.

The FDI branch structure can be described by using two statistical bases: that provided by the Central Statistical Office (CSO) and that provided by the PAFI (see **Tables 12 and 13**). In the former case, the branch structure of FDI is described according to the sections and divisions of the European Classification of Activities and is directly comparable with the data on the structure of the economy, including the structure of industry, documented according to the same classification system. However, the incomplete nature of the information is a very serious drawback. As the CSO says, some of the firms with foreign capital participation refused to submit the required statistical information. For this reason, any analysis based on the CSO statistics might lead to distortions which would be hard to estimate.

The PAFI base which gives information on the largest investors (with investment of at least US$1m seems to be more reliable in documenting the changes in the structure of FDI. These changes occurring in 1994-1996 appeared as follows:

* FDI in Poland is located for the most part in industry, although the share tended to oscillate, amounting to 59.9% in 1994, 63.3% in 1995 and 62.5% in 1996;
* FDI located in finance has a sizeable and steadily growing share, up from 18% in 1994 to 21% in 1996;
* the share of FDI in trade reached the level of about 12% at the end of the 1980s and beginning of 1990s, but has fallen to below 6% in recent years.

The analysis of the share of FDI in each industry in relation to total FDI reveals two main areas of interest, the **food** and **electrical machinery** industries. FDI constantly increases its share in the food industry, both in absolute and relative terms. FDI stock capital in the food industry increased 3.5 fold between 1994 and 1996, and its share in total FDI rose from 16.4% to 21.1% between these years. FDI in the electrical machinery industry increased 2.4 fold in the same period, although its share in total FDI fell to 17% in 1996 compared with 19.6% in 1994.

Other trends are as follows:

* FDI is increasing in the minerals industry (from 3.5% in 1994 to 6.2% in 1996);
* there is a slight fall in the share of FDI in the wood and paper industry (from 6.4% in 1994 to 5.1% in 1996);
* slight oscillations occur in the share of FDI in the chemical industry - this equalled 5.3% in 1996, just 0.5% lower than in 1994;
* FDI has a falling share in light industry (from 3.6% in 1994 to 2.4% in 1996).

Data on the branch structure of FDI are complemented by information on the size of foreign capital in industrial enterprises in relation to enterprises' own funds - see **Table 14**. A high share of foreign capital in industrial enterprises' own funds can be found in the following sections and divisions of the European Classification of Activities:

* radio, television and telecommunication equipment (48.3%),
* waste reclamation (46.8%),
* office machines and computers (44.3%),
* motor vehicles and trailers (28.6%),
* medical and optical equipment, clocks and watches (18.6%),
* furniture; other manufacturing activities (15.6%),
* publishing and printing (15.25),
* food products and beverage (14.6%).

A comparison of the changes which are occurring in the structure of the economy with the structure of invested foreign capital and the share of this capital in enterprises' own funds in each section of the economy leads to the conclusion that FDI is an important factor influencing the structural changes now taking place in the Polish economy, particularly in industry. Two opposing tendencies can be observed. On the one hand, foreign capital becomes a factor supporting changes in the structure of industry towards an increased share for the technologically advanced industries (also called knowledge-intensive industries). On the other hand, the flow of foreign capital perpetuates the existing industrial structure, i.e. labour- and resource-intensive industries, through its high involvement in the food industry and its comparatively large presence in the mineral, cellulose and paper, and furniture industries. Owing to the fact that FDI exerts an indirect impact on the processes of structural change, it is necessary to take into account the influence which FDI has on the host economy in the form of so-called external effects.

Technological external effects resulting from the flow of foreign capital

The host country on the whole expects foreign investors to transfer modern technology and modern organisational methods which on assumption should contribute to growth in labour productivity and improvement in the quality of production. It is also expected that foreign investor's economic activity will contribute to a growth in exports and would thus improve the host country's trade balance. FDI should also boost employment. If we juxtapose these expectations with the motives of enterprises investing abroad, divergences become apparent. Analysis of foreign investors' motivation shows that their basic motives are on the whole to win, maintain or enlarge market share. Other motives are connected with, inter alia, the cost of supply whose importance is dependent on the situation of each firm. It turns out that host countries' expectations with regard to FDI are not necessarily the same as those intended by foreign investors. As a result of FDI, the structure of the economic system of the host country changes in that new economic activity transmits certain external effects. The host country's expectations are largely oriented at these external effects and, to be precise, at the so-called external economies.

There are different classifications of external effects, but the distinction between the technological and financial is of essential importance (Viner, 1931; Meade, 1952; Scitovsky, 1954). Technological external effects occur when the efficiency of production in one enterprise (A) is in part dependent on the size of production or inputs by another enterprise (B). At the same time, the assumption is made that this dependence has a non-market character in that is not reflected in the sale/purchase transactions made between these enterprises. Enterprise A is not able to control the scale of activity conducted by enterprise B; the impact of B on A has an unintended character.

The fact that a firm has specific ownership advantages is one of the prerequisites for it undertaking FDI. The specific ownership advantages include the firm's assets based on knowledge, i.e. technology obtained by R&D outlays, managerial experience gained in the course of the firm's activity, reputation of the product, and identification of consumers with the product acquired by spending on advertising. As a result of the inflow of FDI, the host country may derive advantages from these assets without needing to make a similar investment itself. Beside the conventional effects, this is the basic advantage which the host country derives from the inflow of FDI. It should be underlined that advantages of this kind are either impossible to achieve with other forms of international ties, or are possible but only to a very limited extent.

The existence of a feedback between multinational companies and the revolutionary technological changes in the world economy in the 1980s is unquestionable (World

Investment Report, 1992). Stress is laid on the sizeable number of multinational corporations in the development of computer technologies, new materials and bio-technology. At the same time, progress in advanced technologies affects corporations themselves, their development and strategic alliances such as joint ventures and research consortia.

A further interesting issue is the host country's access to technologies developed by multinational companies. From the UN studies, it follows that access to up-to-the-minute technology is enjoyed first of all by developed countries. For example, within the decade of the 1980s, about 95% of strategic relations concerning technology were made between firms from developed countries (World Investment Report, 1992). Moreover, the relations in which partners from developing (mostly newly industrialised) countries took part were not concentrated so much on leading technologies as was the case of the alliances between firms from developed countries. Over 50% of the latter were concentrated on research and development activity compared with 13% of the alliances in which partners were also firms from developing countries. Thus it follows that less developed countries as a whole do not participate in the creation of the most modern technology generated by multinational companies and do not gain related advantages. Nevertheless, the activity of multinational companies and the resulting flows of FDI can result in these countries being the recipients of technology at different levels of advancement. Transfer of technology by means of FDI may take place:

* in an embodied form, i.e. in the form of goods which are imported by foreign investors to the host country;
* in the form of intangible assets if technology is a free good in the relations between the parent company and its subsidiary;
* through the human factor in the form of know-how when the foreign investor brings in specialists from abroad to manage the project or firm.

The countries of Central and East Europe that host FDI do not constitute any special case in this respect. Transfer of technology may take place in all of the above mentioned ways. Analysing this problem further, two situations can be distinguished:

* when a transfer of technology takes place exclusively between the parent firm and its subsidiary abroad;
* when there is a leakage of technology as a result of a transfer of technology to foreign branches of multinational companies (Das, 1987).

The host country as a whole takes advantage of each of the above situations, whereas local firms only gain benefits in the second situation. The process of learning new technology can be considered in the category of external effects of multinational companies in the host country. They arise through the effect of demonstration and mobility of the labour factor between foreign and domestic firms (Julius, 1990).

If local firms master new technologies in this way, this would be the external effect, ie. advantages in the form of unpaid factors of production which are used by these firms. In addition, there will also occur the second of the technological external effects mentioned earlier, i.e. modification of the environment in which local firms act. As a result of the activity of foreign firms utilizing new and by assumption more advanced technologies than those available locally, as well as more advanced organisational and management methods, native firms face the need to meet the challenge of managing a business is a new way. Meeting these challenges allows them to enter a higher, more advanced technological and organizational level. The benefit derived by local firms is the extra gain of the host country in addition to the gain which results from the pure inflow of technology used in the subsidiaries of multinational companies.

From the viewpoint of the host country, it is important to distinguish between transfer of technology in the area of products and production processes (product and process innovations). The latter tend to leak out more easily than product innovations. This is confirmed by research on transfer of technology by US firms to their foreign branches. Transfer of technology in the area of production processes hastened non-American competitors' access to the technology on average by 3.1 years, but by less than half a year with regard to product technologies (Mansield, Romero, 1980).

With reference to CEE countries, the emergence of external advantages from the transfer of technology within the framework of FDI is dependent upon the scale and structure of the inflowing FDI and on the progress made with systemic transformation. The fulfilment of the latter condition will determine the degree to which the old economic environment will be transformed into a vibrant market environment and the degree to which local firms will be encouraged by these new economic conditions to undertake the effort required to learn new technologies and adapt them to their own needs.

The problem of so-called maladjusted technologies as a result of FDI into less developed countries (Atriakpor, 1988/89) does not seem to be of great importance in CEE countries, which are at a sufficiently high level of development (the second stage by M. Porter classification) so as not to be threatened by the creation of a dual economic structure typical of lesser developed countries, where the transferred technology contributes to the creation of modern enclaves beside the traditional sectors. External advantages will also occur as a result of a transfer of knowledge in the area of organisation, management and marketing gained by the firm hosting investment. They will also be evident in the form of the unpaid factor of production and the modification of the environment in which local firms act.

On the whole, foreign investors have a large contribution to make to the creation of **human capital**, especially in a less developed country. This proceeds through the preparation of employees to carry out tasks more complex than before, leading to a permanent upgrading of staff qualifications. Thanks to the migration of employees between firms, local firms have qualified staff at their disposal without having had to train them themselves. The modification of the environment in which **firms** are acting proceeds through adoption by local firms of the patterns of behaviour typical of foreign firms. This phenomenon may occur not only in less developed countries, but also in countries such as Britain where local firms take over Japanese management techniques as a result of the demonstration effect (Julius, 1990). It is evaluated that British firms have gained considerable productivity benefits since the mid-1980s as a result. It can be expected that technological external effects will also be revealed in the Polish economy as time goes by and progress is made in the transformation process. This will contribute to the growth and development of desirable structural changes.

Table 1 : GDP growth rate 1989-1995

	1989	1990	1991	1992	1993		1994		1995	
	previous year = 100					1990= 100	previous year = 100	1990 = 100	previous year = 100	1990 = 100
GDP (volume index in 1989-1994)	100.2	88.4	92.4	102.6	103.8	99.0	105.2	104.2	107.0	111.5

Source: Official data of the Central Statistical Office.

Table 2 : GDP structure by branches of the national economy, 1990-1993 (in %)

	1990	1991	1992	1993
	in constant 1990 prices			
Total	100	100	100	100
of which:				
Industry	43.6	39.2	39.6	37.8
Fuel and power generation	*6.6*	*5.7*	*4.8*	*4.5*
coal	1.5	1.6	1.3	0.9
fuel	2.7	2.4	2.2	2.5
power generation	2.4	1.7	1.3	1.1
Metallurgical industry	*5.0*	*3.4*	*3.7*	*3.2*
iron metallurgy	3.1	2.3	2.7	2.4
non-ferrous metals	1.9	1.1	1.0	0.8
Electrical machinery industry	*11.6*	*9.1*	*9.6*	*9.5*
metals	2.4	2.3	2.4	2.4
machine-building	3.4	2.8	2.5	2.4
special machinery	0.7	0.5	0.7	0.7
transport equipment	3.0	1.6	2.0	1.8
engineering and electronics	2.1	1.9	2.0	2.2
Chemical industry	*4.0*	*3.5*	*4.0*	*3.9*
Mineral industry	*2.0*	*1.9*	*1.9*	*2.0*
construction materials	1.5	1.4	1.4	1.4
glass	0.3	0.4	0.4	0.4
ceramics	0.2	0.1	0.1	0.2
Wood and paper industry	*2.1*	*2.1*	*2.3*	*2.5*
Light industry	*3.8*	*3.6*	*3.8*	*3.4*
textile	1.7	1.5	1.5	1.5
clothing	1.3	1.3	1.5	1.3
leather	0.8	0.8	0.8	0.6
Food industry	*7.6*	*9.2*	*8.6*	*8.0*
Other industries	*0.9*	*0.7*	*0.9*	*0.8*
animal feed and utilisation	0.1	0.1	0.2	0.1
printing	0.3	0.2	0.3	0.4
other branches	0.5	0.4	0.4	0.3
Construction	9.5	10.9	11.2	9.8
Agriculture	7.3	8.4	7.3	7.1
Transport	4.1	3.6	3.6	3.1
Trade	13.0	15.2	15.0	14.2
Other Services	22.5	22.7	23.3	28.0

Source: Official data of the Central Statistical Office.

Table 3 : GDP structure by European Classification of Activities, 1992-1995 (in %)

Sections and subsections	1992	1993	1994	1995
	in current prices			
Total	100	100	100	100
of which:				
Agriculture, hunting and forestry	6.7	6.6	6.2	6.6
Industry	34.0	32.9	32.2	28.9
Mining and extraction	3.3	3.7	4.2	4.2
Manufacturing activities	26.9	25.2	24.3	21.0
- food products and beverages	*	6.2	5.0	*
- tobacco products	*	0.9	0.9	*
- fabrics	*	0.8	0.9	*
- clothing and furriery	*	1.3	1.1	*
- leather products	*	0.4	0.4	*
- wood and wood products	*	0.7	0.9	*
- cellulose and paper	*	0.3	0.4	*
- publishing and printing	*	0.7	0.9	*
- coke and oil products	*	2.2	1.9	*
- chemicals and chemical products	*	1.5	1.6	*
- rubber and plastic products	*	0.9	0.9	*
- other non-metal minerals	*	1.1	1.3	*
- metals	*	1.1	1.2	*
- metal products	*	1.3	1.2	*
- machinery and equipment	*	1.8	1.8	*
- office machines and computers	*	0.0	0.1	*
- electrical machinery and equipment	*	0.7	0.6	*
- radio, television and telecommunications	*	0.4	0.4	*
- medical and optical equipment, clocks and watches	*	0.4	0.3	*
- motor vehicles, trailers	*	0.9	0.7	*
- other transport equipment	*	0.6	0.8	*
- furniture; other manufacturing activities	*	0.9	0.9	*
- reclamation of waste	*	0.1	0.1	*
Supply of electricity, gas and water	3.8	4.0	3.7	3.7
Transport, storage and communications	6.2	6.1	6.0	6.0
of which:				
- land transport and piping	*	3.0	2.9	*
- post and telecommunications	*	1.8	1.9	*
Construction	7.8	6.5	5.7	5.2
Trade and repairs	13.1	15.0	13.5	13.1
Hotels and restaurants	0.4	0.5	0.6	0.6
Financial services	0.5	0.6	1.0	1.2
Property and firm service	6.5	5.8	6.0	6.8
Public administration and national defence	6.1	5.2	4.5	4.8
Education	3.8	3.2	3.5	3.6
Health service and social security	4.2	3.9	3.5	3.8
Other servicing communal, social and individual activities	6.5	5.8	6.1	6.1
(Balancing Item)	4.2	7.9	11.2	13.3

Source: Official data of the central Statistical Office.

Table 4 : Sales growth rates in industry at start of transformation process
(1989-1992)

	1989	1990	1991	1992
	previous year = 100			
Sales growth rate (in constant 1990 prices)	99.5	75.8	88.1	103.9

Source: Statistical Yearbook of Industry 1994, Central Statistical Office, Warsaw, 1994.

Table 5 : Sales growth rates in industry, 1991-1996*

	1991	1992	1993	1994		1995		1996
	previous year = 100					1990= 100	1992= 100	previous year = 100
Sales growth rate (in constant 1990 prices)	92.0	102.8	106.4	112.1	109.7	123.7	130.8	108.5

Note: *Estimation
Source: Statistical Yearbook of Industry 1996, Central Statistical Office, Warsaw, 1996.

Table 6 : Structure of sales by sectors, sections and subsections of the European Classification of Activities, 1990-1995 (in current prices)

Sections and divisions	1990	1991	1992	1993* A	1993* B	1994	1995
Total	100	100	100	100	100	100	100
of which:							
Mining and extraction	**7.9**	**10.3**	**9.6**	**8.2**	**8.3**	**8.7**	**7.6**
- coal and lignite mining, peat extraction	4.0	6.4	5.8	6.3	6.4	6.6	5.6
Manufacturing activities	**84.2**	**78.6**	**79.2**	**80.7**	**80.2**	**80.8**	**82.8**
- food products and beverages	17.5	19.6	20.6	20.2	20.2	19.8	20.2
- tobacco products	1.1	1.3	1.6	1.8	1.7	1.6	1.7
- fabrics	3.7	3.1	2.9	2.8	2.7	2.8	2.5
- clothing and furriery	2.8	2.8	3.0	3.0	3.1	2.8	2.5
- leather products	1.6	1.5	1.3	1.2	1.2	1.1	1.0
- wood and wood products	2.1	2.1	2.2	2.2	2.2	2.5	2.7
- cellulose and paper	1.4	1.2	1.3	1.3	1.3	1.4	2.1
- publishing and printing	1.4	1.6	2.0	2.2	2.2	2.4	2.5
- coke and oil products	5.2	5.3	6.4	7.1	6.9	5.9	5.3
- chemicals and chemical products	6.5	6.1	5.7	5.6	5.6	6.0	6.5
- rubber and plastics products	2.0	2.1	2.4	2.7	2.6	2.8	3.1
- other non-metal minerals	3.7	3.8	3.5	3.5	3.5	3.8	3.6
- metals	10.3	6.9	5.9	5.8	5.8	6.1	6.3
- metal products	3.4	3.3	3.7	3.5	3.5	3.6	3.7
- machinery and equipment	7.8	6.1	5.0	5.1	5.0	5.1	5.4
- office machines and computers	0.3	0.2	0.1	0.1	0.1	0.1	0.2
- electrical machinery and equipment	2.7	2.4	2.2	2.3	2.3	2.2	2.4
- radio, television & telecommunications	1.6	1.1	1.1	1.2	1.2	1.3	1.3
- medical and optical equipment, clocks and watches	0.8	0.8	0.7	0.8	0.8	0.8	0.9
- motor vehicles, trailers	3.0	2.4	2.7	3.3	3.2	3.2	3.4
- other transport equipment	2.7	2.4	2.1	2.2	2.3	2.5	2.2
- furniture; other manufacturing activities	2.2	2.3	2.5	2.5	2.0	2.5	3.0
- reclamation waste	0.4	0.2	0.31	0.3	0.3	0.3	0.3
- Supply of electricity, gas, steam and hot water	**7.9**	**11.1**	**11.2**	**11.1**	**11.5**	**10.5**	**9.6**
- supply of electricity, gas, steam and hot water	7.3	10.1	10.1	10.1	10.4	9.4	8.8
- water conditioning and conveying	0.6	1.0	1.1	1.0	1.1	1.1	0.8

Source: Statistical yearbook of Industry 1996, Central Statistical Office, Warsaw, 1996.

Note: "Data for 1993 were given in two variants:

A data allow for turnover tax, VAT and excise tax.

Variant B without turnover tax and VAT, but including excise tax.

Table 7 : Average employment in industry by sections and divisions, 1992-1995 (in %)

Sections and divisions	1992	1993	1994	1995
Total	100	100	100	100
of which:				
Mining and extraction	**13.2**	**12.4**	**11.7**	**10.8**
of which:				
- coal and lignite mining, peat extraction	10.7	10.4	9.7	8.9
Manufacturing activities	**79.8**	**79.6**	**80.1**	**81.2**
- food products and beverages	13.3	13.7	13.5	14.0
- tobacco products	0.3	0.4	0.4	0.4
- fabrics	5.3	5.1	5.1	4.8
- clothing and furriery	6.2	6.8	7.1	7.9
- leather products	2.6	2.4	2.3	2.2
- wood and wood products	2.8	2.8	2.8	3.1
- cellulose and paper	1.1	1.1	1.2	1.1
- publishing and printing	1.7	1.7	1.8	1.9
- coke and oil products	0.7	0.7	0.7	0.7
- chemicals and chemical products	4.0	4.0	4.2	4.1
- rubber and plastics products	2.1	2.3	2.5	2.6
- other non-metal minerals	5.0	4.9	4.8	4.8
- metals	4.8	4.9	4.6	4.3
- metal products	4.4	4.2	4.4	4.7
- machinery and equipment	9.5	9.2	8.9	8.6
- office machines and computers	0.2	0.1	0.1	0.1
- electrical machinery and equipment	2.5	2.5	2.6	2.6
- radio, television and telecommunications	1.8	1.6	1.4	1.3
- medical and optical equipment, clocks and watches	1.3	1.2	1.2	1.2
- motor vehicles, trailers	3.2	2.9	3.0	2.9
- other transport equipment	3.5	3.4	3.5	3.3
- furniture; other manufacturing activities	3.6	3.8	3.9	4.4
- reclamation of waste	0.2	0.2	0.2	0.2
Supply of electricity, gas, steam and hot water	**7.0**	**8.0**	**8.2**	**8.0**
- supply of electricity, gas, steam and hot water	5.6	6.5	6.6	6.4
- water conditioning and conveying	1.4	1.5	1.6	1.6

Source: Statistical Yearbook of Industry 1996, Central Statistical Office, Warsaw 1996, and my own calculations.

Table 8 : Labour productivity rate in industry by sections and divisions, 1993-1995 (measured in gross value added at constant prices)

Sections and divisions	Measured in gross VAT		Measured in sales		
	per employee				
	1993	1994	1993	1994	1995
	previous year = 100				
Total	**111.0**	**111.3**	**108.8**	**113.1**	**106.6**
Mining and extraction	**98.2**	**105.2**	**104.4**	**112.1**	**104.2**
- coal and lignite mining, peat extraction	109.2	100.0	102.7	108.8	105.1
Manufacturing activities	**114.6**	**111.5**	**113.4**	**114.0**	**107.0**
- food products and beverages	114.0	105.5	110.2	115.8	102.5
- tobacco products	100.3	107.1	106.0	107.7	99.4
- fabrics	110.4	120.2	117.2	115.3	102.9
- clothing and furriery	109.0	107.4	101.2	107.1	88.6
- leather products	111.9	136.0	108.9	117.4	109.7
- wood and wood products	107.1	114.4	105.1	109.5	96.9
- cellulose and paper	123.2	100.8	111.1	112.1	123.9
- publishing and printing	164.0	106.7	141.4	105.3	104.6
- coke and oil products	106.9	131.2	111.3	106.1	106.5
- chemicals and chemical products	110.3	106.0	108.9	113.5	112.5
- rubber and plastics products	111.0	105.7	111.1	104.7	112.1
- other non-metal minerals	118.0	121.1	112.7	120.0	101.1
- metals	93.1	138.6	102.6	125.1	118.2
- metal products	117.0	98.7	114.4	111.7	105.0
- machinery and equipment	109.2	116.9	115.3	120.6	120.4
- office machines and computers	175.3	205.8	205.0	119.6	151.6
- electrical machinery and equipment	113.8	109.3	114.3	105.5	113.0
- radio, television and telecommunications	189.6	133.5	147.2	138.0	126.4
- medical and optical equipment, clocks and watches	135.7	96.6	129.5	108.0	121.4
- motor vehicles, trailers	135.0	91.0	144.9	109.0	116.9
- other transport equipment	91.4	119.7	114.8	124.0	106.2
- furniture; other manufacturing activities	110.6	113.0	109.2	110.5	106.9
- reclamation of waste	107.0	86.5	100.2	88.4	129.9
Supply of electricity, gas, steam and hot water	**91.1**	**114.2**	**99.7**	**102.9**	**100.4**
- supply of electricity, gas, steam and hot water	89.2	115.3	77.9	103.7	100.8
- water conditioning and conveying	100.8	10	92.1	100.6	99.0

Source: Statistical Yearbook of Industry 1996, Central Statistical Office, Warsaw, 1996.

Table 9 : Stock capital of FDI in Poland and annual flows of FDI in 1989-1996 (US$m)

Year[a]	FDI stock capital		FDI annual flows	
	according to UN statistics	according to the PAFI[b]	according to UN statistics	according to the PAFI[b]
1989	231[c]	-	11	-
1990	320	-	89	-
1991	611	-	291	-
1992	1,289	1,702.4	678	-
1993	3,004	3,041.0	1,717	1,338.6
1994	4,879	4,321.0	1,875	1,280.0
1995	7,389	6,832.0	2,510	2,511.0
1996	-	12,027.7	-	5,195.7

Source: World Investment Report 1995. Transnational Corporation and Competitiveness, UN, New York and Geneva, 1995, p. 99; World Investment report 1996. Investment, Trade and International Policy Arrangements, UN, New York and Geneva, 1996, p. 64

Notes: [a] Data for the end of the year.
[b] PAFI data cover investment of at least US$ 1 million.
[c] Stock capital of FDI in Poland was estimated at US$ 220 million.

Table 10 : Comparison of share of cumulated FDI stock in GDP, 1990-1995 (in %)

Country	1990	1991	1992	1993	1994	1995
Poland	-	0.3	1.7	3.6	5.1	6.2
Hungary	4.5	9.3	13.8	14.5	15.6	-
Czechoslovakia	0.7	2.3	-	-	-	-
						-

Source: My own calculations and World Investment Report 1995. Transnational Corporations and Competitiveness, UN, New York and Geneva, 1995, p. 101; World Investment report 1996. Investment, Trade and International Policy Arrangements, UN, New York and Geneva, 1996, p. 64.

Table 11 : Share of annual FDI flows in investment outlays in Poland, 1990-1995

Country	1990	1991	1992	1993	1994	1995
Poland	0.7	1.8	4.6	12.6	12.6	12.8

Source: My own calculations.

Table 12 : Stock capital of companies with foreign capital participation in Poland, by sections of the European Classification of Activities, 1994-1995 (%)

Sections and divisions	1994	1995
Total - of which:	**100**	**100**
Agriculture, hunting and forestry	**0.4**	**0.4**
Fishery and fish culture..	**0.002**	**0.002**
Industry	**73.1**	**68.2**
- Mining and extraction	0.5	0.4
- Manufacturing activities - of which:	72.6	67.8
- food products and beverages...	21.6	18.6
- tobacco products..	0.9	0.6
- fabrics	0.6	0.7
- clothing and furriery..	2.9	1.5
- leather products	0.5	0.3
- wood and wood products	1.5	0.9
- cellulose and paper..	4.1	2.9
- publishing and printing	4.3	2.1
- coke and oil products	0.2	0.1
- chemicals and chemical products	15.3	8.9
- rubber and plastics products	3.2	2.7
- other non-metal minerals..	5.5	4.4
- metals	2.3	1.1
- metal products...	3.0	2.3
- machinery and equipment	2.1	1.3
- office machines and computers	1.3	0.6
- electrical machinery and equipment..	2.3	1.9
- radio, television and telecommunications...............................	4.9	3.0
- medical and optical equipment, clocks and watches	1.4	1.6
- motor vehicles, trailers	18.1	9.5
- other transport equipment	0.7	0.3
- furniture; other manufacturing activities..................................	3.4	2.3
- reclamation of waste	0.08	0.09
Construction	**1.7**	**2.3**
Trade and repairs...	**15.4**	**20.1**
Hotels and restaurants	**1.3**	**1.2**
Financial services..	**2.7**	**3.7**
Property and firm service..	**0.4**	**0.9**
Public administration and national defence	**4.1**	**2.3**
Education	**0.03**	**0.01**
Health service and social security	**0.03**	**0.02**
Other servicing communal, social and individual activities	**0.8**	**0.8**

Source: Financial Results of Economic Units with Foreign Capital Participation in 1994, Central Statistical Office, Warsaw, 1995; Financial Results of Economic Units with Foreign Capital Participation in 1995, Central Statistical Office, Warsaw, 1996 and my own calculations.

Table 13 : Branch structure of major foreign investors in Poland (1994-1996)

Specification	1994[a]		1995		1996	
	US$m	%	US$m	%	US$m	%
Total Industry	**2638.7**	**59.9**	**4325.6**	**63.3**	**7482.9**	**62.2**
of which:						
- fuel and energy	119.9	2.7	133.3	2.0	182.8	1.5
- metallurgy	43.4	1.0	79.7	1.1	108.3	0.9
- electro-machinery	861.7	19.6	1079.9	15.8	2039.6	17.0
- chemical	255.9	5.8	533.4	7.8	642.4	5.3
- mineral	155.8	3.5	406.5	5.9	748.0	6.2
- wood and paper	280.6	6.4	446.4	6.5	608.4	5.1
- light	159.7	3.6	222.3	3.3	301.2	2.5
- food processing	722.3	16.4	1357.5	19.9	2535.3	21.1
- other	39.4	0.9	66.6	1.0	316.9	2.6
Construction	379.4	8.6	496.2	7.3	607.2	5.1
Agriculture	8.0	0.1	9.0	0.1	15.0	0.1
Transportation	24.9	0.6	29.9	0.4	48.0	0.4
Telecommunication	240.4	5.5	289.7	4.2	587.6	4.9
Trade	259.3	5.9	364.3	5.4	709.6	5.9
Municipal economy	20.4	0.5	22.8	0.3	24.8	0.2
Finance	827.8	18.8	1278.6	18.8	2522.9	21.0
Insurance	4.0	0.1	16.1	0.2	29.7	0.2
Total	**4402.9**	**100.0**	**6832.2**	**100.0**	**12027.7**	**100.0**

Note: a - Data of January, 1995.
Source: Lists of major investors in Poland, PAFI, Warsaw 1995-1997.

Table 14 : Industrial enterprises' own funds in Poland, by sections and divisions of the European Classification of Activities, 1995

Sections and divisions	Total	...of which foreign capital	
	PLZ million	PLZ million	%
Total	**142,331.5**	**6,713.2**	**4.7**
- public sector	114,646.0	235.1	0.2
- private sector	27,685.5	6,478.1	23.4
Mining and extraction	**13,941.4**	**43.0**	**0.3**
of which: coal and lignite mining, and peat extraction	948.8	11.2	0.1
Manufacturing activities	**71,511.1**	**6,665.1**	**9.3**
- food products and beverages	12,547.2	1,827.5	14.6
- tobacco products	808.0	54.7	6.8
- fabrics	1,693.8	70.9	4.2
- clothing and furriery	1,194.0	147.8	12.4
- leather products	362.7	26.4	7.3
- wood and wood products	1,344.7	89.4	6.6
- cellulose and paper	2,567.5	280.9	10.9
- publishing and printing	1,352.3	206.0	15.2
- coke and oil products	4,224.7	14.4	0.3
- chemicals and chemical products	9,715.4	880.3	9.1
- rubber and plastics products	2,792.5	270.5	9.7
- other non-metal minerals	4,189.8	433.1	10.3
- metals	8,165.2	107.4	1.3
- metal products	2,526.0	229.9	9.1
- machinery and equipment	6,285.0	131.0	2.1
- office machines and computers	129.7	57.4	44.3
- electrical machinery and equipment	2,722.5	188.6	6.9
- radio, television and telecommunications	608.5	294.1	48.3
- medical and optical equipment, clocks and watches	841.2	156.5	18.6
- motor vehicles, trailers	3,256.5	932.7	28.6
- other transport equipment	2,439.5	28.7	1.2
- furniture; other manufacturing activities	1,467.4	228.2	15.6
- reclamation of waste	277.0	129.6	46.8
Supply of electricity, gas and hot water	**56,879.0**	**5.1**	**0.01**
- supply of electricity, gas, steam and hot water	48,836.3	0.4	0.001
- water conditioning and conveying	8,042.7	4.7	0.06

Source: Statistical Yearbook of Industry 1996, Central statistical Office, Warsaw, 1996 and my own calculations.

References

J.C. Atriakpor (1988/89), "Do firms choose inappropriate technology in LDCs", *Economic Development and Cultural Change*, no. 3, pp. 557-571.

S. Das (1987), "Externalities and technology transfer through multinational corporations. A theoretical analysis", *Journal of International Economics*, no. 1/2, pp. 171-182.

D.A. Julius (1990), *Global Companies and Public Policy. The Growing Challenge of Foreign Direct Investment*, London, pp. 60-61.

E. Mansfield, A. Romero (1980), "Technology transfer to overseas subsidiary by US-based firms", *Quarterly Journal of Economics*, p. 741, quoted after S. Das, "Externalities and technology transfer through multinational corporations. A theoretical analysis", op.cit., p. 173.

J.E. Meade (1952) "External economies and diseconomies in a competitive situation", *The Economic Journal*, no. 245, pp. 54-67.

T. Scitovsky, (1954), "Two concepts of external economies", *Journal of Political Economy*, no. 2, pp. 143-152.

J. Viner (1931), "Cost curves and supply curves", Zeitschrift fuer Nationalokonomie, vol. III, pp. 23-46, reprinted in Readings in Price Theory, London, 1953, pp. 198-231.

World Investment Report 1996. Investment Trade and International Policy Arrangements, UN, New York, 1996, p. 64.

Lists of Major Foreign Investors in Poland, Polish Agency for Foreign Investment, Warsaw, 1995-1997.

Financial Results of Economic Units with Foreign Capital Participation in 1995 (1996), Statistical Information and Studies, Central Statistical Office, Warsaw.

PANEL II

Regional Cooperation Among Partner Countries - The Institutional Settings

Panelists and contributors:
Katarzyna ZUKROWSKA
Ercan ÖZER
Yuri V. SHISHKOV
Martins LACIS
Pekka SUTELA

POLISH TRADE WITH CEFTA COUNTRIES: IN SEARCH OF PROMISING SECTORS

Katarzyna Zukrowska

Institute of Development and Strategic Studies
Warsaw, Poland

Introduction

Polish trade with CEFTA countries has expanded since the establishment of CEFTA, helping to liberalise commerce and advance systemic reforms. In the period 1993-1997 both the value and volume of trade expanded, accompanied by slight changes in the structure of trade. A continuation of these trends can be expected over the coming years as the date of European Union (EU) membership comes closer.

This paper argues that there are still great untapped reserves regarding trade within CEFTA which could be mobilised by an increase in FDI, thus helping to restructure the economy, to increase intrabranch specialisation, and to positively influence the share of trade in GDP. Moreover, CEFTA countries in the EU would be beneficial for all EU member states since it would increase the competitiveness of different groups of products, including those of declining industries.

Evolution of the CEFTA Agreement

The CEFTA Agreement on the creation of a free trade zone in Central Europe was signed on 21 December 1992 in Cracow and went into force on 1 March 1993. The Agreement was structured after the European Agreements, and although the levels of liberalisation and development were similar among the signing countries, they still differed from the EU. The number of member countries increased with the addition of Slovenia and Romania on 1 July 1997 and by the divorce of former Czechoslovakia. Other countries have demonstrated their interest in accession to the zone, such as Lithuania, Latvia, Bulgaria and Ukraine. The first version of the CEFTA Agreement did not foresee the possibilities of expansion[1].

Different reasons are given by specialists to explain why CEFTA was created. Some argue that CEFTA was established in order to diminish the pressure applied by East-Central Europeans on the EU to expand eastward. Others say that the creation of CEFTA played the role of litmus paper, showing how liberalisation can influence mutual turnover and economic growth. Those who use this argument are focusing on national problems of the economy. A third group consider CEFTA to be an organisation which not only brings the economies of member-states closer together but also improves the position of member-countries in their desire to join the EU. This last view seems to be the most appropriate as it combines the internal and external conditions of integration, which should not be separated.

According to R. Baldwin[2], there are three main reasons behind regional integration. The first assumes that regionalism is an alternative to multilateral liberalisation, which is often considered to be a politically complicated process. The second points out that the USA has withdrawn from its former role of being a locomotive for progress in World trade liberalisation. The third is based on a simple formula that any deepening of integration decreases the "indifferentness" of the neighbouring country regarding regional liberalisation and likewise increases its interest in regional participation. CEFTA fully proves the third argument.

March 1977 marked the fourth anniversary of the establishment of CEFTA. The first commitments which established a free trade zone between Poland, the Czech Republic, Hungary, the Slovak Republic and Slovenia for industrial goods and selectively for agricultural products until the year 2001 have been modified in subsequent years[3]. The first crucial change was introduced by the Amending Protocol to the CEFTA Agreement, launched on 1 July 1994, which has accelerated liberalisation of trade for industrial products and expanded the framework of liberalisation for agricultural products[4]. A second package of changes was introduced on 25 November 1994 during the CEFTA summit held in Poznań, Poland which further abolished some existing barriers in the trade of agricultural products and advanced by one year plans to fully establish a free trade zone in industrial products, with a limited number of exclusions. Thus, the primary schedule of liberalisation, which was launched on 1 March 1993, has been modified on several occasions thereafter.

The liberalisation of trade for industrial products within CEFTA consists of a reduction in customs duties, the elimination of para-tariff barriers, and the elimination of quotas and limits[5]. Concessions are negotiated bilaterally within CEFTA. Despite the fact that Polish customs duties were relatively higher than those in the Czech Republic, Hungary and the Slovak Republic, the Polish market proved to be the most open once temporary customs duties were suspended and protection was limited solely to the undervalued exchange rate of the zloty.

Liberalisation of trade was conducted on four levels, these being within the GATT Uruguay Round, within the free trade zones (European Agreement, EFTA and CEFTA), by tariffication and reduction of para-tariff barriers, and finally through changes in the exchange rate from an undervalued to an overvalued level[6]. Five countries from East-Central Europe (including Poland) participated in the GATT Uruguay Round, which was committed to the reduction in import duties for industrial products by an average of 38%, that is from 16% to 9.9%. This reduction was deeper in Poland than in other CEFTA countries since the starting level was higher. In addition, customs duties were lowered according to the rules imposed by the creation of free trade zones under the European Agreement, CEFTA and EFTA, as well as within bilateral trade agreements.

The current level of external customs duties in Poland is 7.7%, which shows that liberalisation was accelerated in line with the GATT Uruguay Round, similarly as in the case of liberalisation within the free trade zone. Further liberalisation is expected following EU membership which will result in free trade within the single market, lower external customs duties as part of the customs union, and lowered protection for third countries which have association or other trade agreements with the EU.

Since January 1996, customs duties on imports of industrial goods from the Czech and Slovak Republics and Hungary have been abolished. For other goods with lower custom duties, the tariffs were cancelled on 1 January 1997. Regarding imports from Slovenia, custom duties are still applied to some industrial products, while for the majority of goods, a tariff of 50% of the general level is applied. From 1 January 1998, this will no longer be applied. A meeting in April 1996 introduced some arrangements for reducing para-tariff barriers.

The question of the enlargement of CEFTA was solved at the summit in Bern on 11 September 1995 when an Amending Agreement was signed. This introduced article 39a, which stated that each European country can become a CEFTA member. Access, however, is conditional upon signature of an Association (or other trade) Agreement with the EU, membership of GATT/WTO, and upon acceptance by all CEFTA members. These conditions were formulated in the Poznań Declaration in 1994.

The Amending Agreement enabled the expansion of CEFTA to take place resulting in Slovenia's membership on 1 January 1996 and Romania's access on 1 July 1997[7]. Moreover, CEFTA has finally rejected the idea of creating a Permanent Secretariat in Bratislava (as proposed by the Slovak Republic) because there was no need to institutionalise mutual cooperation through the creation of organisational structures.

The Prime Ministers of CEFTA states have signed a common declaration in which they expressed a will to widen economic cooperation into new fields, such as:

* acceleration of negotiations on certification of industrial goods and agricultural products, including mutual acceptance of scientific research results and certificates;
* events to boost investment in CEFTA countries and other promotional activities abroad;
* further liberalisation of service industries;
* continuation of common cooperation within CEFTA (regarding its functioning, the arbitration of disputes, and the interpretation of the CEFTA Agreement itself) by the Common Committee[8].

The enlargement of CEFTA proceeded at the same time as trade barriers were being dismantled among the member countries. Liberalisation in the field of industrial goods was achieved four years earlier than envisaged in the Agreement. Trade in agricultural products is subject to far-reaching concessions introduced on 1 January 1996, the scope of which has been radically widened with countries giving up most custom duties. Concessions introduced for industrial goods are divided into four groups:

* **List A** for those with low sensitivity to competition - "0" duty customs applied;
* **List B** for those with medium sensitivity - custom duties of "0" were applied untill 1 January 1997, after which duties were abolished;
* **List C** for sensitive goods - preferential customs duties, lower than those generally applied, are in force. Since 1 January 1996, custom duties were reduced by 50% and since 1 January 1997 goods falling into this category were traded freely, four years ahead of the scheduled primary goal of 2001 and a year earlier than envisaged in the First Additional Protocol;
* finally, there is a limited group of very sensitive goods which are not covered by preferential tariffs. The list of goods in this category is negotiated bilaterally between CEFTA members.

For agricultural goods, concessions are divided into three groups which are similar to those listed above:

* **Group A** for goods with low sensitivity to competition - "0" customs duty is applied;
* **Group B** for goods with a medium sensitivity to competition - custom duties are higher than "0" but lower than those generally applied;
* **Group C** for sensitive goods for which concessions are granted bilaterally.

The contents of lists A and B are negotiated commonly by all CEFTA members and common duties are applied by all member states. The contents of list C are negotiated bilaterally and custom duties tend to be lower in comparison with the generally applied level. In some cases the custom duties are "0", in other cases preferential custom duties are applied. Finally, there is a narrow group of goods which is not covered by preferential treatment.

Romanian membership is regulated by an Additional Protocol supplementing the Agreement on Free Trade in Central Europe dated 11 September 1995. Article 2 states that Romania accepts all commitments deriving from the CEFTA Agreements. However, the status of Romania is regulated differently in some areas, allowing for a period of adjustment.

Overall, by the end of 1997 CEFTA states will enjoy full liberalisation of trade in industrial goods and deepened liberalisation in agricultural products.

Intra-CEFTA trade

Thanks to the liberalisation of trade within CEFTA, Polish trade with other members in 1995 and 1996 was conducted under the potentially better conditions of mutual access to national markets. Since 1 January 1997, all industrial products were traded freely, while for agricultural products, customs duties were applied only for a limited number of items. The new schedule of liberalisation foresees that in 1997 only 3-5% of the mutual turnover within CEFTA will be protected by custom duties. According to the Ministry of Economy, the protection of agricultural trade fell by 50%. This creates incentives for producers to adjust to free competition and increases mutual turnover.

Trade within CEFTA plays an increasing role in the economies of member states. The geographic structure of Polish exports in 1996 compared to 1995 revealed a decrease in the share of the EU from 70% to 66.3%, an increase in the share of the former Soviet Union (FSU) from 11.4% to 13.9%, and an increased share for CEFTA from 5.4% to 6.1%. No major changes were noted in the structure of Polish imports over the same period, with the EU accounting for 63.9% (1995-64.6%), the FSU 9.5% (9.6%) and CEFTA 5.8% (5.6%). Similarly, as in previous years, a negative balance of trade was recorded with all three areas, but this was balanced by unregistered turnover.

In 1996 Poland exported US$1,473m of goods to CEFTA, 15.3% more than in 1995. Polish imports in 1996 from CEFTA were estimated at US$2,157m, a 24.8% rise over 1995. Thus the share of CEFTA in total foreign trade rose both for exports and imports in both years, although the balance of trade remained negative at US$684m in 1996 against US$380m in 1995. Polish trade with CEFTA in 1996 is shown in **Table 1** below:

Table 1
Polish trade with CEFTA in 1996

	Total turnover US$m	Exports US$m		Imports US$m		Balance US$m	Dynamics 1995=100	
							Exports	Imports
Czech Rep.	1990.0	840.8	57.1	1149.2	53.3	-308.4	120.4	128.9
Hungary	734.8	309.8	21.0	425.0	19.7	-115.2	115.9	120.7
Slovak Rep.	711.3	279.1	19.0	432.2	20.0	-153.1	99.9	113.5
Slovenia	193.3	43.0	2.9	150.3	7.0	-107.3	132.6	145.2
Total	3629.4	1472.7	100.0	2156.7	100.0	-684.0	115.3	124.8

Note: Figures in *(italics)* are percentages (%)
Source: Ministry of Economy, Department of Multilateral Cooperation

The Czech Republic is Poland's main trade partner within CEFTA due to proximity and economic potential. Moreover, both economies complement one another.

Table 2 below analyses the structure of Polish trade with CEFTA in 1995:

Table 2
Structure of Polish trade with CEFTA in 1995 (US$m)

Groups of goods	Czech Republic		Slovakia		Hungary		Total	
	Export	Import	Export	Import	Export	Import	Export	Import
Agriculture products and food (sec. I-IV)	41.9	93.4	15.4	48.4	13.8	95.1	71.1	236.9
Mineral products (sec V)	173.5	73.1	78.3	43.4	41.2	8.6	293.0	125.1
Chemical products (sec. VI-VII)	106.7	242.5	49.6	92.4	41.8	114.8	198.1	449.7
Paper. chips & cardboard (sec X)	21.6	42.7	11.8	37.3	26.0	23.6	59.4	103.6
Textiles and fibre (sec XI)	30.9	43.8	11.0	15.7	8.7	23.8	50.6	83.3
Non precious metals (sec XV)	142.8	131.1	55.4	79.7	89.9	23.4	288.1	234.2
Electromachine industry products (sec. XVI-XVIII)	135.6	177.5	42.0	50.1	34.8	49.9	212.4	277.5
Furniture & lights (sec. XX)	22.9	7.6	4.7	0.8	3.9	1.4	31.5	9.8
Other	22.3	80.0	11.2	13.0	7.2	11.7	40.7	104.7
Total	**698.2**	**891.7**	**279.4**	**380.8**	**267.3**	**352.3**	**1244.9**	**1624,8**

Source: Polish Foreign trade in 1995, Year Report, Warsaw 1996

Polish exports to CEFTA in 1995 were dominated by mineral products (23.5% of total), non precious metals (23.1%), electromachine industry products (17.1%) and products of the chemical industry (15.9%). These four totalled US$ 991.6m, or 79.6% of total Polish exports to CEFTA. Imports from CEFTA countries to Poland in 1995 were dominated by products of the chemical industry (27.7% of total), electromachine industry products (17.1%), food and agricultural products (14.6%) and non precious metals (14.4%). The sequencing of these four groups of goods did not change in 1996, although precise estimations of the value of trade by product group are still not available. Together they made up 73.8% of total Polish imports from CEFTA in 1996.

The structure of Polish trade within CEFTA varies from the pattern observed in trade with developed countries, from where imports are dominated by machines and mechanical equipment; transport and electrical equipment. **Table 3** below shows the structure of Polish trade with CEFTA divided simply between industrial and agricultural goods. For industrial goods, Slovakia registered the highest share of Polish exports and Slovenia the highest share of imports. This can be interpreted as indirect evidence that liberalisation of market access influences the turnover of intra-CEFTA trade.

Table 3
Structure of Polish trade with CEFTA in 1996 %

	Exports		Imports	
	Industrial products	Agricultural products	Industrial products	Agricultural products
CEFTA - of which:	**94.3**	**5.7**	**89.0**	**11.0**
Czech Republic	93.7	6.3	93.4	6.6
Hungary	94.9	5.1	68.2	31.8
Slovak Republic	96.8	3.2	94.0	6 0
Slovenia	93.5	6.5	99.4	0.6

Source: U. Kopeć, Postępy procesu integracji Polski z krajami CEFTA

Basically, trade within CEFTA is dominated by industrial goods. Regarding imports, the share of industrial goods exceeds 93% in each country, whilst for imports, industrial goods comprise a share varying from 68.2% in Hungary to virtually 100% in Slovenia.

Competitiveness of Polish trade

Traditionally, Poland enjoyed a comparative advantage in labour intensive goods. This has changed since 1989. Polish exports are sensitive and react strongly to changes in demand patterns in import markets. This is usually explained by *niche* specialisation and limited intra-branch cooperation which can stabilise fluctuations in trade during periods of depression. It should be remembered that Poland is the best supplied labour market in the region as far as both skilled and unskilled labour is concerned. Low intra-branch specialisation in comparison with other CEFTA countries should improve Poland's future prospects, which may indeed be better than for the Czech Republic or Hungary where intra-branch specialisation is at a higher level. This analysis opposes many widely held opinions to the contrary. Moreover, some experts believe that Polish comparative advantages are exaggerated and will shrink over time, especially when the rate of growth of salaries is taken into account. But if growing salaries are compensated for by a growth in labour productivity, such a conclusion is questionable, both for labour and capital-intensive production. In Poland, the scarcity of supply in the labour and capital markets differ greatly. Poland is considered to be one of the best supplied labour markets, but suffers from a shortage of capital despite the current conditions of growing savings, increasing investment and healthy FDI inflows. **Table 4** below gives an indication of the comparative advantages of various Polish exports to the EU between 1990 and 1995:

Table 4
Comparative advantage of Polish exports on EU markets in 1990-1995

Sector	1990	1993	1994	1995
I. Live animals	4,83	2,41	2,20	1,86
II. Plants	1,92	0,94	0,74	0,69
III. Fats & oils	0,53	0,47	0,22	0,21
IV. Processed food	1,22	0,81	0,70	0,77
V. Mineral products	0,70	0,69	0,80	0,68
VI. Chemical products	1,17	0,68	0,64	0,69
VII. Fibre and plastics	1,06	0,89	0,81	0,91
VIII. Leather goods	0,95	1,06	0,83	0,83
IX. Wood & wood products	1,82	2,51	2,46	2,59
X. Paper and paper products	0,20	0,34	0,40	0,50
XI. Textiles	1,53	2,22	2,17	2,11
XII. Shoes and hats	1,86	1,27	1,05	1,15
XIII. Stone products	2,26	2,11	2,27	2,34
XIV. Precious stones	0,24	0,14	0,33	0,28
XV. Non precious metals	2,52	2,47	2,49	2,27
XVI. Machines & equipment	0,38	0,34	0,37	0,42
XVII. Transport equipment	0,41	1,26	1,03	1,14
XVIII. Instruments, incl. optical	0,11	0,12	0,12	0,12
XIX. Weapons & ammunition	0,20	0,08	0,12	0,08
XX. Other manufactures	2,25	2,80	3,14	3,54
XXI. Art and antiques	0,44	0,11	0,11	0,17

Source: K. Marczewski, Selected aspects of competitiveness of Polish exports, paper presented at meeting of the Board of strategic policy, June 1997.

Table 5 below indicates changes in the competitiveness of these different groups of goods between 1990-1995, presenting direction and areas of change where:
• K = competitiveness,   RCA >1;
• N = lack of competitiveness,   RCA < 1.

Table 5
Changes to the competitive position of Polish exports between 1990-1995

Direction of changes	Changes in competitiveness				Total
	K---> K	K---> N	N---> N	N---> K	
Improvement	4	0	2	1	7
Stabilization	0	0	3	0	3
Fall	3	4	4	0	11
Total	7	4	9	1	21

Source: as in Table 4

Table 6 below shows that competitiveness is predominantly achieved by low prices - a traditional approach. The key role of prices in competition strategy shows that there are vast possibilities for improving overall competitiveness once other areas of improvement are put into force.

Table 6
Forms of export competitiveness in Polish enterprises in 1996

Form of competition	Total number of enterprises in survey	of that number:		
		small	medium	large
1. Price competition	176	55	60	61
- *pure*	*55*	*23*	*20*	*12*
- *with some elements of competition beyond prices*	*121*	*32*	*40*	*49*
2. Other than prices competition	36	6	13	17
- *pure*	*7*	*2*	*2*	*3*
- *with some elements of price competition*	*29*	*4*	*11*	*14*
3. Competition depending on situation	84	37	25	22
4. No answer	4	2	2	0

Source: Inquiry research made by IKiC MGWzZ, November 1996, quoted after K. Marczewski.

Between 1993 and 1995, wages in Polish processing industries rose by 34% in US$ terms, thereby decreasing export competitiveness. This increase was followed by even quicker growth in labour productivity, which resulted in a decrease of unit costs by 19%. Improvements in labour productivity were different in individual sectors of industry. Lower productivity increases were noted in the production of medical instruments, precise products and optical equipment (nearly 80% lower than the average for all processing industries). For textiles, the same indicator was 70%, in furniture production 32%, in electric machines 24%, while in radio & TV equipment it was 21%. Low labour productivity in these sectors indicates a degree of technological and organisational backwardness. This means that the high level of prices should be considered as the main reason behind the lack of competitiveness in these sectors[9].

Declining sectors and sensitive goods

The notion of "sensitive goods" is often erroneously confused with the notion of "declining sectors" of production. Sensitive production is where domestic products successively lose market share to imports from less developed economies. This is usually related to traditionally less advanced (labour not capital intensive) production such as leather goods, textiles, clothes, steel and agricultural produce. Traditionally, such sectors were protected by various trade barriers, the protection being justified on social grounds, particularly the need to preserve employment in depressed regions.

By contrast, declining industries are those which were previously considered as technologically advanced, but such advantage has vanished with the evolution of new products and technologies and through increased competition from economies with lower wage levels. This has happened with newly developed economies which have started to compete in the global economy. Declining industries embrace automobiles, shipbuilding, machine tools and recently also arms. The remedy here is to reduce costs, especially wages, forcing labour to move from sunset to sunrise industries. Such a solution is easy in conditions of high inflation since management can award lower increases in real wages than the rate of inflation. Cutting wage costs is more difficult under conditions of low inflation[10]. This suggests that the speed of decline should accelerate with fulfilment of the Maastricht criteria of convergence, in other words, with low inflation. This in turn creates opportunities for CEFTA countries which can take over some of the orders of declining industries in the EU, having already a pool of skilled labour and some experience in the production of such goods. Such a solution should be considered as advantageous for both the EU and CEFTA.

Nevertheless, this should only be considered as a temporary solution to industrial restructuring in CEFTA. The high rates of growth needed to catch-up with developed countries can be only achieved with further restructuring of the economy, and this means some de-industrialisation as well as the incorporation of advanced technologies into production processes. Furthermore, liberalisation of trade, capital inflow and labour movements are also preconditions for realising the advantages deriving from the globalisation of markets and technology. The realisation of such prospects requires membership in the EU as soon as possible, that is in the year 2000.

Growth simulation models indicate that the rate of future growth of an economy is directly linked with the increase in investment in capital intensive sectors. This can be achieved under three conditions; increased savings, increased rate of investment and rising inflows of FDI. The main question in this context should concern the type of production that attracts investment. The main problem is how to interpret market signals, since investors either make decisions taking into account present (and possibly temporary) advantages, or they rely on future comparative advantages which can in turn be created by contemporary investment decisions.

Generally, opportunities in CEFTA countries should not only be seen in terms of moving from autonomous development and self-sufficiency to a more specialised industrial economy, but should also consider intrabranch specialisation. Multiple opportunities exist in this field since all CEFTA economies are replacing diversified development by a more specialised model in which partners from abroad have a specific role to play. An open economy is a prerequisite for taking advantage of product and technological globalisation. Countries with a lower share of exports in GDP are in a potentially better position to increase openness since production is currently mainly addressed to the home market. This creates opportunities for the internationalisation of production which should be interpreted as being a stimulus towards higher effectiveness and lower unit costs. This indicator was relatively low in Hungary (28.9% in 1994) and Poland (28.5% in 1993 and 24.0% in 1994), while in the Czech and Slovak Republics it was much higher at 52.5% and 65.2% respectively. Some EU countries record similar figures to those of Poland and Hungary. (Italy, Great Britain, Portugal, Germany.) In Japan, it is even lower at 9.5% but is higher in Holland, Denmark and Belgium. This shows the importance of the scale of national markets, but it also indicates that EU economies are still divided into national entities and that the single market has not yet forced a great deal of direct cooperation between companies. Increased competition and deregulation are two factors which could stimulate such cooperation, especially when supported by the requirements of destatisation of the economy, in other words "small government".

This specific finding shows that declining sectors need not necessarily decline if some part of the production process is conducted abroad. Moreover, they could survive for longer periods when the demand in rapidly developing countries is taken into account. Such a solution could apply to the motor industry, shipbuilding and textiles. Demand could be stimulated by increasing consumption in quickly developing post-communist countries and by increasing quality requirements in developed countries.

It becomes clear that such a solution is possible only under specific conditions, these being that post-communist countries need to be incorporated into the integration process as members on equal terms, and that intrabranch specialisation be deepened. The problem cannot be solved by a simple transfer of one type of production from one country to another. Such a solution could create problems with employment, problems that would disappear were production to be shared between countries. This would give a double multiplying effect by stimulating both trade and FDI transfers. CEFTA countries under specific conditions can be considered as good investment markets because their economies were in the past based upon self-sufficiency, just as the defence sector was until recently in the West. Production sharing would open up opportunities for international cooperation beyond those at the national or "East-West" level.

Polish trade in the transition period has revealed that since 1989 the comparative advantage of exports has changed. The primary advantage that Poland has in so called sensitive or declining industries is decreasing, while advantages in sectors which are considered as technically advanced are holding their position. An inflow of FDI into these sectors can improve the situation further. Moreover, improvements in comparative advantage could be stimulated by a more active trade policy, which would in turn stimulate the import of advanced technologies. Such a policy is indeed conducted in Poland, where high-tech sectors are exposed to increased competition (through the suspension of custom duties) rather than being protected. Examples are the suspension of custom duties for imports of electronic components and spare parts for civil aircraft production. Regulations in those fields were introduced in June 1997[1].

The structure of FDI inflows into Poland is changing in that the more technically advanced sectors are slowly gaining ground against other sectors, as **Table 7** below indicates:

Table 7
Sectoral structure of FDI & loans in 1994-1996 in %

Specification	1994	1995	1996
Industry total of which:	59,9	63,3	62,4
electromachinery	*19,9*	*15,8*	*17,0*
food processing	*16,6*	*19,9*	*20,6*
wood and paper	*6,5*	*6,5*	*5,2*
chemical	*5,9*	*7,8*	*6,3*
Financial Services	18,9	18,7	21,3
Construction	8,8	7,3	5,6
Telecommunication	5,6	4,2	4,8
Trade	5,5	5,3	5,0
Others	1,3	1,2	0,9

Source: Foreign Investment Agency.

The structure of investments in the Polish market is changing. In the first period of transformation, FDI dominated in food and agricultural processing industries, sectors that represent a safe and natural strategy. Later, as the economy developed, FDI was attracted more to advanced sectors, especially services. This phenomenon could be seen not only in Poland but also in other CEFTA states.

Investment risk in Poland has improved making the country one of the more attractive investment locations with CEFTA. In 1990, it was in a worse position than either Czechoslovakia or Hungary. Indeed, all the Western studies which analysed investment risks at that time forecast that the situation would change in two years, which is precisely what has happened[12]. Poland was the top CEFTA recipient country of FDI in 1996[13].

Foreign affiliates in CEFTA countries are beginning to play an active role in reducing the region's trade deficit, even though they often are accused of doing the exact opposite (initially importing heavily from their home market before sourcing components from host country suppliers). In fact, exports from companies with FDI are higher than from those which represent national capital. This has been the case in all CEFTA countries[14].

Identifying promising sectors

Criteria that should be taken into account would include profitability, risk, costs per unit, demand and the time over which comparative advantages can be maintained and improved. Economies change and develop rapidly under conditions of intensifying competition, privatisation, deregulation and transformation. Polish studies on competitiveness indicate that wage levels played a more important role in shaping the competitiveness of capital intensive production than in either Hungary or the Czech Republic. This was true for the production of electrical machinery and specialised equipment, automobiles, medical and precise instruments, glass, textiles and radio/TVs. This means that productivity in these sectors was lower in Poland than in Hungary or the Czech Republic. It should be explained that productivity is the relationship of capital to labour. In other words, production in Poland was characterised by a higher effectiveness of labour in terms of the number of manufactured units per hour produced by one worker. Conversely, lower productivity means less units per hour in relation to engaged capital.

Figure 1 below illustrates the winners and losers in Polish industry based upon a comparison between the economic growth performance of each individual sector and average GDP growth:

Figure 1
Winners and losers: difference between sectoral and GDP growth rates 1995-2000

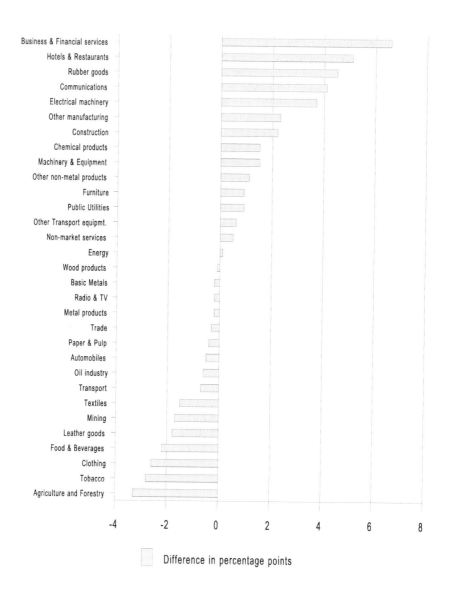

Difference in percentage points

Clearly, each sector could be considered as promising in the longer run, although an individual country might have a definite advantage in producing some types of products rather than others. This stimulates specialisation and is a factor in increasing trade.

Conclusions

The positive correlation between liberalisation of trade and the increase in trade turnover within CEFTA indicates that an improvement regarding market access can positively influence the rate of growth of the economy. This in turn defines the conditions on which future CEFTA members can join the club. New membership need not necessarily be accomplished through gradual liberalisation of access, but by guaranteeing access in line with current CEFTA practice.

Promising industries can easily be found in all CEFTA countries, although a search of this field requires good economic knowledge and a full understanding of the transformation process, which is not always the case with risk evaluation experts from the West. One of the easiest ways of finding promising industries is to study demand on the nascent consumer market. Another is to look for high effectiveness of labour, which is not always clearly indicated by comparative advantages. Studies on transformation show that one should be very careful in interpreting the available statistical data on trade and production. For instance, the growth in the value of exports from Poland in 1995 was not mirrored by a growth in the quantity of exported goods, a circumstance that can in fact be attributed to changes in the exchange rate of the zloty. By the same measure, the deep disparity between exports and imports in 1996 did not illustrate a decline in the quantity of exports but a decline in the value of exports, again the result of exchange rate fluctuations. Practice shows that the elimination of the influence of exchange rates on the value of traded goods is very difficult, and this in turn suggests that all evaluations on competitiveness of different types of production can lead to false conclusions.

The search for promising sectors should be conducted in relation to the effectiveness of labour in different sectors, and this should not be mistaken with levels of productivity. It should also take into account the fact that better prospects exist in locating specific investments in CEFTA countries, the specifity relying on the stimulation of intrabranch specialisation. This should not be understood as industrial policy but as a specific investment strategy applied by the enterprise.

Footnotes

1. Article 36 point 1 of CEFTA Agreement announced that it deals with trade liberalisation among the signatory countries. Point 2 of this article foresees possibilities of creating free trade zones and customs unions, as well as agreements on transborder trade on a scale which should not disturb the conditions of trade of the signatory countries, with special emphasis on the issue of the certificates of origin of traded goods, that are listed in the agreement. This condition has formed the background for creation of the free trade zone between Slovenia and Czech Republic and Slovak Republic in 1993 as well as Hungary in 1994. In 1994 such an agreement was also signed between Czech Republic and Romania.

2. Expanding Membership of the European Union, ed. R. Baldwin, Perti Haaparanta Kiander, Cambridge University 1995.

3. Although not all of the listed countries were CEFTA members from the moment the zone was established. Since 1 July 1997 Romania has also joined the group.

4. U. Kopeć, Polityka handlowa w stosunkach z krajami CEFTA, in: Polska polityka handlu zagranicznego 1994-1995, IKCHZ, Warszawa 1995, p. 197-203. (Trade policy with CEFTA, in: Polish trade policy 1994-1995).

5. A. B. Kisiel-Łowczyc, Środkowo-Europejksa strefa wolnego handlu, (Central European Zone of Free Trade), WUG 1996, p. 162.

6. B. Durka, Polityka handlowa - zakres i formy protekcjonizmu (Trade policy - scope and forms of protectionism), in: Polityka handlowa, zakres i formy protekcjonizmu (Trade policy - scope and forms of protectionism), Report No 14, Warsaw 1996, Rada Strategii Społeczno-gospodarczej przy Radzie Ministrów, p. 25-57.

7. It was decided that a new member can be accepted after finalisation of a full round of bilateral liberalisation with CEFTA members.

8. U. Kopeć, Postępy procesu integracji Polski z krajami CEFTA (Progress in Polish integration with CEFTA), in: Zagraniczna polityka gospodarcza Polski 1996-1997 (Polish foreign economic policy in 1996-1997), IKiC 1997, p.76-87.

9. A. Wziatek-Kubiak, Problemy oceny konkurencyjności polskiego przemysłu (Problems of assessment of the Polish competitiveness), paper prepared for the Board of National Strategy of the Ministerial Committee, 1997, p. 7.

10. L. Thurow, The Future of Capitalism. How Today's Economic Forces will Shape Tomorrow's World, London 1996, p. 188.

11. Rozporzadzenie Rady Minsitrów z 3 czerwca 1997 w sprawie zawieszenia pobierania ceł na niektóre towary dla przemysłu elektronicznego. Dz. U. Nr 61, 18 June 1997, poz. 385; Rozporzadzenie Rady Ministrów z 3 czerwca w sprawie zawieszenia pobierania ceł od niektórych towarów, Dz. U. 17.06.1997 poz. 381.

12. Mapa ryzyka inwestycyjnego. Wyniki pierwszego etapu badań. The map of investment risk, Transformacja gospodarki No.: 39. Gdańsk.

13. UN/ENE secretariat, based on national statistics, quoted after Economic Survey of Europe in 1995-1996, New York Geneva 1996, p. 145.

14. World Investment Report. Transnational Corporations and Competitiveness 1995, UN 1995, p. 110.

15. P. Krugman, Pop internationalism, London 1996.

BLACK SEA ECONOMIC COOPERATION
A TEST CASE

Ercan Özer

Directorate General for Multilateral Economic Relations, Ministry of Foreign Affairs, Ankara, Turkey

Introduction

The Black Sea Economic Cooperation (BSEC) is an idea which found its right timing and milieu in 1992. The amount of enthusiasm it has since generated attests to this. Turkey introduced the idea of a new model of multilateral economic cooperation in the Black Sea region when a series of unprecedented and historic developments were taking place in Central and Eastern Europe. The radical changes in the region and in the World set the scene for the BSEC, and for Turkey as the regional economic hub to initiate it. In other words, the BSEC was a mandate entrusted by history to Turkey and to the countries of the region.

Setting

Owing to its suitable **geographical** location, the region could be integrated with relative ease into the markets of Europe, Central Asia and the Middle East. Regarding **politics**, the Black Sea region has been the scene of tensions, disputes and confrontations in the past, but now welcomes political changes that open up new opportunities for cooperation. The end of the Cold War has given way to a new economic order and more open democratic systems. The **economic** setting comprises a set of complex factors such as revolutionary progress in communications and information technologies; increased mobility of individuals, goods, services, and capital; diffusion of modern technology; and the globalisation of markets. These have all yielded greater interdependence and created more production, investment, trade, technology transfer and financial opportunities for cooperation. Finally, the **cultural** setting of historical familiarity, cultural affinity and linguistic similarity is conducive to mutual dialogue.

Conceptualisation

In conceptualising the BSEC, Turkey was inspired mainly by the dynamics of the rapid process of global transformation which paved the way for a trend of neo-regionalisation, shifting the attention from national strategies to regional concepts. Within this context, Turkey felt the need to contribute to the acceleration of the political and economic transformation taking place in its proximity and came forth with the concept of the BSEC at the end of 1990.

The initial initiative elicited a favourable response from neighbouring countries. Following high level consultations, a series of meetings at expert level were held to draft a document determining the framework conditions of such a regional cooperation. Agreement was reached on the text of the Declaration of the BSEC at the meeting of Deputy Foreign Ministers held in July 1991 in Moscow. This text was later initialled by Foreign Ministers on 3 February 1992 in Istanbul. The formal start to the BSEC process was given by the heads of state and government of the 11 participating states on 25 June 1992 at a summit meeting in Istanbul by signing the "Summit Declaration on the Black

Sea Economic Cooperation". The BSEC train, the private sector as its engine and the creativity and dynamism of private entrepreneurship as its fuel, left the station. The wagons of the train were Albania, Armenia, Azerbaijan, Bulgaria, Georgia, Greece, Moldova, Romania, Russia, Turkey and Ukraine. On 10 December 1992 Poland, and on 17 June 1993 Tunisia joined the BSEC train as observers. These were later followed by Egypt, Israel, the Slovak Republic and two members of the European Union, Italy and Austria. The BSEC Council (which represents the business communities of the participating states) and the Varna based International Black Sea Club were also granted observer status on 10 December 1992 and on 9 December 1993 respectively.

The conception of the BSEC envisages the promotion of an environment conducive to improving and enhancing the economic, technological and social process of participating states and the region with particular emphasis on the encouragement of free enterprise. The promotion of such an environment depends largely on the collective and individual efforts of the countries involved and their private sectors. Such a concept is one that envisions a multilateral economic structure driven by the dynamism and initiative of the private sector. Hence, stimulus is needed to encourage and create a suitable milieu for individual enterprises. The role of government is to facilitate the efforts of the private sector by creating favourable economic, commercial, legal and fiscal conditions. In sum, the aim is to improve the business environment. The governments will undertake and implement joint projects directed at the development of regional infrastructures with the direct participation of the private sector to this end.

Approach

The BSEC approach is a major departure from the earlier static, inward-looking, import-substitution and protectionist policies evident in the region. The BSEC promotes a more dynamic, open, outward-looking export oriented approach. In other words, from a closed regionalism to an open regionalism. This kind of approach promotes international competitiveness, better trade performance, infrastructure building, environmental protection, good governance, cooperation in science and technology, education and training, liberalisation, and structural adjustment. In sum, it aims at dynamic and action-oriented objectives. It envisages intra-regional trade, but not at the expense of extra-regional trade. It promotes the greater involvement of non-governmental sectors and puts more emphasis on the private sector. The new approach stresses the need for the progressive integration of the newly independent states in the World economy.

Strategy

Regional economic cooperation is a long term investment which requires a strategy and farsighted perspectives. The main elements of BSEC strategy are as follows:

* shifting away from rigid integration schemes such as customs unions and common markets towards less binding project-oriented cooperation;
* allowing member countries to progress at different speeds in trade liberalisation;
* permitting member countries to have bilateral preferences with partners sharing common sectoral interests;
* producing jointly the public goods and undertaking commonly the projects which may be too costly for individual members, such as in education, training, research and development, infrastructure, environment, human resource development, energy management, improved flows of information and better communication;
* rationalising the functions, activities and institutionalisation of regional cooperation through clearing and payments arrangements in the transition period, the

avoidance of duplication, operational consistency, and by economising human and financial resources;
* involving the private sector and education and research institutions in the identification and implementation of cooperation projects;
* remaining open for the future participation of new members.

Scope

The scope of cooperation encompasses a variety of areas, notably transport and communications, infrastructure, exchange of economic and commercial information and statistical data, standardisation and certification, energy, mining and the processing of raw materials, tourism, agriculture and agro-industry, veterinary and sanitary protection, health care and pharmaceuticals, environment, science and technology. This wide scope is not limited only to technical issues. Establishing codes of conduct, adopting a grass roots approach to promote the BSEC, taking measures against drug trafficking and terrorism which hinder trade and economic interaction, and increasing cultural and social interaction are other examples of cooperation areas within the scope of the BSEC.

Model

When economic integration and cooperation models are analysed, one cannot put a label on the BSEC. It fits none of them, being a tailor-made product to fit the conditions prevailing in the region and in the World. It is a sui-generis model responding to the needs of our times. The BSEC model is based on the objective desire to develop and diversify existing economic relations among the Participating States by making more efficient use of the advantages arising from their geographical proximity, their traditional ties, the complementary nature of their economies and the large size of their common economic space and market. All projects or initiatives are to be in line with CSCE principles and the dynamics of competitive market economies. It is thus a functional contemporary model designed according to the needs and the aspirations of the region. It has a sound political base and is backed by a strong political will transcending military conflicts. The model has three distinctive features:
* **First**, it introduces a new concept of multilateralism in economic relations among its members and into the region wherein the economic activities hitherto have been bilateral and state-induced. This new approach intends to change this pattern, by setting up a multilateral economic structure based on the potential and dynamism of the private sector. Cooperation is based on private initiatives facilitated by governments, thereby conforming with the aspirations of most participating states to move further towards a market economy and pluralist democracy;
* The **second** distinctive feature of the model is that it aims to create a common economic language among the member countries, thereby enhancing the extent of cooperation and collaboration between and among the private sectors of BSEC states;
* The **third** distinctive feature of the BSEC model is its flexible and pragmatic approach. The speed and the content of cooperation will depend in part upon future developments and will tally with the implementation process of the structural transformation programmes. Cooperation could involve just two or indeed all member states. There is flexibility to increase intra-regional trade, to lower intra-regional trade barriers and controls, and to liberalise external trade. It is open ended in the sense that it does not exclude the use of other external and broader liberalisation exercises. There is flexibility also to expand economic cooperation

through trade and investment but not necessarily involving institutional coordination policies. Thus harmonisation and coherence will be to the extent desired.

Black Sea Economic Cooperation is therefore a comprehensive and project oriented initiative. It is comprehensive in that it includes both multilateral and bilateral relations in all fields of economic activities and also includes the different dimensions of government, parliament, private sector, local administration, academic and civic institutions. Being project oriented, it is more conducive to making productive use of financial and human resources as well as foreign investments. In a wider sense, it is a cooperation scheme which forms a part of the future European and Eurasian architecture. It is a complementary sub-structure and not a substitute for the EU or other European groupings. It is directed towards economic cooperation, at least in the initial phase. It does not necessarily involve a high level of integration. However, it does not exclude this as an eventual outcome. But harmonisation of all economic policies is not an a priori obligation and in no way is the BSEC a supra-national scheme like the EU. Theoretically, economic integration is more likely to be successful among member countries of close or the same level of development, as was the case with the initial members of the EU. But BSEC members differ greatly in their level of economic development which is another reason for it being a regional cooperation rather than a regional integration organisation.

The BSEC envisages free flow of goods, services and factors of production. It encourages interaction amongst the businessmen of the participating states and the easing of travel restrictions. However, it does not aim at a customs union at this stage, whilst the establishment of a free trade area remains only a possibility and a long term goal if the necessary free market preconditions are created. However, taking into account that concrete steps to this end should be made, a Special Meeting of the Ministers of Foreign Affairs was held on 7 February 1997 in Istanbul and a "Declaration of Intent" was adopted for the creation of a Free Trade Area covering the Black Sea Region. Technical work will be done in due course and the modalities for a free trade area will be established.

Institutional Structure

Another characteristic of the BSEC which distinguishes it from other regional economic cooperation organisations is its institutional structure. This structure is built on four main pillars comprising the governments, parliaments, private sectors and local administrations of member states which would assume complementary roles and functions in any regional economic cooperation scheme. Non-governmental organisations and academic institutions can be added to the foregoing as a fifth pillar.

Governments

The BSEC is established by the governments of the 11 full member states. The highest decision making organ of the BSEC is the *Meeting of the Ministers of Foreign Affairs* (MMFA). The sessional chairmanship rotates every six months according to the English alphabetical order. A preparatory meeting of senior officials is held before every MMFA. Permanent or ad hoc subsidiary bodies can be established by the MMFA. At present, no less than 18 *Permanent Working Groups* are in progress, covering areas such as exchange of statistical data and economic information, banking and finance, trade and industrial cooperation, agriculture and agro-industry, transport, communications, energy, environment, science and technology, health care and pharmaceuticals, and tourism. The *Ad Hoc Working Groups* deal with organisational matters, travel facilities for businessmen, promotion and protection of investments, avoidance of double taxation, and legislative information. The intensification of BSEC activities has made it necessary to establish a permanent international secretariat for the BSEC. In accordance with the ministerial decision taken at the First MMFA held on 10 December 1992, the *BSEC International Secretariat* was established in Istanbul.

Parliaments

The foundation of the *Parliamentary Assembly of the BSEC* (PABSEC) on 26 February 1993 added yet another dimension to the sphere of cooperation so that the national parliaments can be induced to pass legislation in line with the decisions of the MMFA. It contributes to the establishment of closer friendly relations among the national parliaments of BSEC countries which is founded on the basic tenets of pluralistic democracy. The establishment of PABSEC represents the institutionalisation of these tenets thus complementing the BSEC and constituting an indispensable component of its evolutionary process. It provides the legal ground for the realisation of principles and goals regarding respect for human rights, the rule of law and democratic values. The PABSEC provides democratic participation in the enactment of legislation needed for implementation of the decisions taken by the BSEC, and thus strengthens parliamentary democracy in the participating states.

Private Sector

The *BSEC Council* was established in December 1992 comprising the business communities of the BSEC. It is in the process of developing proposals, programmes and projects in a variety of fields of cooperation. The BSEC Council has an observer status at the BSEC. The aim of the Council is to contribute to private and public sector cooperation and coordination in keeping with the objectives of the BSEC Declaration. The Council operates through the activities of the Working Groups on energy, transportation, telecommunications, trade and industry, banking, finance and insurance, fair trade practices, harmonisation of commercial legislation, tourism, environment, agriculture, mining, training, business information and technological cooperation. These Working Groups develop proposals, programmes and projects in their domains, and contract feasibility studies. The BSEC Council is mandated to elaborate and work on all project related issues forwarded by the representatives of the participating states. The Council encourages closer operational ties with the EBRD, UNIDO and IFC and other international institutions. The EBRD has decided to participate in BSEC Council activities through a liaison officer.

The BSEC Council has been established to stimulate business cooperation between the participating states of the BSEC and to promote the flow of investment resources into the region. To carry out this objective the Council has established an informal network of focal points throughout the region in order to facilitate the identification, formulation and dissemination of investment project proposals. This mechanism is expected to be the conduit for bringing together potential business partners from within and outside the region.

Municipalities

The *Mayors Conference of the Capitals of Black Sea Countries* held its first meeting on 5-6 April 1993 in Ankara. In the final communiqué, municipal representatives of Black Sea Countries, in line with BSEC objectives, recognised the need to solve ecological problems and expressed their concern for the protection of the Black Sea. They decided to concentrate their efforts on three main areas, namely finance, legislation and management, and environmental issues. They stipulated that activities in the three priority interest areas defined could be carried out on the basis of bilateral and multilateral transfers of knowledge, information, know-how and experience as well as through meetings, seminars and workshops; noting that some of these can be formulated as projects eligible for support from international organisations. They also resolved to provide humanitarian aid in case of major disasters in the region.

The *Black Sea Capitals' Governors and Mayors Round Table* brings together the heads of city administrations of the capitals of the BSEC countries. At Round-Table meetings, the participants exchange views and adopt resolutions on a number of issues concerning urban facilities in their cities as well as on democratic municipal governance towards the fulfilment of BSEC objectives. They concentrate their activities on solving a wide range of issues concerning city transportation, housing, communal services, water supply and sewerage, creating work and recreation for their citizens, developing scientific and cultural potential, protecting the environment, and safeguarding historical and cultural heritage.

The *Varna based International Black Sea Club* was founded on 5 December 1992 by representatives of the cities of Burgas, Varna, Ilichevsk, Konstanza, Nikolaev, Odessa, Piraeus, Thessaloniki, Taganrog and Kherson. The Club aims to create a basis for bilateral and multilateral cooperation among the cities and regions of the Black Sea and the Mediterranean for economic and social development. It has an open-ended participation and observer status in the BSEC.

Accomplishments

Although it is still too early to gauge the results of the BSEC, the achievements so far attest to its dynamism. From my vantage point, the distance covered by the BSEC train since its departure on 25 June 1992 following the signing of the Summit Declaration can only be considered as remarkable.

Within a short time span of three years, the BSEC has completed its institutional structure in all dimensions. In addition to the establishment of international secretariats of the governments, parliaments and private sectors, a *Centre for Exchange of Statistical Data and Economic Information* was set up within the Turkish State Institute of Statistics to collect statistical and economic information, to install a common data base, to harmonise the statistical data collated from different member states, and to provide the flow of information through a network of computer on-line systems. The Centre has already published country files, statistical reference documents and economic indicators.

The agreement on the establishment of the *BSEC Trade and Development Bank* with a capital of SDR1bn (Special Drawing Rights) has been ratified. This bank will finance BSEC trade and investment projects and will be instrumental in providing international credits. The Bank, headquartered in Thessaloniki, Greece, will be operational soon. In addition:

* the scope of the *Balkan Centre for Small and Medium Size Enterprises* established in Bucharest was enlarged to cover all BSEC countries;
* a *Black Sea Regional Energy Centre* was established in Sofia under the SYNERGY program of the European Commission;
* the *Centre for Scientific and Cultural Relations between the Black Sea Countries* was set up in Tbilisi, Georgia.

Moreover, the various working groups have taken concrete steps in their respective fields of activity bringing several projects to the implementation stage, especially in the cooperation fields of transportation, communications and energy. For example, the *Working Group on Trade and Industrial Development* has concentrated its efforts on the avoidance of double taxation and the promotion and protection of investments. Discussions are also underway on agreements related to coastal and inter-regional trade.

Much progress has also been made with the creation and management of free zones, encouraging small and medium sized enterprises, and removing barriers to trade. Technical assistance programs were arranged in 1993 by the *Turkish Small and Medium Size Industry Development Organisation* (SMIDO) to train 20 participants from BSEC countries on entrepreneurship and management of small and medium size enterprises. Technical assistance programs among BSEC countries were also proposed in the *Working Groups on Agriculture and Agro-industry*. In the *Ad Hoc Working Group on Travel of Individuals*, the participating states have made recommendations to facilitate business travel within the BSEC area.

The BSEC movement has also spawned a large number of activities:

* The *Black Sea Trading Company* was established on 1 October 1992 through the initiative of the *Turkish-American Businessmen Association* (TABA) to bring together private sectors and governmental agencies from BSEC associated states and the newly independent states (NIS) of Central Asia, marshalling both trade and project finance from its shareholders and outside institutions at the same time as fostering the growth of business organisations;

* The *Romanian Danube-Black Sea Foundation* established in 1992 aims to develop scientific, cultural and economic cooperation among the littoral states of the Danube and the Black Sea;

* The *Joint US-Turkish Black Sea Trade Mission and Conference* was organised on 3-10 July 1993 sponsored by the *American-Turkish Friendship Council* (AFTC) and the *Turkish Foreign Economic Relations Board* (DEIK) with the cooperation of some business councils from the BSEC countries. A conference and business forum jointly organised on 13-14 October 1992 by the *Middle East Economic Digest* (MEED) and *Interforum Services Limited* brought together government authorities and senior business decision makers who discussed specific projects and investment opportunities in the BSEC area;

* A *Black Sea Business Forum* was organised in April 1993 by the Union of the Free Businessmen of Georgia and the State Council of Georgia;

* The *Conference on Business Opportunities in the Black Sea Region: Challenges and Solutions* was held on 24-26 September 1993 in Tampa, Florida, with the aim of attracting American businessmen and investors to the BSEC area. This Conference was repeated two years later;

* The *Black Sea International Fair* was organised on 2-8 May 1994 in Turkey exhibiting raw materials and industrial products from BSEC countries;

* The first *BSEC International Energy Congress* was organized on 1-6 November 1993 in Ankara by the *World Energy Council* (WEC) to review existing energy resources, to discuss regional problems related to energy, and to examine the possibilities of cooperation;

* The *Convention on the Protection of the Black Sea Against Pollution* was signed on 22 April 1992 by all the littoral states of the Black Sea. There are also ongoing projects in this area such as the *Cooperative Marine Science Program for the Black Sea* (Comsblack), the *Programme of Environment Management and Protection of the Black Sea* (GEF), the *Programme of Monitoring Laboratory Analyses and Management of Information in the Countries Riparian to the Black Sea*, the *Programme on the Interaction between the Danube River and the North-Western Part of the Black Sea*, and finnaly the *Black Sea Regional Programme for Sea Research and Services* (COI);

* The *Convention on Cultural Scientific and Information Cooperation* between BSEC countries (excepting Bulgaria and Greece) was signed on 6 March 1993. The *Black Sea Chamber Orchestra* consisting of 17 musicians from different BSEC countries has been formed;
* The *Black Sea Television Service* established in Yalta, Crimea, is aimed at promoting the idea of a free zone in Crimea, thereby contributing to the atmosphere of cooperation in the BSEC area;
* The *Black Sea : the Zone of Interaction of Civilizations* is a program worked out by the Russian Academy of Sciences;
* The first *The Golden Eagle : The Black Sea Region Movies Festival and Competition* was held on 19-26 September 1992 in Tbilisi. The BSEC *Folklore Festival* was organised in October 1993 in Georgia;
* The *Black Sea University* was established in Constanta, Romania, as a seasonal school offering graduate level courses on issues related to the promotion of BSEC;
* Columbia University, Harriman Institute in the USA and the Centre for International Studies in Bosphorus University in Istanbul have jointly established the *Black Sea Studies Certificate Program*;
* Initiatives to establish BSEC unions for banking, medicine, cardiology and leather producers. The architects of the Black Sea region decided to form an organisation at the end of the *Conference of Architects of Black Sea Region* held on 10-12 October 1995 in Tbilisi. The *Bar Association of BSEC* was established in September 1994;
* A meeting was held in Istanbul on 11-13 April 1997 for the establishment of a *Union of the Red Cross and Red Crescent Associations* of the BSEC participating states and Belarus. A meeting was held on 18 February 1997 in Mangalia, Romania aimed at setting up a mechanism of cooperation amongst the chambers of commerce and commodity exchanges in BSEC Countries;
* A meeting on 3-4 April 1997 in Istanbul was held with a view to establishing a BSEC *Stock Exchange Market*.

Regarding concrete projects, there are completed and ongoing telecommunications projects in the BSEC region:
* *ITUR*, which links Italy, Turkey, Ukraine and Russia by fibre optic cable systems;
* *Black Sea Fibre Optic System* (KAFOS) which interconnects Turkey, Bulgaria, Romania and Moldova;
* *Eastern Black Sea Project* (DOKAP) is a digital microwave radio link covering Turkey, Georgia and Azerbaijan;
* *Trans Balkan Link* (TBL) is a digital transmission track line connecting Turkey, Bulgaria, Macedonia, Albania and Italy;
* *Trans Asia-Europe Fibre Optic System* (TAE) is another fibre optic system linking several countries in the region and beyond;
* *Black Sea Fibre Optic Cable System* (BSFOCS) will provide a fibre optic link between Bulgaria, Cyprus, Georgia, Greece, Russia and Ukraine;
* ADRIA-1 links Albania, Croatia and Greece.

The ITUR project which was launched soon after the establishment of the BSEC in June 1992 was completed on the 14 March 1996. Indeed, 48% of the traffic of ITUR was sold before the project was launched in 1993, thereby financing the project before it was completed. KAFOS was completed in 1996 and DOKAP are also scheduled to be operational in 1997. With regard to **transport**, a combined multi-modal transportation system is being planned which will form a ring corridor around the Black Sea. This will be connected to some of the Pan-European priority corridors in the West and to some Central Asian countries in the East. An electrical energy network project in the region is being developed. There are also other projects in consideration in different fields of cooperation ranging from agriculture to tourism, trade to pharmaceuticals and industry to the environment.

Prospects

As the BSEC is such a young organisation, it is difficult to make a conclusive assessment about its future prospects. An a priori evaluation of the implications of the various regional economic cooperation arrangements is subject to a high degree of speculation. It is very difficult to measure the degree of liberalisation of the member countries. My hypothesis is that the BSEC can become an important regional group influencing the economic, social and political development in its economic space.

The **constraints** to its future development are **geographic** (large and diverse area comprising different nations, religions, sects and cultures where not all members are littoral states of the Black Sea), **political** (historic divisions and disputes still simmer throughout the region) and **economic** (economies in the BSEC region are largely uncoordinated and for the most part underdeveloped). Although economic reforms are progressing in those BSEC countries in the process of transition, there remains much to be done with structural reform and sustainable growth is still some way off. Even though the benefits of reform are becoming more visible, the costs associated with transition are all too obvious. Nevertheless, as the new structures solidify, the supply responses will be more rapid and more efficient and market economic principles will prevail. Limited financial resources are a further constraint and the funding of projects will continue to need back up from the bilateral and multilateral financial organisations. Some BSEC states do not have convertible currencies making both trade and multi-lateral cooperation problematic.

But on a **positive note**, over 320 million people live in the 20 million km^2 of the BSEC region. This is a sizeable market by any criteria and as such is attractive for investment in diversified fields such as transportation, communications, energy and tourism. Owing to locational advantages, potentially large markets in the BSEC region could be integrated with relative ease to the important markets of Europe, the Mediterranean, Central Asia and the Middle East.

The BSEC region also has great potential arising from its unique geographical setting and common heritage. On-going reform and structural adjustment, geographical proximity and transportation facilities across the Black Sea coastline with 200 miles of navigable rivers reaching into the heart of Europe offer advantages incomparable with other regions. The Black Sea Basin has potential for expanding trade from the River Danube to the Ural Mountains. The Black Sea itself is the fourth largest inland body of water in the World. It supports a major fishing industry producing 60,000 tons per annum and employing some 75,000 people. It can also offer substantial tourism opportunities. Moreover, the BSEC region is well endowed with all types of energy such as petroleum, natural gas, coal, minerals and forestry. The member countries also have a wide spectrum of complementary industries and agriculture which should allow them to develop their relative comparative advantages in various economic activities.

Finally, the unifying political will which brings even warring parties together on the BSEC platform is a promising binding factor that could contribute to peace and stability in the region through prosperity. The BSEC is perhaps the only example of its kind where common economic benefits transcend political conflicts and where economic cooperation can serve as a catalyst for political reconciliation.

Conclusion : BSEC and Regional Security

The BSEC has opened a new and special chapter in Black Sea regional history. Established at a time when the Balkans and the Caucasus were facing great unrest and difficulties coupled with ethnic conflicts, the BSEC has proved itself to be a forum where the participating states put aside their differences and undertake joint economic projects for their mutual benefit. It has proved to be a regional arrangement where economic motives transcend political conflicts.

During the five years since its inception, the BSEC has asserted itself as an important confidence building measure and as such is an essential element of peace and stability in the region. The varying national interests, differing political assessments and diverse stages of development of the participating states have not prevented them from seeking common solutions to their problems through dialogue, economic cooperation and by creating an environment conducive to regional stability. The BSEC has helped to create a favourable psychological atmosphere in a region torn by conflicts in all forms and shades. The results are all the more impressive in the face of the diversity of the problems besetting the region. The BSEC represents a strong political will that has the determination of the member states to surmount these problems through dialogue and cooperation at different levels and dimensions including government, parliaments, private sectors, local administrations, NGOs and academicians. The realisation of stability and security requires balanced and parallel progress in all spheres of cooperation: political, economic and cultural. However, the sum of the overall gains, political, economic or otherwise, is more than the sum of economic gains in the BSEC.

Europe is in the process of recasting its defence policy in order to address risks outside the central part of the continent. There is an evident need for a cautious and balanced approach to security problems emanating from the Black Sea region. For their part, European countries and institutions should commit themselves to providing contribution to and dialogue with the BSEC and its individual constituent states. The EU could perhaps establish a special programme for BSEC members. The UN, OSCE, NATO, EU and other European institutions should play their part in addressing properly the various tensions and conflicts in the region.

The variety of risks and divergence of interests of the BSEC participating states make it hardly possible to find a short term formula for a concerted effort to overcome instability and to develop a regional approach to security. Therefore, the members of the BSEC are cautious over the inclusion of a security dimension in their regional cooperation agenda. Some countries and organisations believe that it is important for the coastal states to establish mechanisms for dialogue, and that it is an area in which Turkey, as a full member of NATO, could play a crucial role in assuaging the fears of conflict. Even though time is not yet ripe, Turkey might take a receptive view regarding the formation of a consultative mechanism which would comprise the coastal states of the Black Sea with a political and security content. Such a mechanism would not necessarily have an organic link with the BSEC.

The present security threats in the region are basically generated from ethnic and nationalistic tensions, dissatisfaction with economic and social transition, migration and refugee problems as well as from terrorism and interrelated illegal acts extending beyond regional boundaries. The BSEC is an attempt to develop the necessary roots of long term security and stability in the region by patiently weaving the delicate fabric of peace with the strong threads of economic cooperation. The ground of the region is being cultivated with concrete projects. What we shall reap depends on what we sow. Therefore, European institutions should make positive contributions to render the BSEC more successful. For the success of the BSEC is in the interests of greater Europe.

ECONOMIC COOPERATION WITHIN THE CIS: PROBLEMS AND OUTLOOK

Yuri V. Shishkov

*Institute of World Economy and International Relations
Russian Academy of Sciences, Moscow*

Following the disintegration of the USSR, the leaders of Russia and other post Soviet states naively believed that new opportunities would be opened up for mutually beneficial ties between them. To achieve this, a number of multilateral agreements were concluded, interalia on the principles of customs policy and creating a customs union (10 CIS states, March 1992), on a common monetary system based on the Soviet rouble, and on coordinated credit and monetary policy (8 CIS states, October 1992). All proved to be a waste of time.

Once it became clear that it would be impossible to maintain a single post-Soviet economic space, several CIS leaders hoped that it would be possible to "reintegrate" their national economies on a new market basis. This was to be achieved by the Agreement on Economic Union concluded on 23 September 1993 by 11 CIS states (Ukraine joined later as an associated member). It envisaged a gradual transformation from "free trade association" through customs union and common market to monetary union. To develop this agreement, treaties on free trade areas, on Customs Union, on Payments Union, on common science-technology projects and on a great number of potentially less important subjects were signed. But still there has been no real integration of CIS economies.

At the beginning of 1997 the Managing Secretary of the CIS, Ivan Korotchenja, could present only three real results of CIS activities in the past five years. First, thanks to the CIS, it was possible to manage the disintegration of the USSR in a peaceful manner unlike in Yugoslavia. Second, the long-term interests of each member country were aired in that it became clear who wanted what and how far they were prepared to go to get it. Third, institutional mechanisms and a legal basis were created as a framework within which dialogue between member states could occur[1]. Thus, it is officially accepted that the CIS is as yet no more than an interstate instrument of civilized divorce. To date, it has ensured the more or less peaceful coexistence of former Soviet republics.

Why has the CIS under-performed?

Ivan Korotchenja states that thanks to the efforts of the CIS, "legal channels have been opened for the fruitful cooperation of states in all spheres - from collective security to transport tariffs and from cooperation in space research to searching for a person who does not pay alimony". However, during the five years of the CIS about 800 agreements, protocols and other documents have been signed, yet these legal channels remain unused. Most observers would say that this is because leaders and political elites within these new states do not want to lose newly acquired independence and the power and/or personal material benefit that follows. This is true especially in respect of some Asian CIS states. But this is only a part of the truth. The main causes of failure are rooted in the economic sphere.

Firstly, real integration is only possible between countries with developed market economies where everyday cooperation and economic interaction is going on at grass roots level. Only such cohesion of national economies leads to their gradual transformation into single multistate social-economic organisms on a regional level. This not only leads to economic gain for the member countries concerned, but also makes the process irrevocable. By contrast, the socialist integration of the centrally planned economies within Comecon was based on intergovernmental interaction, artificial prices and virtual, not real, economic gain. The very first push from outside ruined this economic block because connections within it were held together with bad "cement". In essence, Comecon gave only the appearance of integration. That is why real integration within the CIS cannot begin until member countries are much further advanced along the road towards a market economy. At present, this journey is far from finished even in Russia to say nothing of other countries in the CIS. In some member states the non-state sector produces 75% of GDP, whereas in others only 15-20%. Integration of such diverse economies is not possible. Belarus, where the President is attempting to freeze and even reverse the privatisation process, is a case in point. But even when transition within the CIS is complete, the "reintegration" of the Soviet economic space is still not likely to occur because of a number of other reasons set out below.

Second, it is necessary to bear in mind that only national economies that have reached a high level of industrialisation and diversification can integrate. In such countries, the gains of entrepreneurship on a transnational scale become a powerful force in business. Less developed countries with agricultural and raw materials specialisation interact with each other as competitors rather than as mutually complementary partners. Exchange between industries and especially within industries under such circumstances is very poorly developed. Thus there is no material base or economic stimuli for interaction at a higher, national, level. This is confirmed by the empirical experience of economic integration in developing regions of the world. There are about 30 "free trade areas", "customs unions" and "common markets" in Latin America, Africa, South and South-East Asia. Many of them have turned out to be sterile flowers.

In the CIS, some economies are very much more industrialised than others, as **Table 1** below demonstrates. On this basis, the CIS cannot be considered as a prime candidate for economic integration.

Table 1
Structure of GDP and per capita income levels in CIS - 1995

Countries	Share in GDP (in %)			GDP per head	
	Agriculture	Industry	...including machine building	US$ in PPP	Index
Russia	9.2	28.2	5.1	4,224	100
Belarus	12.0	25.6	6.0	3,119	74
Ukraine	13.6	34.7	5.6	2,291	54
Kazakhstan	12.1	23.4	1.7	2,274	54
Uzbekistan	28.5	16.4	1.5	1,989	47
Armenia	43.5	29.1	3.7	1,866	44
Moldova	39.0	21.0	2.3	1,852	44
Turkmenistan	34.9	24.9	0.4	1,610	38
Azerbaijan	26.8	21.8	0.8	1,273	30
Kyrghyzstan	40.3	15.5	1.5	1,228	29
Georgia	45.6	17.4	1.0	940	22
Tajikistan	21.7	35.3	1.5	815	19

Sources: Statistical Handbook 1995. States of former USSR, Washington 1996; EIU Country Report: Russia 4th quarter 1996, p.37-38

However, of even greater importance is the structure of industrial production. In the CIS, the overwhelming share is accounted for by the extraction and processing of raw materials and fuel. But the industry that ideally provides for deep diversification of production and wide ties between and within industries is machine-building, which throughout the CIS accounts for at most 6% of GDP and in most cases substantially less than that. As far as high-technology industries are concerned, almost all are concentrated in the three leading CIS countries. Of the 60,000 most advanced enterprises within the Soviet defence complex, 70% were located in Russia, 17% in Ukraine and 4% in Belarus. All other Soviet republics accounted for only 9%[3].

The relative backwardness of most CIS countries vis-à-vis the four leading CIS states is mirrored by per capita income disparities of 4-5 fold. This huge difference is in part due to slow progress with market reform and also because of military operations on the territories of Tajikistan, Georgia and Azerbaijan. But the difference will not narrow quickly because of demographic dynamics. Over the next 20 years, the growth of the population in Azerbaijan and Kyrghyzstan will be 2.8 times higher than in Russia, in Tajikistan - 3.5 times, in Uzbekistan - 3.6 times, and in Turkmenistan - 3.9 times[4]. Indeed, the CIS has a "North" and a "South" of its own. To prevent this disparity from increasing, rates of economic growth in the "South" would need to be at least two and perhaps even four times higher than in Russia, which is not a likely prospect. Real integration between the "South" and "North" of the CIS is not a realistic prospect, even in 10-15 years.

Third, the transition from planned to market prices has changed the relative values and effectiveness of former close ties between Soviet republics. A trade that may have been profitable before reform has now become unprofitable. Moreover, every CIS country can chose between partners not only within the CIS but also in the "far abroad". The whole system of economic criteria has changed from one based on command planning to one based on comparative advantages. This has led to a considerable reorientation of trade flows for all CIS countries (see **Table 2** below) with the share of regional trade contracting by more than 50% over the last five years. For Russia, intra-CIS trade has contracted by over 70%.

Table 2
Intra-CIS trade as a proportion of total trade - 1991 and 1993 to 1996 (%)

	1991	1993	1994	1995	1996	Change 1996/1991
Russia	74.1	25.3	22.9	21.9	21.0	0.28
Uzbekistan	87.5	60.5	57.9	40.0	27.0	0.31
Armenia	85.1	71.8	59.6	52.3	35.8	0.42
Azerbaijan	88.6	53.5	53.7	36.7	39.6	0.45
Georgia	92.2	73.1	58.2	44.1	44.1	0.48
Tajikistan	85.3	31.3	33.8	47.2	50.6	0.50
Ukraine	82.5	55.9	64.0	57.4	58.7	0.71
Kazakhstan	87.0	72.5	59.2	59.7	61.4	0.71
Moldova	83.2	76.9	72.6	65.2	63.6	0.76
Kyrghyzstan	87.9	74.7	65.8	66.9	65.5	0.75
Belarus	87.2	75.3	64.0	69.3	65.7	0.75
CIS as a whole	*78.0*	*39.3*	*35.4*	*32.9*	*34.2*	*0.44*

Source: Statistical Handbook 1993. States of the Former USSR, Washington 1994; Foreign Trade Statistics in the USSR and Successor States, Washington 1995, p.148, 151; Mezhgosudarstwennyj statisticheskiy komitet. Statisticheskij bulletin) M. 1996, N3, 1997, N4.

Moreover, the share of mutual trade of CIS countries in their joint GDP has fallen even faster: from 19.2% in 1990 to 5.2% in 1996. For Russia, the figures are 14.7% to 3.6%. (See **Figure 1** below.)

Figue 1: Intra-regional exports of CIS states as proportion of GDP (%)

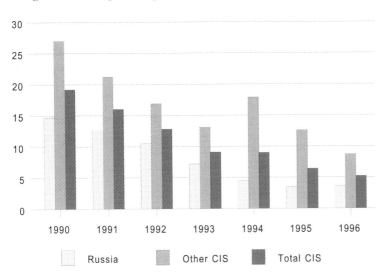

Note: GDP and inter-regional exports have been calculated in $ on PPP basis.
Source: EIU Country Report: Russia. 4th Q. 1996, p.37-38; Foreign Trade Statistics in the USSR and Successor States. The World Bank. 1995, p.148-150; Economic survey of Europe in 1996-1997, Appendix tables B-1, B-10; Russian Economic Trends, 1997, N1, p.95.

This means that the former pattern of interlocking national production processes is rapidly weakening. CIS economies, especially Russia, are becoming more and more isolated from each other, despite all the agreements and declarations about "reintegration" from the CIS bureaucracy.

Fourth, there is no symmetry between CIS states either in economic size, political influence, military-technical capacity or in overall potential. Basically, Russia dominates with 69% of CIS GDP, 72% of exports and absolute dominance in military-technical potential. By contrast, the EU is more a partnership of equals. In 1958, Germany had 36.2% of GDP of "the six", France - 32.8%, Italy - 18.5%[5]. Thus small countries could manoeuvre within this triangle and successfully lobby for their own interests. When Great Britain joined the EC this equilibrium became even more stable.

Under these circumstances and taking into account Russia's imperial past (as well as her far from irreproachable present policy towards some CIS countries), small CIS states have more than enough grounds to be against super-state institutes which Moscow would dominate. Thus most CIS member states are strictly against the idea of a customs union and other supra-national bodies, preferring to conduct economic relations with CIS neighbours through bilateral consensus instead. It comes as no surprise therefore that even the CIS statute was not signed by three members - Moldova, Ukraine and Turkmenistan. In January 1996, Ukraine, Turkmenistan, Azerbaijan, and Armenia did not sign the common decision of the Heads of States Council on the formation of a customs and payment union[6]. In Spring 1997, the agreement on the "Conception of Economic Integrating Development of the CIS to 2000" has only been signed at the Head of State level by the chairman of this Council, one Boris Yeltsin. Thus for the foreseeable future, the CIS will not have effective institutes for multilateral cooperation. This will have consequences both economic and political.

Probable Perspectives

It is clear that the "reintegration" of the post-Soviet economic space within the framework of the CIS will not be possible for some time. Even external political events, such as NATO enlargement to the East, will not bind the CIS closer together.

How thus will economic relations develop between CIS countries? First, despite the above-mentioned trends, Russia remains the centre of gravity for all national economies of the CIS, excepting Turkmenistan. Given the poor conditions for normal multilateral trade and payment relations, the less developed CIS states support their economic relations with Russia and other more developed CIS states on a bilateral basis in the form of the so called "hub and spoke" model (see **Table 3** below). This hampers the development of multilateral economic ties within the CIS, but does not prevent member states from developing economic ties on a bilateral basis with other countries beyond the CIS.

Table 3
Export trade flows within the CIS (% of total exports to CIS)

	Years	Russia	Ukraine Belorussia Moldova	Kazakhstan	Middle Asia	Caucasus
Russia	1991	-	56.7	10.2	20.4	12.7
	1993	-	61.0	17.2	11.7	10.1
	1994	-	73.5	15.6	8.2	2.7
	1995	-	72.7	17.0	8.5	1.8
	1996	-	72.0	16.4	9.3	2.3
Ukraine	1991	66.7	14.3	4.3	9.4	5.3
Belorussia	1993	74.4	13.6	3.0	5.4	3.6
Moldova	1994	75.7	15.7	1.6	5.8	1.2
	1995	79.4	14.0	1.5	4.4	0.7
	1996	80.2	13.2	1.7	3.1	1.8
Kazakhstan	1991	60.8	15.0	-	21.5	2.7
	1993	70.2	12.4	-	14.0	3.4
	1994	80.8	8.1	-	9.0	2.1
	1995	79.9	6.9	-	12.3	0.9
	1996	80.4	7.6	-	11.5	0.5
Middle Asia	1991	57.2	15.0	11.2	10.4	6.2
	1993	36.9	27.7	15.9	13.5	6.0
	1994	35.2	18.8	13.4	27.8	4.8
	1995	27.9	34.2	13.9	13.1	10.9
	1996	34.5	14.6	20.0	23.4	7.5
Caucasus	1991	65.0	17.1	5.2	7.9	4.8
	1993	53.6	20.1	8.4	10.5	7.4
	1994	52.4	22.0	3.5	16.9	5.2
	1995	48.5	24.2	3.9	7.7	15.7
	1996	45.1	7.7	3.8	16.1	27.3

Source:Statistical Handbook 1995. States of former USSR, Washington 1995, tables 3,8; Foreign Trade Statistics in the USSR and Successor States, Washington 1995, p.150; (Sodruzhestvo Nezavisimych Gosudarstv 1995. Satisticheskiy ezhegodnik) M., 1996, p.64-65.

There have been significant changes in the geographical structure of export flows within the CIS over the past five years. Exports from Ukraine, Belarus, Moldova and Kazakhstan were notably re-oriented away from other regions of the CIS and towards

Russia. Russian exports mirrored this shift, moving away from the Caucuses and Middle Asia and towards the European CIS and Kazakhstan. This confirms that certain factors are working towards the economic integration of Russia with a small group of relatively developed CIS countries - Belarus (in 1996 Russia accounted for 52.2% of its foreign trade), Ukraine (44.4%), Kazakhstan (49.5%). It remains possible that Moldova (Russia accounted for 50% of its foreign trade) may at some stage join these three.

But even the above-mentioned 4-5 CIS states cannot begin the process of real integration when the right conditions for it to succeed do not exist. Besides, Russia itself as the centre of gravity must not only overcome its deep social-economic crisis but must also become a developed and prosperous country. A sick economy is not attractive to neighbours who are just as ill. Moreover, political tension within the CIS must be eliminated along with any residual territorial disputes. Such disputes in the recent past have pushed Ukraine towards NATO and the EC.

CIS states in Middle Asia and the Caucusus are gradually reorientating their exports from Russia to Middle Asian markets. This confirms the assumption that this group is neither ready nor prepared to integrate with European partners in the CIS. They will look to their own forms of shallow economic interaction within the subregion, as well as in a wider geo-economic context. Institutions for this have already been created: in 1994 the Commonwealth of Central Asian States was created with the participation of Kazakhstan, Uzbekistan, Turkmenistan, and Kirghyzstan. Before this, in February 1992, these four states plus Azerbaijan entered the Organization of Economic Cooperation created in 1964 by Iran, Pakistan and Turkey.

Efforts to force the creation of a Customs Union between Russia, Belarus and Kazakhstan (1995) - and to extend it to include impoverished Kyrghyzstan (1996) - will not help to further integration between this small group of CIS countries in the future. As to the Union between Russia and Belrus (April 1996 and May 1997), this is doomed to failure so long as the current and retarded state of Belarusan economic and political reform persists. Bilateral treaties signed by the two Presidents merely represent a political game and can only frighten other countries away from further rapprochement with Russia.

If in the coming years Russia can achieve high rates of economic growth, re-establish its high technology industries and improve the welfare of its population, it could begin to realize the existing integration potential of the 4-5 European countries of the CIS. As to the other CIS states, some could join later as associated states. But if Russia fails to become an attractive centre of gravity then the disintegration of the post-Soviet economic area will become **irrevocable** and CIS countries will reach out for other centres of gravitation in Europe (including the EU) and in Asia (including China and the Middle East). The share of the EU in the foreign trade of Ukraine has already increased from 6.3% in 1992 to 13.5% in 1995, in that of Belarus from 16.4% to 17.8% and in that of Moldova from 2.8% to 12%[7]. The EU share in Russian trade turnover rose from 16.4% in 1992 to 35.7% in 1996[8].

Inability to integrate economically would not necessarily preclude the close military-political union of all or a considerable part of the CIS, especially in the face of a growing threat from Islamic fundamentalism. But the enlargement of NATO to the East is unlikely to become a factor influencing the political unity or integration of CIS states. In the global market place, economic relationships between states are now conducted according to more complicated rules which leaders of CIS states have not considered up to now and, I am afraid, do not completely master today.

Footnotes

1. Nezavisimaya gazeta) 17.01.97.

2. Ibidem.

3. Izwestiya, 15.03.96.

4. Forecast of the experts of IMEMO.

5. *European Economy*, N14, 1982 (November), p.195.

6. Informazionnyj bulleten Mezhdunarodnogo ekonomicheskogo komiteta M., 1996, N3,p.41.

7. Calculated upon: Statistical Handbook 1995. States of the Former USSR, 1993 and 1995.

8. Calculated upon: Russian customs statistics data.

ECONOMIC COOPERATION AMONG THE CBSS COUNTRIES

Mārtiņš Lācis

Secretariat of the Council of Baltic Sea States, Ministry of Foreign Affairs of the Republic of Latvia

Summary and Introduction[1]

In their efforts to foster regional identities, region-builders most often rely on historical myth and symbols to evoke common aspirations. Typically, these myths are based on history which precedes the national distinctions in the area, e.g. in Germany, the Baltic Sea Region is known as the "New Hansa", after the North German Hanseatic League which dominated trade in the Baltic area in the Middle Ages.

The Council of the Baltic Sea States (CBSS) was established in 1992 to serve as an overall regional forum to promote cooperation and coordination among the Baltic Sea States following the removal of the "Iron Curtain". The CBSS encompasses a wide range of goals and various areas of cooperation. This paper, however, will focus on the main projects and forms of economic cooperation.

The main goal of the developed countries is the extension of their export markets. In order to carry out this goal within the countries of the potential market, it is necessary to ensure political stability, adequate economic legislation, as well as to remove border obstacles and develop transport, communications and services. The main goals of the countries in economic transition are their economic development, attracting investment, upgrading their industries as well as receiving practical contributions towards meeting the necessary requirements to start accession negotiations with the EU.

According to previous experiences of cooperation and taking into consideration the various goals outlined above, the following conclusion can be drawn - **an effective cooperation between the two groups of countries is possible within the "points of intersection"**. For example, with the development of transit routes through the Baltic States and the Kaliningrad oblast of Russia. Interests of trade extension ensure an opportunity to cooperate in the field of developing transport corridors.

The economic development of the Baltic States, Kaliningrad and Poland fosters greater optimism within the business community than within the governments of the countries concerned. While business focuses on economic potential and development opportunities, governments value the work which has to be done to bring both legal frameworks and macroeconomic indicators up to EU requirements.

Economic cooperation within the region helps and promotes the development of democratic institutions, the improvement of legislation, environmental protection and cross-border cooperation. Because the goal of the Baltic States and Poland is to become EU members, economic cooperation will facilitate this process.

General Description of the Region

The Baltic Sea Region (BSR) shares several common traits as well as obvious differences in its organization, scope of activities and modes of working. Nevertheless, a prominent common denominator is that it is composed of countries and provinces formerly divided by the Iron Curtain. The BSR consists of the littoral states surrounding the Baltic

Sea, i.e. Denmark, Estonia, Finland, Germany, Latvia, Lithuania, Poland, Russia and Sweden. In addition, Norway, Iceland and the European Union are members of the Council of Baltic Sea States, bringing the total number of participating countries and entities to 12. However, in terms of practical cooperative effort, the area is more limited, as some parts of the participating states are more Baltic-related than others. In Germany, the Länder of Hamburg, Schleswig-Holstein and Mecklenburg-Vorpommern are the real participants in practical terms, as are the five coastal wojewodships of Poland and the Leningrad and Kaliningrad oblasts in Russia. With around 60 million inhabitants, the area is densely urbanized and produced a combined GDP of US$1,000bn in 1991.

The BSR has historically been a very important trading area, not least because the Baltic Sea has been at the crossroads of different cultural and economic regions within Europe. However, during most of this century, normal trade was prevented by the existence of command economies in several countries. Now, once again, the preconditions for increasing trade exist. In all the former command economies, the process of change to market economics is under way. Some countries have been able to progress faster than others. Various significant changes in economic and social life have been made in the last six years, but all the requirements of a fully functioning market economy have not yet been realized.

In recent years, trade between BSR countries has increased by approximately 20% per year. For example, Estonia's exports in the Region amounts to some 70% of its total exports. But although trade, investments and business cooperation between BSR countries differ, in general, business shows great interest in expanding into all markets of the Region. The BSR can definitely be considered as an area of economic growth.

There are at present very large differences in relative living standards among the countries of the Region. But GDP growth in Latvia, Lithuania, Estonia and Poland is expected to be 3-6% in 1997. In Russia, GDP growth could also resume, thus heralding an overdue recovery of the Russian economy. In the western part of the BSR, several countries have problems with economic imbalances. Their growth rates are presently too low to substantially reduce unemployment.

The Council of the Baltic Sea States (CBSS)
In the Baltic Sea area, a certain amount of cooperation on sectoral matters has been in evidence for several decades. Particularly in the environmental field, joint action has been in progress since the signing of the Convention on the Protection of the Marine Environment in the Baltic Sea in 1974. Nevertheless, it was only with the inauguration of the CBSS that the term "Baltic Sea Region" came into usage, making this the first new Region in northern Europe. The CBSS forms the anchor point for the BSR. It was founded at the meeting of the Foreign Ministers of the littoral states held in Copenhagen in March 1992. The Declaration establishing the CBSS consists of four main parts:
* **Part I** lays out the political framework for regional cooperation;
* **Part II** concerns itself with the actual CBSS and identifies six specific areas to which particular attention should be paid. These are -
  * *Assistance to new democratic institutions,*
  * *Economic and technological assistance and cooperation,* including the promotion of economic growth and development of market mechanisms in the former planned economies, as well as the intention to promote economic assistance in these economies in the initial phase,
  * *Humanitarian matters and health,*
  * *Environment and energy,*

- *Culture, education, tourism and information,*
- *Transport and communications,* focusing on the development of a communication infrastructure and other transport links;
* **Parts III and IV** emphasized the openness of the cooperative effort and ways to implement the ideas in the Declaration, stating that particular attention should be paid to economic and technological assistance and cooperation.

There are currently three Working Groups and Committees of Senior Officials under the auspices of the CBSS. These are:
- *Working Group on Economic Cooperation* (Chair 1996/97 : EU Commission);
- *Working Group on Assistance to Democratic Institutions* (Chair 1996/97: Denmark);
- *Working Group on Nuclear and Radiation Safety* (Chair 1966/97: Finland).

These Working Groups are composed of specialists within the stated areas from relevant ministries of the member states. Their tasks are to formulate status reports and forward suggestions for action within their areas of competence and to serve as a knowledge basis for the Committee of Senior Officials and the Council. The Working Group on Economic Cooperation (WGEC) coordinates member countries' joint economic development projects.

Regional Economic Cooperation Projects

An important step for coordinating efforts by member countries was the adoption of **Action Programmes** at the Council meeting in Kalmar, Sweden, in July 1996. These programmes are seen as representing a step forward for regional cooperation since they indicate the direction the cooperative effort is likely to take in the coming years by delineating a number of priority areas.

The ambitious goal for the programme of *Economic Integration and Prosperity* is to develop the Baltic Sea Region into an integrated, competitive and dynamic area of sustained growth through the creation of a regional market for trade, investment and cooperation. This programme has five components: *Economic Integration and Transition*, which aims to liberalise trade, improve the business climate and promote land reform; *The Baltic Sea Region and the European Union*, which helps to advance the gradual integration of Estonia, Latvia, Lithuania and Poland into the EU; *Transport*, which seeks the removal of obstacles to the cross-border flow of goods, the establishment of transport corridors, the upgrading of ports, and an improvement to telecommunication facilities; *Spatial Planning*, focusing on an intensification of efforts for regional development whose initial aims are to enhance spatial cohesion and to overcome earlier divisions by contributing to balanced growth within the region; and finally *Energy*, concentrating on environmental aspects of energy production and use, including both electricity, natural gas and nuclear installations.

Several hundred bilateral and multilateral projects both large and small have been prepared and many have already been implemented. The first results of the sub-programme on economic integration indicate substantial progress in establishing free trade areas (i.e. common transit procedure for Estonia, Latvia and Lithuania). Most favoured nation treatment (MFN) as a minimum standard for trade relations among CBSS members will be achieved only when Russia grants MFN status to Estonia. Free trade for non-agricultural goods already applies amongst most of the member countries. Some BSR states have even introduced free trade in agricultural goods.

The European Commission has agreed to contribute towards the drawing up of a "macroeconomic identity" for the BSR. The objective is to form an idea of the economic potential of the Region as a whole in which radical changes in economic development in the coming decades are to take place. The progress of change depends on the success and speed of transition. Progress in the largest country in the Region - Russia - will no doubt be very significant in determining the future development of East-West traffic.

One of the main factors contributing to the growth of trade and the development of East-West traffic is the growth of GDP in the countries involved. The so-called catching-up model (which assumes the elimination of differences between countries due to faster growth in the countries in transition of 5% per annum against 2.5% annual growth in Germany, Denmark and Sweden) indicates that trade among these countries and Russia may triple by the year 2000 and increase tenfold by 2010, which in absolute terms (constant prices), means an increase by US$33bn up to the end of the present decade and US$84bn in the following decade respectively. This is another example of the potential of the Region and indicates excellent opportunities for further cooperation.

A modern system of land and other real estate property registration is essential and the process of land reform and creating a real estate market is to be continued. Nordic countries provide efficient assistance to the Baltic States and Poland by training personnel and supplying them with modern technology. Further development of land, sea and air traffic is being achieved through enhanced infrastructure, bearing in mind the environmental aspects.

These are a few examples of regional cooperation projects under the auspices of the CBSS. However, this is not sufficient to describe the CBSS as a preparatory class for European integration, as sometimes occurs. Such integration will not be possible until much more emphasis is placed on the economic dimension and on contributions from outside for the improvement of our infrastructures. In this context, it must be recalled that to progress smoothly through the pre-accession negotiations, the European Union associates will have to demonstrate not only that they are amending their legislation in accordance with EU directives, but are also succeeding with their general economic development.

Footnote

[1] The views expressed in this paper are those of the author and do not necessarily reflect the opinion of the Ministry of Foreign Affairs of the Republic of Latvia or the Council of Baltic Sea States.

References

Cooperation in the Baltic Sea Region, the Barents Region and the Black Sea Region. A documentation report. Erik Hansen (ed.), Oslo, 1997.

The Stockholm Declaration on Growth and Development in the Baltic Sea Region. Baltic Sea Business Summit. Stockholm, 1996.

Business' Priorities and Concerns in the Baltic Sea Region. Baltic Business Advisory Council. Kiel, 1997.

Action Programmes for the Baltic Sea States Co-operation. Fifth Ministerial Session. Kalmar, 1996.

Baltic Sea Region Initiative. Communication from the Commission. European Commission, Brussels, 1996.

Current and future EU policy on the Baltic Sea Region with specific reference to local and regional aspects. Opinion of the Committee of the Regions. Brussels, 1996.

Presidency Declaration. Baltic Sea States Summit. Visby, 1996.

Transition Report Update, EBRD. London, April 1997.

Regional Cooperation in the Baltic Sea States Area. Bertelsmann Wissenschaftsstiftung. Conference on the Baltic States integration into the European Union. CBSS CSO Chairman's Report. Tallinn, June 1997.

ECONOMIC COOPERATION IN THE EASTERN BALTIC SEA REGION: A FINNISH VIEW[1]

Pekka Sutela

Department of Economics, University of Helsinki
Advisor to the Board, Bank of Finland

This paper deals with the Finnish experience and views on regional economic cooperation primarily in what can be called the Eastern Baltic Sea Region (EBSR for short), comprising Finland, the three Baltic countries and (North-Western) Russia[2]. For a wider view, other regions may also be touched upon. The Baltic Sea Region includes in addition to the above countries, Sweden, the northernmost parts of Poland and Germany, Denmark, Norway and, due to historical reasons, also Iceland. Altogether, this is a region of 50-60 million inhabitants. The Euro-Arctic region, on the other hand, includes the northernmost provinces of Norway, Sweden, Finland and the northern part of north-western Russia. The emphasis in this paper will, however, be on the EBSR.

Background: Finnish economic relations with the USSR

The share of the Soviet Union in total Finnish foreign trade averaged 16% in 1953-1990. This share peaked at about 25% in 1983-1985, as the price of oil, the major Soviet exportable, surged and the US$, the pricing currency, was strong. In 1986-1990, as both oil and the US$ became weaker and the Soviet economy stagnated, Finnish exports to Western markets boomed and those to the USSR declined, not only relatively by falling to 12.7% of all exports, but also absolutely, declining from Finmark (FIM)18bn (current) in 1985 to less than FIM13bn in 1990.

The high level of Finnish-Soviet trade was not due to the bilateral trade and clearing system then in existence. Rather, the Soviet authorities used the bilateral trade system for political reasons to maintain a higher Finnish share in Soviet imports from the West - 10-15% in the 1980s - than would have been warranted by Finnish competitiveness. As this political preference became absent or nonoperative, Finnish exports to Russia were bound to decline even without the Soviet collapse. The fact that Finland has again become one of the major non-CIS trading partners of Russia reflects not only geographical proximity but also the benefits of Soviet-era traditions.

The Soviet Union inherited a few previously German-owned enterprises after the war, but showed no interest in further investment in Finland. Neither were the Finns encouraging such investment. Finnish companies built a few large-scale projects in Russia, but had no investment in the USSR. After joint ventures became possible in the late 1980s, about 350 Finnish-Soviet joint ventures were registered by early 1991[3].

In numbers of joint ventures, Finland was third after Germany and the USA. Almost all Finnish establishments were minor. Experiences of joint ventures were mixed and most were converted to fully or majority owned Russia-based companies when this became possible. Cooperation with a Soviet co-owner was often complicated and joint ventures were rarely able to enjoy a level playing field.

The collapse of the Soviet economy in 1991 together with the abolishment of bilateral trade led to a collapse of Finnish exports to the USSR from almost FIM13bn in 1990 to FIM4.5bn in 1991[4]. The share of the former Soviet Union and the Baltic States[5] in Finnish foreign trade bottomed out at about 6% in 1992. Because misunderstandings on this point abound, it is necessary to emphasise that this was an important, though not the major reason, for the Finnish economic crisis which wiped-out 13% of GDP in 1991-1993. After collapsing in 1991, Finnish exports to Russia stagnated in 1992 and only started to grow in 1993. This growth still continues. After annual growth of about 100% in 1993 and 50% in 1994, growth was only 6% in 1995 but 34% in 1996. Finnish enterprises are confident that this growth will continue, largely irrespective of the state of the Russian macro economy. Russian figures differed widely from these Finnish statistics especially in 1993-1994 and again in 1996. A particularly large part of imports seems to have escaped Russian statistics and the tax man in those years.

As elsewhere, Finnish foreign trade with the USSR was with Moscow, i.e. with the central authorities and state-owned foreign trade organisations. True enough, the so-called border trade outside the centralised protocols also existed, but its share remained minor. Seen from the Baltic viewpoint, something like 80-90% of their trade was with the non-Baltic USSR immediately before independence was restored. The rest was divided between intra-Baltic trade and trade with the non-Soviet abroad. Even the 5-10% of trade with developed market economies was handled by Moscow and Leningrad-based Soviet foreign trade organizations. This was the hub and spoke trade structure typical of centre-periphery relations.

The reorientation of Baltic trade flows after 1991 was fast and sweeping. Though statistics - especially concerning transit and trade with the CIS - are less than perfect, an interesting picture emerges[6]. In 1993-1995 total exports from all three Baltic countries expanded rapidly but unevenly. By 1995, Estonian exports-per-capita of about US$1,200 equalled that of Hungary, whilst those of Latvia - US$500 - and Lithuania - US$750 - were on a par with Poland. Only Estonia can probably be characterised as a case of export-led growth. Altogether, Baltic exports were US$5-8bn in 1995. Their imports totalled US$7.3bn. One would expect a trade deficit in a fast growing economy as investment goods are shipped in. The statistically measured growth performance of the Baltic countries is however quite modest[7] and the evidence of a particularly large share of investment goods in their imports is less than convincing[8]. The trade deficits - in 1996, 22% of GDP in Estonia, 15% in Latvia and 11% in Lithuania - therefore give rise to serious concern[9]. Also current account deficits - about 10% of GDP in Estonia and estimated at 7.0% of GDP in Latvia and 8.7% in Lithuania in 1996[10] - are clearly excessive.

Geographical trade reorientation has also been more uneven than sometimes assumed. The share of the CIS - mostly Russia - in foreign trade is still more than half in Lithuania, about a quarter in Latvia and slightly more than a fifth in Estonia. Quite probably, these figures are underestimates. As foreseen early on[11], intra-Baltic trade has remained decidedly modest. No bilateral Baltic trade share reaches 10% and minerals are usually the prime traded good.

Roughly, the fifteen EU member states account for 40% of Lithuanian, 50% of Latvian and 60% of Estonian foreign trade. Estonian EU trade is strongly dominated by Finland and Sweden with a combined 40-50% share of all foreign trade. In Latvia, these two countries account for less than a fifth of all trade and in Lithuania only for a few percentage points. In the two more southerly Baltic countries, the share of the twelve non-Nordic EU members rose rapidly to about 30% of all trade. Thus the overall trade orientation of the three Baltic countries actually differs to some extent. Lithuania trades with Russia and the non-Nordic EU in that order; Latvia with the non-Nordic EU and Russia; and Estonia with Finland, Russia and Sweden. Germany, the overwhelming economic power of the Baltic Sea region, is in addition to Russia the only important trade partner common to all the

Baltic countries with bilateral trade shares of at least 10% and usually higher with each of the countries. For Germany, on the other hand, the whole Baltic Sea region is decidedly a secondary trade area with about an 8% share of all trade. Indeed, the trade dominance of Germany in the region is such that two thirds of the foreign trade of the Baltic Sea region countries is accounted for by Germany. Of intra-region trade, Germany has about 35%, while Russia and Finland trail with a 10% share each. Such trade within the region is, with a share of 60-70% of total trade, crucial for the Baltic countries. Finland has almost 40% of its total trade with the region, mostly with Germany and Sweden. For Russia, the figures are 18% for exports and 25% for imports.

Baltic foreign trade balances clearly deteriorated in 1996. The situation was worst in Latvia, where real export growth was just 1.1%, while imports, particularly those of inter-mediate consumption goods, boomed by 13.6%. In Estonia exports almost stagnated in dollar terms while imports grew almost by 10%. Only in Lithuania did both imports and exports seemingly grow robustly in dollar terms, by 17% and 14% respectively.

Foreign investment figures in the region remain controversial. In the World Bank view, Estonia, the smallest of the three countries, had by end-1995 attracted about one half more foreign direct investment than the two other countries combined[12]. Most of the investment comes from Sweden and Finland. The flow to Latvia has been about one half of the Estonian level. After declining in 1995, it picked up in 1996 and may have been as high or higher than in Estonia, where the 1996 level was only about one third[13] or one half[14] of the one reached in 1994-1995. Investment flows to Lithuania have remained modest. In Latvia, Denmark and Britain are relatively major investors, as is Germany in Lithuania. It is interesting to note, in view of Germany's dominant trade position, that it is nowhere in the Baltics the main investor. There is also major Russian investment in each of the countries which is probably underestimated in the statistics.

Activities of Finnish enterprises in Russia and the Baltics in 1991-1996: An Overview

Like other countries, Finland had difficulties in following the speed of the collapse of the USSR and the birth of the new Russia. During the last months of the USSR, a new treaty on the fundamentals of Finnish-Soviet relations was negotiated to substitute for the 1948 Treaty of Friendship, Cooperation and Assistance. New Russia soon adopted the same treaty. In January 1992, a new most favoured nations based trade agreement was signed, confirming that trade should be on market conditions. A separate treaty was soon signed concerning cooperation in the so-called neighbouring areas, originally the regions of Murmansk, Karelia, St. Petersburg and its environs, but later widened to embrace also the Arkhangelsk region. These were quite nonspecific treaties, mainly notable for con-firming the adherence to IMF and GATT principles in trade. But they also provided for a degree of continuity while underlining the change in rules and institutions. As Finland became an EU member, the Korfu agreement became the defining set of rules for Finnish-Russian economic relations.

Finnish trade relations with the Baltic countries have been based on market principles since these countries liberalised their foreign trade in 1991-1992 (Estonia and Latvia) and 1993 (Lithuania). Soon after, these countries negotiated free trade agreements with EFTA and in 1995 signed Europe agreements with the EU. The Europe agreements still remain to be ratified by all the EU countries. The Baltic countries agreed upon free trade in indus-trial goods in 1994 and in agricultural goods in 1996. A customs union is planned for 1998.

Tables 2-4 give the level and structure of Finnish trade with the whole geographical area of the former Soviet Union(FSU). Table 5 does the same for the three FSU Baltic

States alone. Russia accounts for the major share, some 67% of this trade. The Baltics account for one quarter. As an export market, the Baltics have risen to about 60% of Russia, while the non-Russia CIS, mainly Ukraine and Kazakhstan, are far behind. As Russia accounted in 1996 for slightly less than 7% of Finnish foreign trade, the share of the FSU (geographical area) has returned to be almost equal to what it was in 1990. The intensity of Finnish trade with Estonia, in particular, is quite phenomenal. Finnish exports to Estonia are worth about US$600 per Estonian. This is higher than per capita exports to wealthy Sweden, and compares with the figure of about US$15 for Russia. Indeed, a number of gravity model studies imply that Finnish-Estonian, Finnish-Latvian and Swedish-Estonian trade flows in early-to-mid 1990s were higher - in some cases much higher - than their potential levels as forecast by factors such as GDP and distance[15].

A relatively large share of Baltic trade consists of East-West transit, basically oil, oil products and other primary products from Russia to the West as well as different commodities from the West to Russia. Measured in tons, an overwhelming majority of Russian trade through the Baltic Sea uses Baltic harbours, in particularly Ventspils, Tallinn, Riga and Kleipeda. Estimates regarding the impact of transit on GDP are at times quite high, but remain very unreliable as well as sometimes politically laden. Somewhat peculiarly, many Russians tend to see transit through the Baltic harbours as a waste of money and even as a political risk. Plans for additional harbour capacity in St. Petersburg and the Leningrad region abound, but resources are scarce. Therefore, dependence on Baltic and partially also Finnish harbours will continue[16].

In the early 1990s, many Finnish authorities believed that the country should become the major gateway between World markets and Russia. Such hopes were partially based on the fact that the small number of harbours remaining in Russia were already congested and on the generally poor shape of the road network connecting Russia and Europe. But there were also exaggerated hopes of economic recovery in Russia, especially in the North-Western regions. It is now generally understood that although the neighbouring areas remain part of the Finnish home market, St. Petersburg and environs are probably relatively declining regions due to their heavy dependence upon military-related production and research that Russia will not be able to maintain. Fortunately, no major infrastructure investment has been made on gateway grounds, and though some may be forthcoming - the Helsinki/St. Petersburg/Moscow transportation link is an EU priority - they need proper justification.

The role of St. Petersburg in many Finnish calculations has also failed on another account in that the city has lost all the battles that it has taken up against Moscow. It has a declining economic base, it has not become Russia's leading financial centre, nor a special economic zone, and it has been unable to defend military production, research and development. Relative to St. Petersburg, Moscow is a boom city. But St. Petersburg still has several million inhabitants[17], many representatives in Moscow decision-making and a crucial geographical position. A regional approach to Russian foreign economic relations may become topical in the near future, since the general opening up of the Russian economy has either failed or - to the degree that it has taken place - might prove unsustainable due to rising protectionist pressures. Thus, thinking in terms of special economic zones might well come back, and if so, St. Petersburg would be a prime candidate and Finland - as well as potentially at least Estonia - would be uniquely positioned to utilise it. A related feature is the growth in outward processing. Finnish textile companies employ in this way some 4,000-5,000 people in North-Western Russia. This is however an activity which is particularly dependent on the vagaries of the Russian tax and customs regimes. In

Estonia, the situation is naturally much more stable. A Finnish electronics component company is in fact by far the largest Estonian exporter.

Available statistics on direct investment in Russia leave much to be desired[18]. It seems that of all Finnish foreign investment, only a couple of percentage points have gone to Eastern Europe as a whole. Russia has been next to Estonia as the second most popular target country in the region. Poland comes next. Within Russia, St. Petersburg and the Leningrad region are the most frequent sites, with about 60% of Finnish investment projects. If the figures available are comparable, Finnish investment in Russia was in 1990-1995 less than 2% of all foreign investment received by the country. Finland, which ranked third among the early founders of joint ventures, now probably ranks 10-12 in terms of cumulative investment flows and 8-10 in terms of numbers of foreign owned companies. It is only in neighbouring, small and poor Karelia that Finns are the most important investors. In St. Petersburg, Finns rank third.

Most foreign investment in Russia goes to the energy and construction sectors. Hardly any Finnish investment does. Finnish investment has gone primarily into the service sectors. Only 9% of projects were by the end of 1994 in the production of goods. Most of the investment is in small-scale establishments with less than 10 people employed. This also helps to explain why perhaps only one half of all Finnish enterprises active in, for example, St. Petersburg are recorded in official Finnish sources. There are only a few Finnish direct investments in Russia employing hundreds of people. These are descendants of early joint ventures in furniture and cables. Their experience, as well as that of all Finnish investment in Russia, is mixed. In 1995 investor expectations were less optimistic than in 1993[19]. Learning has thus taken place. The instability and unpredictability of the administrative, legal and political environment - in particular taxation - is regarded as the foremost problem. Crime is much less of a problem. Overall, though some investment is clearly successful, the Finnish attitude towards investment in Russia is clearly much less optimistic than that concerning trade.

Even in forestry, the backbone of Finnish industry, no large-scale investment has taken place. The former Finnish paper mill in Svetogorsk, now a few kilometres outside the border, is owned and operated by a Swedish group, who have serious problems. The same is true of several other forestry investments in Russia. The Finnish forest industry fells and imports large amounts of roundwood from Karelia. This single export revenue of the Karelian republic is however endangered by environmental concerns particularly in Germany, a crucial market.

Instruments and policies in Finland's economic policy vis-à-vis Russia

The role of government policies in current Finnish-Russian trade is marginal, especially when compared with Soviet state trading. Since Finland became a member of the EU in 1995, foreign economic policy vis-à-vis Russia is exercised through three main channels: EU trade policy, the Finnish-Russian Commission for Economic Relations, and the Policy on Neighbouring Areas. On the Finnish side, the Ministry of Foreign Affairs has main responsibility for all these three channels although other officials - in particular the Ministry for Trade and Industry - also participate.

The Finnish-Russian Commission for Economic Relations

Finland decided in 1991-1992 that a government-level political framework would be needed for trade and cooperation with the new market-oriented Russia, since the role of political decision-making would remain important. Therefore, the Finnish-Soviet Commission for Economic Relations was transformed into a Finnish-Russian

Commission. On the Russian side, it was for quite some time chaired by Deputy Prime Minister Oleg Davydov (who spent years in Finland building the Loviisa atomic power station), on the Finnish side by a Cabinet Minister nominated to oversee "Eastern Trade" (currently Mr. Ole Norrback, Minister for European Affairs). The Commission has three permanent working groups (trade, energy and traffic) and several ad hoc working groups (investment, entrepreneurship, shipbuilding, standards and certificates, Bashkortostan, Nenetsia and the Komi Republic). The number of working groups is radically smaller than with the USSR, when the Soviet planning system made it convenient to have a formal forum for any industrial branches of importance in trade. The rise of the regional approach is also notable. Several other Russian regions have also been interested in having an ad hoc working group of their own. The competence of the Commission is also narrower than with the USSR. Trade policy competence is with the EU, and there is no longer any state trading. Although getting the Russians to attend a meeting is often not all that easy, the Commission is regarded as a useful conduit for contacts, information and negotiations.

Typical trade barriers in Russia include various demands for certificates, slow-downs and arbitrary fees at the border, arbitrary fees set by the militia, arbitrary taxation of foreign-owned companies, unstable legislation etc. These issues are regularly raised in the Commission and at other meetings. Indeed, they may be the single most laboursome set of issues facing Finnish foreign trade authorities. EU channels have also been used for communicating Finnish worries to the Russians. Part of the problem is spontaneous devolution of decision-making in Russia; another the existence of various authorities in Russia that may hinder trade (not primarily foreign trade authorities, but the customs, the militia, the tax police, the Ministry of Communications etc). It is understood that progress in these matters - and it has taken place - will always be slow and complicated. Russia will never become an easy operational environment. Common history and experiences may have nurtured in Finns the stamina needed to do business in Russia.

Finland and EU policy vis-à-vis Russia

When Finland became a member of the EU in 1995, trade policy competence moved to Brussels. The EU-Russia PCA has thus supplanted earlier Finnish-Russian agreements. The PCA is also more detailed and contains a better formula for solving eventual disagreements than the earlier Finnish-Russian agreements. As Finland adopted EU external tariffs, Russia claimed compensation alleging losses of about FIM250m annually. This demand was later dropped, as Finnish calculations only amounted to a tenth of the Russian figure and Russia was not entitled to such compensation, not being a member of GATT.

Finland has been an active participant in the preparation of EU strategies for Russia and the Baltic Sea Area. It has a strong position in TACIS, and has argued successfully for making the environment a TACIS priority, for making cross border activities acceptable in TACIS and for making TACIS-Interreg cooperation possible. Arguably Finland is the only EU member with a specific interest in cooperation with Russia. Inter alia, this arises from the 1,300 km of common border.

Policy on neighbouring areas[20]

As Western assistance to Russia became topical in 1991-1992, Finland decided to concentrate its efforts on the neighbouring areas (Karelia, Murmansk region, St. Petersburg, Leningrad region and later also Arkhangelsk region). The need for concentration was obvious given the relative scale of any conceivable Finnish efforts. The neighbouring areas were also a natural choice for reasons of Northern know-how, earlier experience, logistics and security. On the other hand, these are in the main poor, even impoverished areas, and Arkhangelsk region was later added as a priority primarily due to the energy resources of Nenetsia. Clearly, there are now valid reasons for looking in more detail at several other regions of Russia as well. This is evident on several levels: business relations, trade and investment promotion, and even diplomatic representation. Within the neighbourhood areas, the emphasis has shifted from the Republic of Karelia to St. Petersburg and the Leningrad oblast.

Because of the relative poverty and often poor development prospects of many of the neighbourhood regions, it is increasingly argued in Finland that the country has become a prisoner of the initial geographical priorities set. But on the other hand, only concentration on the geographically adjacent regions allowed for the peculiarity of experience of the past five years. Cooperation with the neighbouring areas is a many-layered web reaching from grassroots civil society, aid and cooperation, to formal state policies. Only in 1996, as a new Strategy on Neighbourhood Areas was accepted, was a decision reached to coordinate these activities by the Ministry of Foreign Affairs. Formerly, even government ministries had quite independent and uncoordinated policies.

The amount of financial aid given by the state was FIM440m in 1990-1996. In addition, there were guarantees for about FIM50m. Adding other finance, the recent annual volume of neighbourhood areas projects has been around FIM200-250m. Altogether, a wide variety of about 400 projects have been implemented, and about 120 projects are currently being implemented. Many of them - such as support for private farms in Karelia - have been failures, other - especially in education, energy and environmental matters - have been more successful. The major contribution of this policy has been the direct contacts that thousands of Finns and Russians have built. This has created a large bank of practical knowhow and experience. Any small Helsinki Ministry of a few hundred employees will have tens of people practically involved in this cooperation, and the same is true of regional administrations and the civil society. The political benefit involved is obvious, but such practical expertise also helps in attracting outside finance from the EU and international financial institutions.

Orientations for the future

The Government of Finland published the first part of its futures report to parliament in late 1996[21]. This report contains a relatively frank discussion on Russia's future. It notes the exceptionally difficult starting point of Russia's reform, and also the problems Russia has had in settling on a reform policy. The weakness of the Russian state is emphasised, and this is also reflected in a lack of consistent reform strategy, especially in the uncertainty concerning the long-term competitive advantages of the country. The peculiarities of the political system may impair the predictability of the system, but although the key features of Russian capitalism are already visible, the current favourable political and economic trends could still be jeopardized. Fast growth is not to be expected in Russia. Therefore, although the Finnish Government does regard Russia as a major player in the European economy, the analysis presented in the report clearly seems inconsistent with any major new public sector efforts to increase trade and investment in Russia. The official Finnish view on Russia's future is sombre; the private one often even more pessimistic. But as the trade figures show, success stories also exist.

A Baltic economic region?   From the Hanseatic League to a Euroregion

The idea that the Baltic sea rim might be a distinct economic region seems to go back to the idea of a new Hanseatic league, raised by the (Social Democratic) regional leaders of Northern Germany as a counterweight to the perceived southerly orientation of

(Christian Democratic) Germany. German unification and the moving of the capital to Berlin were also seen as a boost to the northern and Baltic regions of Germany. Though the exact contents of the idea remained to be specified, leaders, especially of the Baltic states, were eager to seize the opportunity to emphasise their traditional Baltic Sea Europeanness. In 1995, the idea was made official in that Sweden and Finland joined Germany and Denmark as members of the European Union, the three Baltic countries signed Europe Agreements and applied for membership in the Union[22], a decision was made on the temporary application of the Corfu agreement with Russia, and the Baltic region was mentioned in the communique of the Cannes Summit[23].

Baltic Sea regional cooperation has long roots, especially in such natural areas as environmental protection[24], transport and safety at sea. Altogether, it is estimated that there are about 70 different Baltic Sea region cooperation bodies. Some are old, but most have been established in the 1990s. Their participants range from universities via labour unions to chambers of commerce and other civil society organisations. Reflecting both a link to the tradition of Nordic cooperation and current realities, the major institution for regional cooperation, the Council of Baltic Sea States, includes also Norway and Iceland on one hand and the European Commission on the other. Thus, the Baltic Sea region is not merely a creation of Brussels Eurocrats but an outgrowth of long existing links and processes. Naturally, EU political and financial support is also of great importance for the success of such cooperation. PHARE assistance alone has reached more than ECU125m for the three Baltic states, Latvia being the largest recipient. On the other hand, Baltic cooperation has so far not received the kind of major boost from EU developments and policies that were expected by the optimists. The Baltic Sea region does not have the same priority as the Mediterranean, and this will be reflected in future enlargement talks. Adopting the Northern German viewpoint, one again notes that while German trade with the Council of Baltic Sea States increased by a quarter in 1991-1995, the trade of Schleswig-Holstein with the region at best stagnated[25].

One highly probably direction in further regional cooperation is infrastructure, and energy supply in particular. The Nordic electricity providers have been utilizing trans-border links since the early 1960s. Links with Germany are also well-established. There also exist links between Estonia and Russia, Estonia and Latvia, Lithuania and Latvia as well as between Poland and Germany. A ring link around the Baltic Sea is technically feasible and might become reality within the foreseeable future. Other current discussions concern natural gas. The idea of diversifying Finnish (and possibly Baltic) gas supplies to include Norway (in addition to Russia) has so far stumbled on the unwillingness of Sweden to increase purchases from Norway. Meanwhile, another possibility has surfaced. Within ten years or so, the West European gas deficit has to be fulfilled whether from Algeria or Russia. One of the possible routes for Russian gas would be via Finland to Germany either through the Baltics or utilising the Baltic Sea seabed. But there are other possibilities as well.

In road transport, a Via Baltica route from Helsinki (and St. Petersburg) through the Baltic countries to Warsaw has been under development since 1985. The connection is operational, but growth in traffic has been less than hoped for, partially because some of the border crossings involved have formed bottlenecks. These problems are now basically a matter of the past, and it remains to be seen whether traffic will increase sufficiently to justify necessary further investment. There is also a parallel rail connection, but it is only used for passenger traffic. Maintenance of the connection is currently endangered by the small amount of traffic and the financial problems of the Baltic railroads.

Concluding Comments

The Baltic Sea region is not a single market. It consists of a number of countries or regions[26]. Even in the process of European integration, a unified market is not in sight. Poland and possibly Estonia will become Union members in the foreseeable future. Even the road to free trade with Russia remains a long one. But still, the context of the Baltic Sea region is no longer the long-forgotten times of the Hanseatic League but European integration.

This emphasised, one has to point out an important caveat. In some dimensions at least, a true civil society network of relations is crucial. From the Finnish point of view, this is true of the relations with Russian neighbourhood areas, but especially concerns the grassroots integration between Southern Finland and Northern Estonia. In just a few years, the amount of passenger traffic between Helsinki and Tallinn has bypassed the long-established flow between Helsinki and Stockholm. A similar phenomenon can be seen in the large number of cooperation bodies and initiatives linking the Baltic Sea region countries on different levels.

Perhaps somewhat paradoxically, such links between Finland and Russia are only possible on the basis of stable governmental relations and borders that remain exceptionally well guarded on both sides. Though experiences cannot be readily transferred, one should ask whether something similar should not be needed to a greater extent than is now available over such borders where development of cooperation still poses great challenges. This seems to concern, in particular, Russian-Baltic relations, but also to some extent intra-Baltic and Lithuanian-Polish relations. There has been much progress, but there is still a long way to go, even if one were to admit that the closeness of Nordic cooperation and prospective Finnish-Estonian integration are products of exceptional historical and linguistic circumstances.

From an economic point of view, it is also interesting to note that in most cases trade integration is much more pronounced than foreign direct investment. The small size of most of the markets involved is one natural explanation, but one also has to remember that the Eastern Baltic shore countries still have much to do to attain the standards of politico-economic stability (and EU Pillar Three aspects) that investors would take for granted elsewhere in Europe. Market integration in finance, telecommunications and services is still relatively underdeveloped.

Table 1
EBRD's Evaluation on the Progress of the Baltic and the Russian Economies

	Estonia	Latvia	Lithuania	Russia
Large-scale privatization	4	3	3	3
Small-scale privaization	4.5	4	4	4
Enterprise restructuring	3	3	3	2
Price liberalization	3	3	3	3
Trade & foreign exchange system	4	4	4	4
Competition policy	3	2	2	2
Banking reform & interest rate policy	3	3	3	2
Securities markets & non-bank financial institutions	2	2	2	3
Extensiveness & effectiveness of legal rules on investment	4	4	2	3
AVERAGE	**3.39**	**3.11**	**2.89**	**2.89**

Table 2
Structure of Finland's trade with the area comprising the Soviet Union 1989-1996 %

EXPORT	1989	1990	1991	1992	1993	1994	1995	1996
Food and beverages (0-1)	2.6	6.2	7.2	11.6	15.1	17.9	11.0	12.2
Crude material and mineral fuels (2-4)	3.9	3.6	3.7	6.5	3.0	5.1	7.0	8.3
Chemicals and related products (5)	6.6	7.6	14.3	8.6	6.4	6.4	7.2	9.2
Machinery and transport equipment (7)	50.2	45.2	38.9	42.8	41.8	33.1	34.8	32.7
Paper and paperboard and articles thereof (64)	19.1	17.4	8.4	2.7	2.8	3.8	7.4	7.4
Textiles and clothing (65, 84, 85)	5.7	5.8	5.7	7.8	6.7	6.5	6.0	5.2
Other manufactures and articles (6, 8, 9)	11.9	14.2	21.8	20.0	24.2	27.2	26.6	25.0
TOTAL	100.0	100.0	100.0	100.0	100.0	100.0	100.0	100.0
IMPORT								
Food and beverages (0-1)	0.3	0.2	0.3	0.8	0.6	0.6	0.3	0.4
Wood (24)	7.5	7.6	7.5	10.5	11.3	10.7	16.4	11.7
Metalliferous ores and metal scrap (28)	1.5	1.5	3.1	6.2	6.9	5.0	5.0	5.6
Energy (32-35)	69.4	69.2	72.0	58.2	53.8	48.3	38.9	47.0
Crude materials (2-4, except 24, 28, 32-35)	0.6	0.6	0.3	0.6	0.7	0.9	1.2	1.0
Chemicals and related products (5)	3.2	3.5	4.8	5.3	7.8	8.2	8.3	5.8
Machinery and transport equipment (7)	9.0	7.9	5.4	4.2	2.9	4.2	5.9	6.3
Iron, stell and non-ferrous metals (67, 68, 69)	3.4	3.9	3.4	5.0	7.6	10.1	13.9	8.7
Textiles and clothing (65, 84, 85)	0.4	0.4	0.8	2.6	4.0	4.9	5.7	5.9
Other manufacturers and articles (6, 8, 9)	4.7	5.2	2.4	6.6	4.4	7.1	4.4	7.6
TOTAL	100.0	100.0	100.0	100.0	100.0	100.0	100.0	100.0

Source: Official Statistics of Finland, National Board of Customs

Table 3
Value and structure of Finland's trade with Russia, the Baltic States and the other FSU countries in 1992, 1994 & 1996 - FIM m

EXPORT	1992			1994			1996		
	Russia	The Baltic States	Other FSU	Russia	The Baltic States	Other FSU	Russia	The Baltic States	Other FSU
Food and beverages (0-1)	356	133	41	1850	462	41	1678	501	148
Crude material and mineral fuels (2-4)	101	186	13	163	453	51	611	832	41
Chemicals and related products (5)	270	51	71	509	301	31	1188	498	76
Machinery and transport equipment (7)	1293	529	142	2468	1647	246	3328	2510	427
Paper and paperboard and articles thereof (64)	91	24	11	282	173	50	951	331	132
Textiles and clothing (65, 84, 85)	230	124	2	371	466	25	424	569	5
Other manufactures and articles (6, 8, 9)	679	175	64	2351	1082	143	3127	1516	147
TOTAL	**3020**	**1222**	**344**	**7994**	**4584**	**587**	**11307**	**6787**	**976**

IMPORT	1992			1994			1996		
	Russia	The Baltic States	Other FSU	Russia	The Baltic States	Other FSU	Russia	The Baltic States	Other FSU
Food and beverages (0-1)	26	35	0	13	55	0	11	36	5
Wood (24)	658	113	29	1128	182	18	1296	171	51
Metaliferous ores and metal scrap (28)	289	180	8	474	131	10	654	60	5
Energy (32-35)	4312	9	123	5840	22	119	5503	18	570
Crude materials (2-4, except 24, 28, 32-35)	36	9	1	73	28	14	86	47	0
Chemicals and related products (5)	358	27	12	865	13	40	692	20	35
Machinery and transport equipment (7)	276	34	11	286	235	12	229	572	16
Iron, stell and non-ferrous metals (67, 68, 69)	310	21	51	1142	42	58	1001	80	39
Textiles and clothing (65, 84, 85)	56	139	1	117	482	1	110	648	3
Other manufacturers and articles (6, 8, 9)	397	96	11	643	219	12	650	327	10
TOTAL	**6718**	**663**	**247**	**10581**	**1409**	**284**	**10232**	**1979**	**734**

Source: Official Statistics of Finland, National Board of Customs

Table 4
Value and structure of Finland's trade with Russia, the Baltic States and the other FSU countries in 1992, 1994 & 1996 - %

	1992			1994			1996		
EXPORT	Russia	The Baltic States	Other FSU	Russia	The Baltic States	Other FSU	Russia	The Baltic States	Other FSU
Food and beverages (0-1)	12	11	12	23	10	7	15	7	15
Crude material and mineral fuels (2-4)	3	15	4	2	10	9	5	14	4
Chemicals and related products (5)	9	4	21	6	7	5	11	7	8
Machinery and transport equipment (7)	43	44	43	31	35	42	29	37	45
Paper and paperboard and articles thereof (64)	3	2	3	4	4	9	8	5	13
Textiles and clothing (65, 84, 85)	8	10	1	5	10	4	4	8	0
Other manufactures and articles (6, 8, 9)	22	14	19	29	24	24	28	22	15
TOTAL	100	100	100	100	100	100	100	100	100
IMPORT									
Food and beverages (0-1)	0	5	0	0	4	0	0	2	1
Wood (24)	10	17	12	10	13	6	13	9	7
Metalliferous ores and metal scrap (28)	4	28	3	4	9	4	6	3	1
Energy (32-35)	64	1	51	53	2	43	54	1	78
Crude materials (2-4, except 24, 28, 32-35)	1	1	0	1	2	5	1	2	0
Chemicals and related products (5)	5	4	5	8	1	14	7	1	5
Machinery and transport equipment (7)	4	5	4	2	14	4	2	29	2
Iron, stell and non-ferrous metals (67, 68, 69)	5	3	21	11	3	20	10	4	5
Textiles and clothing (65, 84, 85)	1	21	0	5	34	0	1	32	0
Other manufacturers and articles (6, 8, 9)	6	15	4	6	18	4	6	17	1
TOTAL	100	100	100	100	100	100	100	100	100

Source: Official Statistics of Finland, National Board of Customs

Table 5
Finland's trade with the Baltic States (Estonia, Latvia and Lithuania) in 1992, 1994 & 1996 - FIMm

	1992				1994				1996			
EXPORT	Est.	Lat.	Lith.	Total	Est.	Lat.	Lith.	Total	Est.	Lat.	Lith.	Total
Food and beverages (0-1)	78	27	28	133	370	49	43	462	376	67	58	501
Crude material and mineral fuels (2-4)	121	63	2	186	287	152	14	453	641	260	31	932
Chemicals and related products (5)	44	5	2	51	234	38	23	295	339	88	72	499
Machinery and transport equipment (7)	379	79	70	528	1188	295	164	1647	1863	353	290	2506
Paper and paperboard and articles thereof (64)	18	4	2	24	108	48	18	174	182	96	52	330
Textiles and clothing (65, 84, 85)	109	9	6	124	392	40	34	466	498	34	37	569
Other manufactures and articles (6, 8, 9)	149	14	13	176	797	174	111	1082	1169	173	176	1518
TOTAL	898	201	123	1222	3376	796	407	4579	5068	1071	716	6855
IMPORT												
Food and beverages (0-1)	35	0	1	36	53	0	2	55	28	0	8	36
Wood (24)	62	42	9	113	114	62	6	182	117	54	0	171
Metalliferous ores and metal scrap (28)	176	2	0	178	105	19	7	131	46	7	6	59
Energy (32-35)	4	4	0	8	1	21	0	22	0	0	18	18
Crude materials (2-4, except 24, 28, 32-35)	6	3	1	10	24	1	3	28	27	18	2	47
Chemicals and related products (5)	23	1	4	28	8	1	4	13	12	1	7	20
Machinery and transport equipment (7)	29	3	2	34	224	9	2	235	554	14	4	572
Iron, stell and non-ferrous metals (67, 68, 69)	20	0	1	21	41	0	1	42	75	1	5	81
Textiles and clothing (65, 84, 85)	113	12	15	140	374	30	78	482	524	43	81	648
Other manufacturers and articles (6, 8, 9)	75	10	12	97	177	17	25	219	276	26	26	328
TOTAL	543	77	45	665	1121	160	128	1409	1659	164	157	1980

Source: Official Statistics of Finland, National Board of Customs

Footnotes

1. Parts of this paper utilise an earlier paper on Finnish-Russian economic relations written for the Instituto Affari Internazionali, Rome.

2. The EBRD view on the progress of transition in the Baltics and Russia is summarised in Table 1. See EBRD Transition Report, October 1996.

3. Laurila, Juhani: "Experiences of Finnish-Soviet Joint Ventures", Bank of Finland Bulletin 66 (1992): 3, 6-9.

4. Rautava, Jouko and Juhana Hukkinen: "Russia's Economic Reform and Trade Between Finland and Russia", Bank of Finland Bulletin 66 (1992): 4, 3-7.

5. Any terminology used in this paper for reasons of brevity and convenience is not intended to imply that the Baltic states had ever been legal parts of the USSR.

6. Lainela, Seija and Pekka Sutela: The Baltic Economies in Transition, Bank of Finland A:91, Helsinki 1994; Korhonen, Vesa: "The Baltic Countries' Changing Foreign Trade Patterns and the Nordic Connection", Review of Economies in Transition (Bank of Finland) 1996:3, 17-32.

7. Again, the statistics are generally unreliable, but if one accepts the figures used in the European Commission Economic Reform Monitor, the top Baltic growth performance so far is Lithuania's 3.5% in 1996, this being the only country in the region to have ever topped 3% in GDP growth. In 1996, four Central European countries grew faster than the best Baltic country.

8. Latvia is a case in point. According to the Ministry of Finance, "the share of capital goods (in imports - PS) is inadequate, and the growth rate in this sector is very slow". Biletens Latvijas Republikas Finansu Ministrija 1997: 1, 44.

9. Pautola, Niina: "The Baltic States and the European Union Enlargement: Achievements and Challenges", in Kari Liuhto, ed.: The Baltic States and the European Union Integration, Institute for East-West Trade, Turku School of Economics and Business Administration, Turku 1997, pp.53-90.

10. For Estonia, see Esti Pank/Bank of Estonia Statistical Datasheets June 1, 1997, for the other countries see Biletens Latvija Republikas Finansu Ministrija 1997: 1, 50, citing figures by Deutsche Morgan Grenfell. In the latter source, the estimate for Estonia is only 4.5%.

11. Sorsa, Piritta "Regional Integration and the Baltics: Which Way", Policy Research Working Paper 1390, the World Bank, Washington D.C., December 1994.

12. World Development Report 1996, The World Bank, Washington D.C. 1996, Figure 3.2, p.64.

13. EBRD Transition Report Update, April 1997, p.42.

14. Eesti Pank/Bank of Estonia Statisitical Datasheets June 1, 1997, Table 29. The halving of net direct foreign investment was a consequence of an increase in Estonian investment aborad from EEK29.1m to EEK480.9m together with a decrease of inward investment from EEK2,312.9m to EEK1,665.7m. The decline took place in investment into capital stock, which dropped by about four fifths, while investment in net loan capital increased.

15. For references see Korhonen, Vesa: op.cit., 1996.

16. Finland has a harbour capacity that is similar to that of the Baltic Sea Eastern coast (Russia and the Baltics) combined. The shortest route from Arkhangelsk region to Western Europe goes via the harbours of Northern Finland. Due to high costs, Finnish harbours are basically competitive only in high-value goods. An oil pipeline is also planned from Kirishi refinery to Porvoo in Southern Finland.

17. Though the population is growing older and is expected to decline by about a million by 2020.

18. Laurila, Juhani and Inkeri Hirvensalo: "Direct Investment from Finland to Eastern Europe: Results of the 1995 Bank of Finland Survey", Review of Economies in Transition (Bank of Finland) 1996: 5, 5-25; Borsos, Julianna and Mika Erkkilâ: "Foreign Direct Investment and Trade Flows Between the Nordic Countries and the Baltic States", Research Institute of the Finnish Economy, Discussion Papers No.540, Helsinki 1995.

19. A similar change had not taken place concerning investment in Estonia.

20. Technically, the Baltic countries are also regarded as part of the neighbourhood areas, and the amounts of money used for cooperation with them are similar to the ones used in Russia. However, this paper only discusses assistance to Russia.

21. Finland and the Future of Europe, Prime Minister's Office Publications Series 1996:4, Helsinki 1996.

22. Poland naturally has had a Europe Agreement since 1991 and applied for membership in 1994.

23. Kivikari, Urpo: Hansan perilliset, Otava, Helsinki 1996 is a Finnish view on Baltic Sea economic region, also available from the same publisher in Swedish, English, German and Russian.

24. For a discussion in a wider context see Darst, Robert G.: "Bribery and Blackmail in East-West Environmental Politics", Post-Soviet Affairs 1997:1, 42-77.

25. Weyrach, Peter M.: "Baltic Region Economic Development and Cooperation" (in Finnish), Suomen Lâhialueet 1996:4, 10-15.

26. Setting the borders is not simple, as seen above. Only historical reasons explain why Iceland is at least in some connections an insider while Belarus and the Pskov region are outsiders.

PANEL III

Regional Cooperation Among Partner Countries - A Sectoral Approach

Panelists and contributes:
Michael KASER
Friedemann MÜLLER
Alexander A. ARBATOV
Tony SCANLAN

REGIONAL COOPERATION AMONG CENTRAL ASIAN ECONOMIES

Michael Kaser

Institute for German Studies, University of Birmingham

A region of five states

It was a sign of Central Asian political cohesion that in 1993 the governments of the five states declared themselves to constitute 'Central Asia' (in Russian usage, *Tsentral'naya Aziya*) rather than the four states of literally 'Middle Asia' (*Srednyaya Aziya*) plus Kazakhstan. The previous year, when a United Nations mission was present in Tashkent at the moment of their admission to UN membership (March 1992), the acronym CARK had been coined (Central Asian Republics and Kazakhstan) which mirrored the Soviet classification of the two as separate 'large economic regions'.

There had, however, been sound historical reasons for 'Middle Asia' to be taken as an economic entity, because (ignoring uninhabitable mountains and deserts) three of the states - Tajikistan, Turkmenistan and Uzbekistan - with southern Kyrgyzstan were based on settled agriculture, chiefly in the basins of the two great rivers renowned in antiquity, the Amu Darya (the classical Oxus) and the Syr Darya (the classical Jaxartes), and the Turkmen oases. However, desert again apart, much of Kazakhstan and northern Kyrgyzstan depended economically on nomadic steppe and semi-arid pasturing and upland transhumance. The only natural barrier to migration and invasion was the eastern mountains (with the Chinese Empire beyond them), and the entire zone was hence open to cultural, political and military impact from the south (Persians, Indian and Arab), the west (Romans) and the north (Mongols and Russians). But in four millennia of an exchange economy, the region has been divided by customs frontiers only in the past five years: on that vast historical scale the issue of economic re-integration has been posed in a period of a mere 0.1% of the time.

A short way of putting the historical reason is that the region has an imperial rather than a balkanized past: it was part, and at times the metropole, of great empires: to name but a few, the Persian Emperors, Alexander of Macedon and Ghengis Khan ruling from outside, the Khorezmshahs and Timur from within. Tsarist Russia took Kazakhstan in the first half of the last century and 'Middle Asia' in the second half, leaving only Bukhara and Khiva in semi-independence. When the successor Soviet state effected the 'national delimitation of Central Asia' in 1924, it drew political, not economic, frontiers. Under the Five-year Plans, the allocation and distribution system was uniform throughout the 'socialist sixth of the world'; of the few economic powers allowed purely Republican ministries, none were discriminatory against other Union-Republics. The rouble was the single currency but the exchange of goods and services among Union-Republics did not depend on money: transactions were on official quota or informal negotiation, each with no concern for inner-Soviet frontiers.

The basis of those relationships was swept away by the events of late 1991 and early 1992 - the collapse of the USSR and general price decontrol. In that last year of Soviet existence, gross budget transfers from the Union exceeded domestic tax revenue in three republics (Kyrgyzstan, Tajikistan and Uzbekistan), and were substantial in Turkmenistan and Kazakhstan (8% and 5% of GDP respectively). Without such inflow and no mechanism for public borrowing, budget deficits could only be monetised; the gap was of course widened where state expenditure proportionately grew (Kyrgyzstan, Tajikistan and Uzbekistan). The coincidental liberalisation of most wholesale and retail prices (after seven decades of largely arbitrary fixed pricing) further fuelled inflation, even to hyperinflation. Widely different rates of inflation in 1993 (they were still bunched together in 1992) and national quantitative controls applied in response to the many supply/demand imbalances that arose quickly disarticulated the previously-unified channels of production and consumption.

The residuary body of the former Soviet Union, the Commonwealth of Independent States (CIS), sought to restore trade and payments relations within the new market environments by rational use of the existing common currency, the rouble, and in October 1992 three of the Central Asian states (Kazakhstan, Kyrgyzstan and Uzbekistan) joined with Armenia, Belarus and Russia to plan for an Interstate Bank of the CIS. It was argued both within the countries and by international advisers that the advantages of a single currency should not be readily discarded - an exemplar in the Maastricht Treaty envisaging Economic and Monetary Union for the EU had been signed in December 1991 - but within the space of a few months (May to November 1993) the CIS Bank proposal was a dead letter and the five states had separate currencies[1].

The common post-independence shocks
In their early years each of the Central Asian states suffered triple shocks and their variant responses further widened the disaggregation of the economic region:

- The fiscal shock required measures towards the equilibration of public-sector revenue and expenditure in matters over which Union-Republican governments had exercised little control or discretionary power. Thus taxes appropriate to a market economy had to be formulated, the relevant tax base surveyed and registered, and expenditures had to be radically restructured;

- The management shock required new institutions and staff to run them for political independence and for a market economy, both changes being simultaneous and *de novo*. The dispersion of property rights from state and collective ownership proceeded at a different pace in each state, multiplied the number of economic agents which the state had to tax or regulate, and introduced foreign investors with whom few officials previously had had to deal;

- The recession shock of declining production and investment retarded macroeconomic stabilization and (partly due to differential government protection) varied from country to country. Calibrated against 1989, measured GDP in 1996 in Uzbekistan was as high as 84%, but as low as 37% in Tajikistan. The other three states were around half[2].

For the first year and a half of independence, the five governments partly protected themselves at Russian expense. Their new Central Banks (the former Union-Republican offices of the USSR Gosbank) and the specialised state banks (corresponding branches of such as Promstroibank and Vneshekonombank) extended to domestic entities credits with scant concern for ability to service the loans; indeed, such supportive funding was little more than outright subsidization and an exacerbation of inflation. It was the IMF's conditions to Russia for a US$1.5bn Systemic Transformation Facility in 1993 which precipitated the break-up of the rouble zone. The Central Bank of Russia (CBR) was required to target its base rate and monetary emission to an appreciation of the real rate of exchange: change in the rouble-dollar rate was to be half that of domestic inflation. The CBR would have had to control the money supply of other CIS central banks still using roubles[3]. Bilateral negotiations between the CBR and the Russian Government on the one hand and each of the Central Asian authorities on the other showed mutual policy incompatibility, except, as already noted, for Tajikstan, where an economically weak administration controlling only part of a territory in civil war depended on continued Russian support.

As part of the establishment of their economic autonomy, the newly-independent governments formulated customs tariffs, introduced exchange controls and applied their own regulations to foreign investment. The common external tariff of the former USSR and the central planning of state-owned enterprises had directed trade predominantly among the Union-Republics, but after independence the burgeoning private sector sought markets wherever profit beckoned. Between 1991 and 1995 the share of mutual trade in the aggregate GDP of CIS members fell from 14.4% to 4.0%[4]. Between 1991 and 1996 the percentage share of the CIS in trade turnover (imports plus exports) fell in Uzbekistan from 87.5 to 27.0, in Tajikistan from 85.3 to 50.6 and in Turkmenistan from 90.6 to 51.0; lesser declines were exhibited by Kazakhstan (87.0 to 61.4) and Kyrgyzstan (87.9 to 65.5)[5]. Payments arrears also contributed to the fall in intra-CIS trade for two reasons: one was the increase of arrears generally as recession made a differential impact on buyers and on sellers; the other was the approximation to world prices for such transactions after long isolation from the relativities prevailing outside the USSR or selected partners (CMEA members and politically-favoured developing countries).

Finally, the impact of foreign direct investment (FDI) differed from state to state, and three countries opened special economic zones. The EBRD calculates that between 1989 (when more liberal Soviet joint-venture legislation came into force) and 1996 Kazakhstan received US\$2,761m and Turkmenistan US\$444m - below only that into Azerbaijan (mainly in oil and gas finance) in per capita terms (US\$56, 32 and 80 respectively); the other Central Asian states received less Uzbekistan US\$342m, Kyrgyzstan US\$146m and Tajikistan US\$55m (per capita a mere US\$2, 7 and 2 respectively). There are three special economic zones in Kazakhstan, four in Kyrgyzstan and seven in Turkmenistan, with a principal objective to encourage foreign investors to establish manufacturing facilities therein, imports and exports being duty-free. Disparities in attracting FDI and the facility of tax-concessional zones would divert or create trade in the medium, rather than the short, term, but they were further breaks with the uniformity that had marked external economic relations in Soviet Central Asia.

Rebuilding economic relations within the CIS

Remedial measures to seek to minimise the decline in intra-CIS trade were early on members' agenda. At the general CIS level, an Economic Court was authorized in July 1992 but it only started work in mid-1994 and not all members subscribe[6]. In October 1992 an agreement was signed in Bishkek by eight CIS members to establish a payments union to prolong the use of the rouble as a common currency, but when this was overtaken by the separation of currencies, a series of CIS treaties were negotiated to attempt economic reintegration. First came that on the Establishment of Economic Union (September 1993), then two together, on the Establishment of a Payments Union and the Establishment of an Interstate Economic Committee (October 1994) and finally on an Interstate Monetary Committee. Together, these treaties were intended to assure a common customs regime, a multilateral payments mechanism and the facilitation of transnational enterprises. The Interstate Monetary Committee first met in February 1996 and set up a secretariat, but although presented with a draft for a mechanism for mutual payments by the Russian delegation at its second meeting (October 1996), no CIS-wide convertibility has been - nor is soon likely to be - achieved. The reasons are all too obvious - the considerable settlement arrears that have accumulated between CIS members, the divergent movements of exchange rates (in real terms, some have appreciated, others depreciated), exchange rate determination (some are unitary, some dual, some controlled, others floating) and finally their degree of liberalisation (ranging from free capital and current accounts to arbitrary control).

Recognising the immediate problems, a CIS leaders' meeting in Moscow in April 1997 resolved on a longer-term 'Concept of Economic Integration of CIS States'. The resolution recognises that each member should independently determine the extent of its participation in each of three stages - a free trade area, a customs union and a payments union. No 'single market' (on the EU model) assuring free movement across member frontiers of labour and capital is apparently envisaged (as took place within the confines of Soviet central planning). Between 1989 and the beginning of 1996 some 4.2 million people moved within, between and from the five Central Asian republics, driven by political, economic and ethnic factors, and following the general abolition of residence permits[7]. Such migration has been slackening, but a fully-free labour market within the CIS would require non-national residents to have the same rights as nationals - as is the case within the EU; Kazak and Uzbek legislation does not permit dual nationality. Capital movements are still subject to control in Central Asian states, save in Kyrgyzstan, but the agreement by Kazakhstan and Uzbekistan to accept IMF Article VIII on current account convertibility (not yet implemented in Uzbekistan) is a step towards it. In fact, the limitation on transnational capital flow arises more from national constraints on ownership of land and of privatised state enterprises.

Cooperation across CIS frontiers

At a humbler level, a large number of functional bodies have been set up under CIS auspices to foster and enhance mutual cooperation - on banking, railways, agriculture, engineering, coal-mining, oil and gas. Relations more profound than trade contracts are being re-established through 'financial-industrial groups', which are particularly numerous between Kazakhstan and Russia (in ferrous and non-ferrous mining and metallurgy, heavy engineering and telecommunications), with some between Uzbekistan and Russia. The more grandiose infrastructure projects are all bilateral or trilateral with participation by the private-sector corporations involved. The Central Asian states especially seek to diversify their export markets away from the CIS, but need to cross CIS territory to do so. Kazakhstan has described itself as 'a country at the heart of East-West rail lines'[8]. These comprised the newly-exploited railways between Turkmenistan and Uzbekistan to the Iranian network and from Russia across Kazakstan into China; a Kazakhstan-Turkmenistan-Iran link is also under construction, such that, with four major trunk-lines already into Russia and thence to Europe or to the Northern Pacific, Central Asian freight has a range of options to ocean ports. One minor issue that has caused conflict has been the charges levied by the Tajik authorities for trains crossing Tajik territory between parts of Uzbekistan in the Fergana Valley.

The relevant governments have substantial equity in all the oil and gas pipelines connecting CIS states. Those originating in Central Asia include one already settled - the Caspian Pipeline Consortium (CPC) for a line, to be operated by Russia's Transneft, from the north-west Kazakh oilfields to the Russian Black Sea port of Novorossisk - and one still to be finalized - the Kazakhstan Pipeline Consortium to take other Kazakh oil under the Caspian, collect Azerbaijan crude, and exit at the Georgian port of Supsa on the Black Sea. Kazakh oil is to transit Turkmenistan to northern Iran, the United States government conceding on its sanctions against Iran because the transaction is only a swap for southern Iranian oil on a US company account. The gas pipelines built in the Soviet period to take Uzbek gas into Russia will be supplemented as new deposits are exploited, but the only major agreement (of May 1997) involving other CIS transit is for Turkmen gas to be routed through Iran to supply Turkey and thence Georgia; the agreement overlaps an earlier Iran-Turkey contract for Iranian gas and may supersede plans for a pipeline under the Caspian to transit Azerbaijan and Armenia into Turkey. Russia already supplies Turkey via Ukraine, Romania and Bulgaria and if Turkey becomes over-supplied, Turkmen gas could be sold on to European users.

Intergovernmental agreements on water have been more controversial and in significant cases rational usage and appropriate charges have yet to be negotiated. The principal cotton-growing state, Uzbekistan, uses 76% of the total freshwater resources available within itself and from neighbouring countries (compared with Kazakhstan's 30% and Kyrgyzstan's 24%)[9]. Irrigation methods for cotton plantations have grossly wasted water and drained into waterways a noxious mix of chemicals. Intergovernmental negotiations particularly concern the shrinkage of the Aral Sea, the timing of water release and charges for water to rationalise consumption[10]. An agreement between Kazakhstan, Uzbekistan and Kyrgyzstan of May 1996 provided for scheduling the flow of the Syr-Darya, and one between Turkmenistan and Uzbekistan of January 1996 regulates the lower Amu-Darya; if the peace agreement holds in Tajikistan, an agreement may become possible over the upper Amu-Darya. Conflict arises not only on the amount of water released but its timing: Kyrgyzstan and Tajikistan want to retain water for autumn and winter hydroelectricity generation, whereas the downstream states need it in spring and summer for irrigation.

Environmental problems

The water allocation problem has generated Central Asia's worst environmental damage - the drying out of the Aral Sea, which now holds only one-quarter of its 1960 volume as a direct result of the diminution of the annual input of water from the Amu-Darya and the Syr-Darya from 60 cu. km to 5 cu. km. Water pollution from farm chemicals, soil salination from inefficient canalization and airborne salt from the dessicated bed of the Aral Sea are further problems, now the subject of an agreement between the five Presidents and the World Bank in March 1997: although agreement on the Tajik contribution is awaited, the other four countries will devote 0.3% of their fiscal revenue to an International Fund for Saving the Aral Sea, to which the World Bank will over four years contribute US$380m.

At least two other environmental problems have international dimensions. One is the emission of fluor by the South Tajik Aluminium Works at Tursunzade causing fluorosis downwind of the plant in Uzbekistan. Contamination problems arise from the chemical warfare installations and test grounds near Aralsk in Kazakstan and could affect neighbouring areas of Uzbekistan. Radiation from the Semipalatinsk nuclear-weapon test 'polygon' (disused since 1963) has required the movement since Kazakh independence of nearly 200,000 people elsewhere in the republic and 116,000 to other countries; the neighbouring Altai region of Russia has also been affected by the residual radiation[11]. The World Bank and the EBRD have made environmental protection part of their lending programmes and the latter is advising each government on a National Environmental Action Plan.

Two integration unions

The inadequacy to date of CIS-wide collaboration has led governments to seek small-er groupings for more intensive economic integration, of which the most inclusive, but domestically-disputed, is the Customs Union of Belarus with Russia. In Central Asia, a tri-lateral agreement was signed in 1994 on a 'united economic zone' of Kazakstan, Kyrgyzstan and Uzbekistan, and some progress has been achieved in harmonizing rates of value-added tax and on double taxation[12]. Kazakhstan and Kyrgyzstan are members of a quadrilateral customs union embracing also Belarus and Russia, established in March 1996; a threat by Kazakhstan in early 1997 to leave, due to problems of tariffs in the tran-sition period before projected tariff harmonisation, appears to have been withdrawn. Kazakhstan raised some tariffs to the Russian level which protected Russian production, but of course resulted in dearer imports: domestic interests made Kazakhstan cut them sharply, and hence (as is also the case with Belarus) allowed Russian buyers to import more cheaply than through their own country's entry-points.

Central Asian complementarities

Prospects for integration among the five central Asian states depend on their econom-ic complementarities. They all need to generate more value-added to their rich natural-resource exploitation and to enlarge other sectors - especially services - to employ their expanding working age population (15-64 years of age): by 2010 it will in four of the republics be between two-fifths and two-thirds larger than it is now[13]. Demographic move-ment is less dynamic in Kazakhstan, where a large Slavic population has long had a lower fertility. Because a high proportion of the active labour force is occupied in agriculture (one-third or more in four states, other than Kazakhstan) and the post-independence reces-sion has brought redundancies in many industrial plants geared to a Soviet-wide and non-cost-conscious clientele, underemployment may add seven million people to the 11 mil-lion projected from demographic growth. Some industries are already established which could be redeveloped in a policy of diversification, but they had their origin in a centrally planned economy which assured them of outlets by and large irrespective of their produc-tion or transport costs. To nurture some of them into a competitive relationship with imports may require a period of protection when WTO membership is negotiated and as the two customs unions with some of the states are finalized. Utilisation of crude oil and natural gas in refining and petrochemicals is already being undertaken. Other examples include processing Uzbek wool into high-quality textiles and to make fabrics, carpets and blankets for export; and a Turkmen plant to weave high-quality denim. Financial and tourist services are expanding. Foreign investment is increasing domestic value-added, especially among consumer goods which use local materials, and may be a sound mode of assuring that the trilateral and quadrilateral customs unions evoked for political reasons do not bypass the signals of competition and profitability.

Footnotes

1. The Kazakh tenge, the Kyrgyz som, the Turkmen manat and the Uzbek sum were national units; Tajikistan maintained use of the Russian rouble until 1995.

2. These are the estimates shown in EBRD, *Transition Report Update 1997*, Table 1. Those of the UN ECE, *Economic Survey of Europe in 1996-1997*, Table B.1 are lower, except for Kyrgyzstan (slightly higher) and Turkmenistan (much higher, because it reflects the Turkmenstan Statistical Office's revaluation of oil and gas to world prices by 73% in 1992-3, a change which strictly should not influence an indicator of real economic activity).

3. Ukraine had already disengaged and Kyrgyzstan was in the process of doing so.

4. See paper by Yuri Shishkov (Panel II).

5. See Table 2 of paper by Yuri Shishkov (Panel II).

6. This section draws on Mark Webber, *CIS Integration Trends: Russia and the Former Soviet South*, London: Royal Institute of International Affairs, 1997.

7. UNHCR, *CIS Conference*, Geneva, HCR, 1996, p. 5. A few residence permit controls have been retained (e.g. for Tashkent) to inhibit urban unemployment and shanty dwelling.

8. *Financial Times*, 11 July 1996 (Supplement on Kazakhstan, p. vi).

9. World Bank, *World Development Report 1997*, Table 10 (no data for Tajikistan or Turkmenistan).

10. On rationalizing water consumption by user charges, see Michael Kaser, *The Economies of Kazakhstan and Uzbekistan*, London, Royal Institute of International Affairs, 1997, pp. 61-2, and EBRD, *Transition Report 1996*, pp. 42-3.

11. UNHCR, *CIS Conference*, p.15.

12. From a detailed survey of its subsequent operation, Heribert Dieter, 'Regional Integration in Central Asia: Current Economic Position and Prospects', *Central Asian Survey*, vol.15, no.3/4, 1996, pp.369-386, has high expectations of the 'trilateral union' and points out that its Interstate council has funding from the European Union.

13. UN ECE, *Economic Survey of Europe in 1996-1997*, Table 4.3.2: the 1995-2010 increments are projected at 64% for Tajikistan, 53% for Uzbekistan, 52% for Turkmenistan and 42% for Kyrgyzstan, but only 21% for Kazakhstan.

COOPERATION IN THE FIELD OF ENERGY

Friedemann Müller

Senior Research Associate, Stiftung Wissenschaft und Politik, Ebenhausen, Germany

Introduction

The day the Founding Act between NATO and Russia was signed, the International Herald Tribune ran a front page headline "NATO and Russia: The Gazprom Factor" and quoted in this article an executive from *Gazprom*:

> *"Why are you guys so concerned about the enlargement of NATO to the East? I can assure you that the enlargement of NATO to the East will be more than compensated for by the enlargement of Gazprom to the West[1]."*

Is this the new security guarantee for Russia? Will it provide stability for Europe? There is no doubt about the territorial "enlargement of *Gazprom*". However, the structure of the energy sector and the rules of the game have changed in Europe, both East **and** West during the 1990s. Competition is growing, cooperation and diversification have become more intensive, dependencies have changed fundamentally. The transformation of the energy sector in Europe reflects different movements during the millennium's last decade:

* the transformation of the economies in the Former Socialist Countries (FSCs);
* deregulatory measures providing more competition in the energy sector within the EU and beyond;
* the linking of East and West after the end of the cold war.

Europe is still in the midst of these processes. The results are still unclear. It is, however, quite clear that future challenges such as the enlarged EU's need to be competitive in a globalised market and the necessity of dealing with global environmental issues, particularly the climate change problem, make a completely modernised and restructured energy sector as necessary as the agreement on common rules for the whole of Europe.

Transition of the Energy Sector in Former Socialist Countries : A Mixed Record

The energy sector received special treatment in all Central and East European FSCs during the transition process. The basics of the transformation to a market economy, which are price liberalisation, privatisation and demonopolisation, have not been applied without delays and exceptions, indeed, no continental European country has completely achieved these targets in the energy sector. First steps were taken in Western Europe in the 1950s. However, these processes only gained real momentum through the EU Single Market and globalisation effects which did not gain prominence until the beginning of the 1990s. In Western Europe, price liberalisation has been taken furthest, while privatisation has been given second priority. Demonopolisation in the field of electricity and natural gas has begun due to a major effort on the part of the EU Commission. However, the process is far from being completed[2]. Those FSCs which have signed Europe Agreements (EA countries) and wish to negotiate EU membership after 1998 have no comparable timeframe to adapt their energy sectors to competitive market conditions. They therefore have to adjust to Single Market rules under immense time pressure. Those countries that are not preparing for EU membership, mainly in the CIS, will certainly need a longer transition period. **Price liberalisation** is not being carried through consistently in any of the FSCs. Free prices, such as the price of coal in the Czech Republic, are the exception[3]. An overwhelming majority of energy prices are regulated to prevent social unrest. The old reliance on subsidised energy prices as a substitute for an efficient social policy is still deeply rooted in all the transition countries[4]. The effect is that energy consumption per GDP unit is several times higher than the EU average. This is particularly extreme in countries like Ukraine where economic recovery is substantially hampered by the high energy import bill. At the same time, low energy prices prevent the emergence of a profit-oriented energy saving industry (regulators, insulation, etc.) and serve to discourage foreign investment. There is, however, a growing awareness of this problem. In countries like Hungary serious efforts are being undertaken to adjust energy prices to a market level.

The progress made with **privatisation** by different countries varies greatly, with Hungary being by far the most advanced country. By 1995, privatisation was already well advanced. For example, the state's share of the country's vertically integrated oil and gas company, *MOL*, has been reduced to 55%[5]. In Poland, plans to privatise power generators as well as the oil, natural gas and coal production sectors are partially combined with efforts at demonopolisation. However, progress is still insufficient. The Czech Republic has attracted some foreign investors, mainly in the field of oil refineries. All other EA countries are lagging behind. In Russia, the natural gas monopoly *Gazprom* is formally privatised with a state share of 40%; the remaining shares are divided among the company's management, the employees, and local distribution companies, with 9% of the shares reserved for sale to selected foreign investors. Russian oil production is divided into 12 companies producing between 0.16m (*Onako*) and 1.02m (*Lukoil*) barrels per day (b/d) in 1996 with a state share between 0% (*Sidanco*) and 100% (*Rosneft*). The state's stake in *Lukoil* is 11%[6]. Russia will continue to operate and negotiate joint ventures for shared production in huge oil and natural gas projects[7]. The really big deals, however, were contracted by Kazakhstan and Azerbaijan with Western oil consortia. Even Turkmenistan, whose transformation lags behind, has recently signed a number of contracts with Western companies to develop its natural gas fields.

Demonopolisation is the least advanced aspect of the transition process. In Russia, to the extent that the oil companies compete at all, they do so in international markets (Kazakhstan) rather than domestically. The gas market (*Gazprom*) like the oil (*Transneft*) and electricity transportation (*Unified Energy Systems*) are formally organised in monopolistic structures. Even the big fight between Deputy Prime Minister Nemtsov and *Gazprom* over the company's adaptation to market rules ended (temporarily) with Nemtsov's declaration of success: "the largest company in Russia has finally come under state control"[8]. Other FSCs have not made major efforts to introduce domestic competition. By virtue of its privatisation progress and its relatively high share of foreign capital, Hungary is better prepared than other countries to take this step in the foreseeable future[9].

Former Socialist Countries : From Dependency to International Competition

After the breakdown of the Soviet empire and the dissolution of the Council for Mutual Economic Assistance (COMECON) in June 1991, the East Central European countries were forced to completely reorganise their energy supply structures. In 1990 the Soviet Union had an almost complete monopoly in the natural gas trade with these countries and a very high share of the oil trade[10]. While Russia tried to maintain the level of its energy deliveries to Western countries, it reduced its deliveries to the EA countries drastically due to the decline in production. Russian oil exports to East Central European countries were cut by more than half between 1990 (45.7 million tons {mt}) and 1994 (21.0mt) whilst deliveries to the Baltics were reduced to one-fourth of their previous level (11.5mt in 1991 to 3.7mt in 1994)[11].

The EA countries themselves had no reason to maintain the former monopolistic supply source of Soviet/Russian deliveries since the price advantage in comparison to world market prices had disappeared[12]. Moreover, substantial declines in the size of their economies (of between 25-40%) in the early 1990s combined with energy efficiency improvements implemented since about 1994 have reduced import demand. There is a clear interest in modernising the energy sector in accordance with Western type structures and in diversifing supply.

Nevertheless, **Poland** signed a natural gas deal with *Gazprom* in 1996 which adds another 14 billion m³ to the already 8 to 10 billion m³ of natural gas it buys from Russia annually. This will cover virtually all Poland's demand for gas of 24 billion m³ after 2010. There is, however, a difference between this and former dependence structures. Firstly, the newly built *Netra* pipeline from Wilhelmshafen to Berlin which will probably be connected with the Polish network could substitute supply deficits. Secondly, the fact that this new deal with *Gazprom* is part of a major Russian-European deal delivering Yamal natural gas via Belarus and Poland to Western Europe means that the dependence between Russia as supplier and Poland as transit country will be a mutual one.

The **Czech Republic** has followed a different policy. In March 1997 it announced a long-term gas supply contract with Norway for at least 3 billion m³ annually to be supplied by three Norwegian companies. This would be in addition to the current 9 billion m³ provided by *Gazprom*. Trade Minister Dlouhy hailed it as a way to make his country "strategically independent from eventual possible Russian economic pressure"[13]. He therefore declined an offer of supply by West European companies (*Nederlandse Gasunie NV* and *Wingas*) which are linked by joint ventures to *Gazprom*. The Czech Republic is already sufficiently connected with the West European natural gas network to avoid dependence on any single operator.

Bulgaria, traditionally the country most dependent on the Russian energy supply, announced recently that Russia is charging too much for its gas and that it is looking for alternative suppliers[14]. Extending the Western pipeline system to East Central Europe will allow them to buy natural gas from West European sources in the foreseeable future.

Romania has made special efforts to establish a network of alternative options for the supply of energy to South East Europe. Romanian firm *Romgaz* signed a contract in 1996 with Hungarian and Norwegian companies to establish a pipeline link via the modernised Hungarian network to the EU[15].

Slovakia, however, relies completely on Russian natural gas and has extended this relationship by planning a fifth pipeline linking these two countries to be constructed by the year 2000. This pipeline will also increase Slovakia's huge transit capacity (85 billion m³ p.a.) for Russian gas to the West[16]. It makes Russia's strategic dependence at least as high as that of Slovakia.

Ukraine's dependence on Russian gas is almost complete. While some natural gas is delivered by Turkmenistan, there has been to date no real alternative to the Russian transportation network. The high cost of energy imports which overall amounted to US$16.95bn in 1995 means that Ukraine's debt to *Gazprom* (as well as to Turkmenistan) has accumulated, thereby increasing its dependence on Russia despite efforts to diversify at least the oil supply[17].

The most dramatic change in terms of geopolitics and international economics is taking place in the Caspian Sea area where three Newly Independent States (NISs),
Azerbaijan, Kazakhstan and Turkmenistan, are trying to gain wealth and independence
through the exploitation and sale of their oil and natural gas reserves. The fact that all three
NISs are landlocked forces them to cooperate with their difficult neighbours. But Russia
is keen to preserve the status-quo which it considers to be the centrepiece of the CIS and
tries to benefit from the natural and geographical conditions[18]. The situation is complicated by the interest of other countries like Turkey, Iran and even Pakistan in profiting politically and economically from this emerging region. Even the United States is intervening
as a major political player in the shaping of transport infrastructure by isolating Iran and
supporting Turkey[19]. The situation is further complicated by the fact that transit routes must
cross regions of conflict. This holds true for the Nagorny Karabakh region, Chechnya, as
well as Afghanistan. Nevertheless, from the dynamics of the oil rush there emerged a number of contracts and consortia involving different companies from Russia, the NIS and
Western countries, an important training field for post cold war economic cooperation[20].

Oil, coal and electricity trade between Russia and the EA countries is no longer a matter for concern on the grounds of dependence. Coal trade was always negligible, whereas
the oil trade has decreased sharply due to Russia's reduced capacity and a better supply
system through alternative pipelines. The integrated electricity network of the COMECON
countries has disintegrated to a large extent. Insofar as there is an interest in trading electricity, linking up with the European system is much more attractive.

Cooperation Between East and West : New Opportunities Under New Conditions

The diversification and partial reorientation of EA countries' energy supplies towards
Western European countries (Norwegian natural gas, oil through pipelines from the West)
has already been discussed. The most dynamic involvement, however, is taking place in
the field of infrastructure and capital investment. Numerous pipelines linking East and
West in Europe and the current planning of further construction are preconditions for more
diversification, less dependence and more competition. Europe as a whole is moving
towards an integrated network for the transportation of oil, natural gas and electricity. The
capital for this is not only flowing from West to East, but also to some degree vice versa.
The natural gas giant *Gazprom* is extending its transport routes and capital shares towards
Western Europe. It has founded two joint ventures with the German company *Wintershall*
(*WIEH* and *Wingas*), that have gained a 10% share of the gas delivery market in Germany
and now own portions of the pipeline networks on German ground. The main capital transfer, however, is directed from West to East. Hungary has sold major shares of its natural
gas and electricity distribution companies to Western companies. One source of Western
firms' interest is the different price and quality structures of electricity within EA countries
and between EA and Western countries. This might lead in the longer run to major trade
in different qualities of electricity at different prices. Romania counts on significant
Western capital inflows to regenerate its exploration and production of oil and natural gas
both in on-shore and off-shore fields. Due to a lack of modernisation investments, production has been declining since the 1980s[21]. The domestic pipeline system also needs renovation with Western technology and capital. In the Czech Republic local suppliers are
cooperating with Western companies to build power stations, both nuclear and thermal[22].

The quantitatively biggest attractions for Western capital are Russia and the CIS countries to the south. Project planning for oil and natural gas production in the Russian Arctic,
on the Sakhalin peninsula and around the Caspian Sea suggests an aggregate investment

potential of more than US$100bn[23]. The risk factor for investments made under still unstable legal conditions is, of course, high[24].

Interdependence in Europe : An Opportunity for Meeting Future Challenges

The energy scene in Europe has changed during the 1990s faster than in any previous decade. In 1990, two separate systems with totally different market and price structures were linked only through natural gas and oil deliveries from the Soviet Union to the West. Today, the Eastern systems are now adjusting to the Western system, which in turn is moving towards demonopolisation and more competition. Whereas the West's dependence on Soviet energy deliveries was a major concern and a cause of Atlantic dispute in the early 1980s, it is no longer an issue today. Like the West Europeans, most EA countries have made great progress in diversifying their supply structure. The end of the cold war provided an opportunity for closer cooperation and the taking of at least the first steps towards an all-European network with interdependent capital structures, pipelines and electricity networks. These are preconditions both for diversification and for the option to exploit market conditions which includes new product diversity, especially in the electricity sector.

To support this growing interdependence, the EU initiated as early as 1990 negotiations for a European Energy Charter as a regulatory regime defining common rules and market behaviour. The Charter was signed on 17 December 1991 by all OECD countries and all FSCs as a declaration of intention[25]. According to the Charter, a legally binding "Treaty of the Charter" was to be negotiated over a period of three years and this was signed in December 1994[26]. It has not yet been ratified by all signatory states[27]. Russia, for example, is presently in the midst of the ratification process. This Treaty of the Charter is an excellent example of how to deal with the deficiencies of the regulatory framework in international relations during a time of increasing exposure to globalisation[28]. The very fact that it could be successfully negotiated between former adversaries is a good sign considering the need for further agreements on regulatory regimes. This is particularly relevant in the case of environmental problems linked to energy production, transportation and consumption. Transboundary pollution and climate change effects due to fossil energy consumption desperately need an effective regime that reduces the externalisation of costs. The necessity of such a regime is acknowledged in principle in the Charter as well as in the Treaty of the Charter.

There is still a long way to go to accomplish the goals of an integrated European energy market and an adequate regime on energy-related environmental issues, although the progress since 1990 does provide grounds for some optimism. There is no concrete force that wants to stop this process. It is no zero-sum game, there will be no loser and all players expect to benefit. To some extent, **this growing interdependence is a sort of security guarantee. It drives Europe towards greater stability.**

Footnotes

1. International Herald Tribune, May 27, 1997, p.1.

2. Adrian *Brown*, Towards a single European market for energy: recent European Union developments, Petroleum Economist, Vol.63, No.1 (1996), Supplement; Georg C. Goy, Chancen für eine gemeinsame europäische Energiepolitik, Deutsches Institut für Wirtschaftsforschung, DIW Wochenbericht, Vol. 63, No. 41 (10 October 1996), pp.659-662.

3. Josef *Seják*, The Czech Republic: Combining Market Economy and Environmental Protection, in: Friedemann Müller, Susanne Ott (eds.) Energy and Environment in Central and Eastern Europe, SWP-S 414, Ebenhausen (November 1996), (pp.59-111), p.60.

4. According to the Russian Ministry of Energy „10% of the richest Muscovites receive 50% of energy subsidies in the city", OMRI, Daily Digest No. 32, Part I (February 14, 1997).

5. Eastern Europe. A Rocky Road to the Market Economy, Petroleum Economist, No 10 (October 1996), pp.52-53.

6. Petroleum Economist No. 2 (February 1997), pp.6-8.

7. In 1996 40 joint ventures with foreign participation produced 22 million tons or 7.7% of Russia's oil output, according to Finansovye Izvestiya, March 27, 1996.

8. NTV, May 12, 1997 quoted in Monitor, Vol III, No.97 (May 16, 1997).

9. Jeff *Freeman*, Energy - Hungarian Utility Privatization Moves Forward, OMRI Transition, Vol. 2, No. 9 (May 3, 1997).

10. Friedemann *Müller*/Rudolf *Botzian*, Abhängigkeit der europäischen Länder von Rußland und der GUS im Energiesektor, in Wolfgang Heydrich et al. (eds.), Sicherheitspolitik Deutschlands: Neue Konstellationen, Risiken, Instrumente, Nomos Verlagsgesellschaft, Baden-Baden (1992), pp.475-499 (tables 1-5).

11. Hermann *Clement*, Integrationspolitik und -entwicklung im ehemaligen RGW-Raum, Osteuropa-Institut München, Working papers No. 194 (December 1996), p.87.

12. Russia still offers preferential prices to Ukraine, however also in this bilateral trade the price advantage is diminishing.

13. International Herald Tribune, March 19, 1997, p.13.

14. Monitor Vol. III, No. 93 (May 12, 1997).

15. Striking the Balance Between East and West, Petroleum Economist No. 11 (November 1996), pp. 11-14.

16. ibid., p.14.

17. Volkhart *Vincentz*, Zur außenwirtschaftlichen Entwicklung Rußlands und der Ukraine, Osteuropa-Institut München, Working Papers No. 197 (December 1996).

18. A. *Vasilenko*/V. *Razuvaev*, Neft i meshdunarodnye otnosheniya, Mirovaya Ekonomika i Meshdunarodnye Otnosheniya, No. 12 (December 1996), pp.56-64.

19. Rosemarie *Forsythe*, The Politics of Oil in the Caucasus and Central Asia, Adelphi Paper 300, Oxford University Press. London (1996).

20. The problem is broader discussed in Fond im. Fridrikh Eberta, Kaspiyskaya nefty i meshdurarodnaya bezopasnost', Moscow 1996, or in Heinz Kramer and Friedemann Müller, Relation with Turkey and the Caspian Basin Countries, in Robert Blackwill, Michael Stürmer (eds.), Allies Divided: Transatlantic Policies for the Greater Middle East, MIT Press, Cambridge MA., 1997 (in print).

21. Romania - Energy sector opens its arms to the West, Petroleum Economist, No. 3, (March 1996). p.47.

22. Martin *Czakainski,* Deutsch-tschechische Kooperation auf dem Vormarsch, Energiewirtschaftliche Tagesfragen, Vol 46, No.10 (October 1996), pp.661-662.

23. Petroleum Economist No. 12 (December 1996), pp.4-6; Supplement to Petroleum Economist , Gas in the CIS 1996 (October 1996), pp.41-43.

24. Andrej A. *Konoplyanik,* Rußlands Energiesektor zwischen Krise und Transformation: Der Bedarf an ausländischen Investitionen, SWP-AP 2959, Ebenhausen (June 1996).

25. Text of the Charter: Europe Documents, No. 1754, Brussels (December 21, 1991).

26. The Energy Charter Treaty, Bundesrat Drucksache 963/96, (August 16, 1996).

27. All FSCs and all European OECD countries signed the Treaty, also Japan and Australia, however not the United States and Canada.

28. Thomas Waelde, International Investment under the 1994 Energy Charter Treaty, Journal of World Trade, Vol. 29, No.5 (October 1995) pp. 5-72.

Bibliography

Adrian Brown, Towards a single European market for energy: recent European Union developments, Petroleum Economist, Vol. 63 (1996), Supplement.

Hermann Clement, Integrationspolitik und -entwicklung im ehemaligen RGW-Raum, Osteuropa-Institut München, Working Papers No. 194 (December 1996), p.87.

Energy Charter, Europe Documents, No. 1754, Brussels (December 21, 1991).

Fond im. Fridrikh Eberta, Kaspiyskaya nefty i meshdunarodnaya bezopasnost', Moscow 1996.

Rosemarie Forsythe, the politics of oil in the Caucasus and Central Asia, Adelphi Paper 300, Oxford University Press, London (1996).

Georg C. Goy, Chancen für eine gemeinsame europäische Energiepolitik, Deutsches Institut für Wirtschaftsforschung, DIW Wochenbericht, Vol. 63, No. 41 (October 10, 1996), pp. 659-662.

Andrey A. Konoplyanik, Rußlands Energiesektor zwischen Krise und Transformation: Der Bedarf an ausländischen Investitionen, SWP-AP 2959, Ebenhausen (June 1996).

Heinz Kramer, Friedemann Müller, Relations With Turkey and the Caspian Basin Countries, in Robert Blackwill, Michael Stürmer (eds.), Allies Divided: Transatlantic Policies for the Greater Middle East, MIT Press, Cambridge MA. (1997), pp. 175-202.

F. Krawczynski, J. Michna, Effektivität westlicher Hilfe im Energiesektor, Energiewirtschaftliche Tagesfragen, No. 1-2 (January 1997) pp.20-23.

Friedemann Müller, Rudolf Botzian, Abhängigkeit der europäischen Länder von Rußland und der GUS im Energiesektor, in Wolfgang Heydrich et al. (eds.), Sicherheitspolitik Deutschlands: Neue Konstellationen, Risiken, Instrumente, Nomos Verlagsgesellschaft, Baden-Baden (1992), pp. 475-499.

Friedemann Müller, Susanne Ott (eds.), Energy and Environment in Central and Eastern Europe, SWP-S 414, Ebenhausen (November 1996).

Peter Rutland et al., Energy, Transition, Vol.2, No.9 (May 3, 1996), pp. 6-29.

The Energy Charter Treaty, Bundesrat Drucksache 963/96 (August 16,1996).

A. Vasilenko, V. Razuvaev, Neft i meshdunarodnye otnosheniya, Mirovaya Ekonomika i Meshdurnarodnye Otnosheniya, No.12 (December 1996), pp. 56-64.

Volkhart Vincentz, Zur außenwirtschaftlichen Entwicklung Rußlands und der Ukraine, Osteuropa-Institut München, Working Papers No. 197 (December 1996).

Thomas Waelde, International investment under the 1994 Energy Charter Treaty, Journal of World Trade, Vol. 29, No.5 (October 1995), pp. 5-72.

THE ROLE OF RUSSIA ON THE EUROPEAN ENERGY MARKET

Alexander A. Arbatov

Chairman, Committee for Productive Forces and Natural Resources, Russian Academy of Sciences, Moscow

A significant part of the post-war history of the USSR has been the growing export of energy resources to the European market. This was promted not only by large reserves, boosted in the 1960s and 1970s by the discovery of huge oil and gas deposits in Western Siberia, but also by the fact that energy was one of the few competitive sectors with which the Soviet Union could compete in World markets. In **Table 1**, the export dynamics of this trade during the Soviet era is presented.

Table 1
Fuel Exports from USSR from 1950 to 1991

	1950	1960	1970	1980	1985	1988	1989	1990	1991
OIL (m.tonnes)	0.3	17.8	66.6	119.0	117.0	144.2	127.3	109.0	60.5
- as % of total production	0.8	12.1	18.9	19.7	19.7	23.2	20.8	19.1	11.8
OIL PRODUCTS (m.tonnes)	0.8	15.4	29.0	41.3	49.7	61.0	57.4	50.0	43.9
NATURAL GAS (bn.m3)	-	0.2	3.3	54.2	68.7	81.3	93.2	110.0	104.1
- as % of total production	-	0.5	1.7	12.5	10.7	11.0	13.0	13.5	13.0
COAL (m.tonnes)	1.1	12.3	24.5	25.3	28.3	39.4	37.5	35.4	26.0
- as % of total production	0.4	3.3	5.1	4.6	5.0	5.0	5.0	5.0	4.1

It is evident that exports of oil and gas grew at a much faster pace than for coal, exports of which had stabilised by 1970 with minor fluctuations thereafter. However, the start of accelerated growth in gas exports lagged behind oil by about 10 years. Not only has an absolute increase of physical volumes taken place, but a growth in the share of exported fuel as a proportion of total output was also noted.

The fast growth in **oil** exports in the middle of the 1970's was explained by two circumstances, namely that prices rose on the World market and because of the development of West Siberian deposits that have entered their period of maturity. In the 20 year period from 1960, annual exports of oil and oil products have grown from 33.2 million tonnes (mt) up to 160mt, representing a 4.8 fold increase and annual average growth of 8.5%. In this period, oil production grew 4.1 fold (annual average growth rate of 7.6 %). Thus no sharp changes in the ratio between domestic consumption and exports were observed in this period.

This picture changed during the next decade. Between 1980-1988, oil production increased to 624mt (annual growth rates averaged 0.4%) with export of oil and oil products reaching 205mt in 1988 (average annual rates of increase were approximately 3.2%). Thus the rate of growth in oil exports was 8 times greater than that for internal oil production, indicating essential shifts in the structure of oil utilisation. Growth in production costs due to a deterioration in the quality of the resource base and a lack of investment has resulted in a fast decline of oil export volumes, which dropped by 17mt in 1989 back down to the 1986 level. Exports in 1991 were just 60.5mt.

The dynamic of **gas** exports was in many respects similar to that of oil, but with a 10 year delay and without the sharp decreases of recent years. In the decade 1970-1980, export gas deliveries grew 16.4 fold (annual average growth rates of 32%) whereas annual production growth was only 8.2%. In the beginning of the 1980's, gas exports were constrained by a shortage of transport capacity. But following the completion of the "*Urengoi - Uzhgorod*" gas pipeline, the growth of gas exports speeded up again. In the 1980s, annual growth rates in gas production averaged 7.5% in the USSR, while those of export deliveries were 6.3%. In other words, exports were already lagging marginally behind production. In general, gas exports have stabilised with a slight tendency towards a slow reduction in volumes emerging which could be explained by domestic consumption growth at that time.

The export of **coal** remained stable for an extended period, marked only by a slight growth as a proportion of production volumes.

The accelerating growth of energy production and export was closely connected with the internal economic and international political situations in which the USSR found itself during this period. Internally, there was a rigid system of centralised planning known as the "command" economy in which the only purpose of enterprises was to fulfill quantitative output targets. Production was then distributed in a centralised way at prices established by the state that reflected neither consumption value nor opportunity cost. Thus wide disparities between internal Soviet and external World market prices developed which led to widespread waste of resources.

The main purposes of the Soviet economy were as follows:
* maintenance of the material and technical conditions for military build-up;
* economic support for socialist countries and other friendly regimes;
* maintenance of minimal living standards for the population;
* provision and maintenance of nationwide infrastructures.

Given these constraints, most industrial enterprises lost money. The situation was aggravated by the lack of incentives to promote enterprise efficiency. The Soviet economy was thus approaching a crisis whose features were already evident in the 1970s despite official efforts to hide reality behind falsely optimistic statistics. By the end of the 1980s, it had become impossible to hide the deep malaise within the Soviet economy. That this economy kept afloat for as long as it did can be attributed to the high level of fuel exports which were achieved in the 1970s and 1980s. These revenues counterbalanced a sharp deficit in foodstuffs and consumer goods whilst also making it possible to procure the sophisticated equipment and high technology needed to maintain top-grade military potential.

Deliveries of fuel on very concessionary terms to a number of countries that followed the Soviet lead allowed the USSR both to expand its influence through creating dependencies whilst also allowing these client states to profit (at the USSRs expense) by re-exporting Soviet fuel at World prices.

The export growth of Soviet energy took place under conditions of deformed pricing. Artificially low internal prices made export profitability very high compared to domestic sales thus intensifing the export effort. A real growth in production costs due in part to production complications became hidden, both behind the distorted and low prices for domestic industry, as well as behind the growing export revenues. By the end of the Soviet era, export of energy played a dual role. On the one hand, the existing regime could be preserved from collapse despite its economic inefficiency. On the other hand, the difficulty in maintaining production and export volumes as the best reserves became depleted due to their intensive exploitation demonstrated that a change of policy with regard to energy resources had become unavoidable. Such a change has now taken place.

Russia has inherited the lion's share of the Soviet Energy complex. The structure of the primary part of this heritage - the Oil and Gas Complex (OGC) - is shown by **Figure 1** below:

Figure 1: Russian / other CIS shares of Soviet OGC (%)

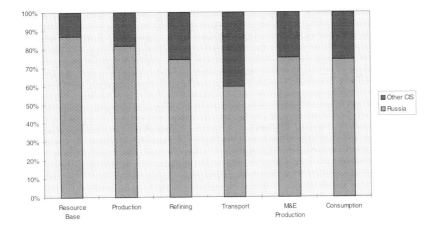

The new situation has developed in different ways for oil, gas and coal. Thus the problems of production and export for these three energy sectors should be considered separately.

Oil

Russia's oil economy has changed considerably due to the increased costs of production resulting from the accelerated exploitation and near exhaustion of the richest deposits. By the beginning of the 1990s, the share of exploited deposits with costs that far exceeded the industry's average production cost accounted for 11-12%. Regarding non-exploited deposits that had been discovered in the second half of the 1980s, the ratio is 38%. Among the probable category of reserves, the share of "superexpensive" certainly exceeds 50%. In the 1980s, average oil output per well has decreased 2.3 fold. In Western Siberia, the ratio was more than 5 fold. The average resource base in the West Siberian deposits has decreased from 149mt at the beginning of the 1980s to just 19mt at the beginning of the 1990s.

Oil production growth rates have not corresponded to those of technical renovation and re-equipping of the oil industry, which has resulted in a significant physical depreciation of the equipment stock. By the beginning of the 1990s, one-half of all machinery and equipment in the oil industry was more than 50% worn-out and only 14% met World standards. About 70% of drilling installations were produced in 1950-1957 and are outdated. Moreover, conditions in the World oil market have also developed adversely for exporters in that stabilisation of demand by the main consumers has combined with the growth of oil production in non-OPEC countries to depress prices. The situation is aggrevated by Iraq, struggling to escape sanctions, which now has permission to sell limited quantities to ease humanitarian problems. Furthermore, some OPEC countries are pressing for quotas to be increased. Notwithstanding seasonal fluctuations, oil prices have developed in such a way that a levelling-off or even a small decrease could be the best that exporters can expect in the immediate future.

These and other problems have resulted in a sharp fall in oil production in the 1990s now that centralised investments have been all but terminated and that old management structures have been partially or completely destroyed. See **Table 2** below:

Table 2
Total Oil Production and Exports to non-CIS in 1991-1996. (mt)

	1991	1992	1993	1994	1995	1996
Production	461.6	394.6	354.0	317.8	306.8	301.1
Exports (non-CIS)	54.0	68.1	80.0	90.9	93.0	102.1

But, as can be seen in **Table 2**, oil exports to outside the CIS grew steadily over the same period due to the considerable drop both in domestic consumption and in exports to the CIS and the Baltic States. **Table 3** below refers:

Table 3
Domestic Oil Consumption and Exports to the FSU in 1991-1996 (mt)

	1991	1992	1993	1994	1995	1996
Domestic Consumption	303.7	266.0	234.0	197.0	182.7	178.4
Exports (to FSU)	117.4	75.5	47.6	37.8	31.1	17.5

Despite all these problems, the Russian oil industry still possesses many strengths in terms of physical reserves, technical resources (in the form of existing production and refining capacities, transport and distribution infrastructure) and professional potential. These should allow Russia to stay among, and perhaps even move up the league table of, the leading oil producing nations of the World.

An important and unique feature of the Russian oil industry is that it functions on the basis of two essentially different price systems for crude oil. For example, while retail prices on the internal market for non-ethylene gasoline A-92 have reached and even exceeded those in the USA, crude oil prices remain much below World levels. After numerous increases and having reached the maximum possible level given current demand, the domestic price still does not exceed 60% of the World price (including excise duties). Reaching the World price level is a remote prospect. Therefore, Russian oil companies and enterprises will have to work under conditions of economic reality, which, given the price differential, stimulates the maximisation of crude oil exports. However, the existing technical constraints of the transport system - which is already close to saturation and requires expansion - place a physical limit on the further expansion of oil exports. Besides, export-oriented oil production jeopardises the existing oil products supply system, the reconstruction of which is vital for the whole economy. The export opportunities of Russian oil refineries are also restricted by virtue of high industrial costs that make them uncompetitive, despite the fact that they buy crude oil at low internal prices. Thus, the average price of a set of oil products obtained from one tonne of crude oil at Russian oil refineries is 25-30% lower than the World average. The main problem facing the Russian oil industry is thus one of finding the optimum balance between exports (within the limits of transport provision) and domestic supply to refineries for the production of oil products both for domestic demand and profitable export.

In 1995, the Russian oil industry began to stabilise as production and consumption came into balance. While the reason for the sharp fall in oil production was the reduction in investment between 1991-1993, in 1994 the decisive factor behind continuing decline had become falling domestic demand and export transportation constraints. This trend bottomed-out in 1995 when the decrease in oil production was only 3.5 % (10.2% in 1994) with export growth of 2.3%. In 1996, the fall in oil production remained about the same (3.8%), while exports increased by 9.8%. So the oil industry has obviously stabilised following such a dramatic production fall. But what of the future? This is especially important in view of the large potential natural resource base, which, with appropriate investment, could in time ensure considerably larger production volumes than at present.

In theory, the Russian oil industry could in ten years time and under ideal economic conditions produce more than 400mt of oil per year. However, reality would suggest future oil production levels somewhat lower than this figure, in part because domestic demand is unlikely to recover rapidly. Even assuming that a return to a centrally-planned economy were possible, it would take place without its major driving force - centrally planned investment from the national budget. Any government attempt to revert to centralised state management would lead to another economic crisis and the continuance of industrial recession, including in the oil industry. Under this scenario, oil production could by the end of the Century drop to 200mt per year or even lower. Oil would be extracted only from the richest deposits whilst oil exports would be restricted to the level necessary to meet import requirements. But under a scenario of successful economic reform that brought rouble convertibility and World market prices, the total volume of oil production would be determined by the state of the investment market, i.e. by a comparative yield of investments made in the oil industry against that in other sectors of the economy.

The emergence of industries in Russia more profitable than oil or raw materials is unlikely until the year 2000 at the earliest. But given a favourable course for reform, they could emerge in the first years of the next Century. At about that time, the first appreciable results of energy saving could be expected. Thus, by the beginning of the 21st Century, oil production could be constrained both by a reduction of investment and a slowing down in internal demand. But, to counterbalance these factors, a reviving economy with growing demand (although, as mentioned above, demand could be less than otherwise expected) combined with technical renewal of the industry (which would lower real operating costs) could encourage production growth.

The counterbalance of these two tendencies should limit internal consumption to 200mt per year until 2000. Only by 2010 could the growth in domestic consumption to a maximum of 240mt per year be expected. Total demand will be determined both by the opportunity to export at World market prices along with the level of deliveries to former Soviet republics. Exports to the World market are now limited by the existing transport system, which is at present capable of transporting only about 110mt of oil per year to customers outside the FSU. **Table 4** below refers:

Table 4

Export of Russian Crude Oil in 1994

Market	Volume (million tonnes)	Share of total (%)
Central Europe	21.0	16.7
CIS and Baltic States	37.8	30.1
Mediterranean	12.3	9.8
Eastern Europe	10.0	8.0
America	2.5	2.0
Northern Europe	32.0	25.5
Other	9.5	7.6
Total	**125.6**	**100.0**

This system could be expanded and exports thereby increased. However, the growth in production costs and competition for capital from other emerging industries could push investment away from projects to expand transport infrastructure, as well as from the repair and maintenance of the network which is necessary to keep exports at or close to existing levels. Thus it is more likely that annual export volumes will remain steady at about 100mt, and these would mainly comprise products produced by joint ventures and foreign companies.

Annual deliveries to the former USSR republics upto 2000, given their continuing poor economic situation, are expected to remain steady at between 20-30mt, maybe 35mt at most. Some growth in deliveries could be expected thereafter, but they would be at World market prices. Thus existing oil exports to the West could in the future be diverted to CIS markets.

In brief, the most probable upper level for oil production in Russia is 330mt in 2000 and 360mt in 2010. These figures could of course alter due to the influence of both **negative** factors (such as the continuing fall of production and demand, the shortage of investment resources and slow progress with energy saving) and **positive** factors (such as greater investment in more efficient industries, the success of energy saving, and an increase in solvent demand both in Russia and elsewhere in the FSU).

Natural Gas

Following the disintegration of the USSR, the gas industry has found itself in the best situation, not only among Russian fuel-energy sectors but also relative to all other industries. This was due to the largest proven reserves in the World (35% of global total) combined with the *Unified Gas Supply System* which integrated natural gas production and transport to a uniform technological and economic system throughout Russia. This system was also connected with the gas supply systems of a number of states to the south-east and to the west, including twenty European countries.

In the first half of the 1990s, *Gasprom* did not require serious investments either for the development of new natural gas producing regions, or for the construction of new transport infrastructure facilities. Against the background of a general investment crisis in Russia, the opportunities for stable output within the gas industry were quite good. Thus gas exports to Europe have increased in recent years. (See **Table 5** below) But at the same time, gas exports to the CIS and Baltic States decreased considerably.

Table 5

Russian Gas Exports (excluding FSU) in 1992-1995 (bn m³)

Destination	1992	1993	1994	1995
Western Europe	60.72	62.00	67.10	71.40
Eastern Europe	33.94	33.90	33.73	40.30
Middle East (mainly Turkey)	4.44	5.00	4.97	5.70
Total	**99.10**	**100.90**	**105.80**	**117.40**

Despite export success, overall gas production fell slightly over this period because of the reduction in internal consumption and a fall off in deliveries to former USSR republics due to their indebtedness. See **Table 6** below.

Table 6
Russian Natural Gas Deliveries to the FSU in 1992 and 1995 (bn m³)

Destination	1992	1995
Ukraine	77.6	52.8
Belarus	17.7	12.9
Moldova	3.4	3.0
Kazakhstan	1.7	0.0
Estonia	0.9	0.7
Latvia	1.6	1.2
Lithuania	3.2	2.5
Total	**106.0**	**78.1**

The decrease in internal consumption by 3% in 1993 and by 5% in 1994 did not affect production by very much, basically owing to increased exports. In 1994, production was only 1.8% below that in 1993. Available capacities will permit production to increase when growth in demand and consumption occurs, which is expected after 1997. Indeed, a stabilisation of consumption could occur this year.

As distinct from the World oil market, the gas market has a regional character and is based on large long-term agreements. This is explained by the high costs of gas transportation which requires large investment projects. These can only be justified if long-term stable and reliable deliveries are ensured. This also explains the significant involvement of the government in gas projects and agreements.

It is common practice for gas importing countries to diversify their sources of supply, both for political (ie. strategic) and economic reasons. The lack of such a choice is a crucial factor for some countries. In the case of the newly independent states of the former USSR and some East European countries, the Russian export option is to some extent the only one. For the countries of Central Europe, economics works in favour of Russian supply. In West European countries, the stategic need to diversify supply assumes greater importance.

A new phenomenon has appeared in the international gas market, that of a growing discrepancy between contractual and actual physical volumes of gas deliveries. Such a discrepancy makes the compromise between the economic efficiency of gas deliveries and their reliability (in case of political upheaval) difficult to achieve. This is why the international gas supply system involves support, agreements and guarantees at the multinational level. Indeed, the gas trade is now the most important aspect of regional international cooperation in the energy sector.

The price of gas, though connected with that of oil, does not have a direct correlation in that it depends upon the ratio between prices for crude oil and mazut (or gasoil). Usually, the price of gas is established pursuant to market value, i.e. having regard to the price of the closest competing fuel, which, depending on the particular market, could be gasoil, mazut or coal. Thus gas prices do not wholly depend upon the interrelation between supply and demand, and do not therefore fully reflect gas production and delivery costs.

In some cases, the price is established in response to costs and includes the price on the border (which is agreed between the importer and the exporter), transport charges, and distribution and storage expenses. There has recently appeared a new factor in gas pricing - a so-called type of competition known as 'gas-gas', under which a competitive transit market between the sellers to replace non-flexible long-term contracts on gas deliveries can be created. This is now well established in North America, although not yet in continental Europe.

When comparing competitive kinds of fuel used in the power sector, gas has recently been quite frequently compared with coal, whereas oil products continue to be the main competition. Forecasting gas prices must also take account of mutual relations between supply and demand. The driving forces behind the demand for natural gas in Europe are as follows:

* use of natural gas for power production since it has some advantages over competing fuels;
* lower capital investments compared to coal or nuclear fuel, shorter term of realisation, more flexible production process;
* advantages of gas over other fuels as a lesser pollutant of the environment;
* socio-economic development in Eastern Europe, which requires expansion of gas use and the further replacement of other types of fuel.

Future supply will be based on the expansion of existing production capacities, the commissioning of new facilities, the construction of new pipelines, and the implementation of liquefied gas projects.

Surveys recently financed by the EBRD show that from 1994 to 2000, demand for gas in Europe will be provided largely by local production at a price of US$2-3.25/mBTU as well as by imports from the former USSR and Northern Africa at a price of US$2.50-3.00/mBTU. However, when evaluating additional demand for natural gas of 57 billion m^3 by 2005 and 100 billion m^3 by 2010, gas supply costs might increase considerably since this demand can be only met by gas transported through expensive new systems. Even allowing for low production costs (of US$0.50mBTU), long-distance delivery cost (to the European market) can be as much as US$2.50-3.50/mBTU and even more, particularly for new projects which could range up to US$4/mBTU, thus matching the LNG price in Asia. **Table 7** below gives an evaluation of future Russian gas prices on the Ukrainian border:

Table 7
Future Russian Gas Prices (on Ukrainian border)

	1995	2000	2005	2010
US$ per million BTU	1.97	2.35	2.64	2.95

Taking into account these price factors and the possible development of supply and demand, Russian natural gas supply would be as in **Table 8** below:

Table 8
Future Russian Gas Supply (in billion m³)

Coal

The coal industry is in the most depressed state of all fuel industries in Russia. This is explained both by problems of transition which have accelerated the growth of production costs, and by the changing role of coal in the Russian power industry. For several years the demand for coal has continued to decline, although employment in the coal industry has remained steady. Subsidies granted to the coal industry even now account for 1.2 % of Russian GDP and rank second after agriculture as heavy burdens on the national budget. According to the World Bank, the future "viable core" of the Russian coal industry would be about two-thirds its current size with total employment being less than half of today's level.

Before its demise, the USSR was not the World's largest coal exporter, but was nonetheless a large and stable provider for global markets. However, both production and exports have fallen since 1991. See **Table 9** below;

Table 9
Russian Coal and Coke Production and Export (non CIS) - 1991-1996

	1991	1992	1993	1994	1995	1996
Production (million tonnes)	340.0	323.1	293.8	262.0	252.1	247.9
Export (million tonnes)	26.0	24.7	18.6	14.5	17.7	18.0

Within this overall decline, exports to the Far East, especially to Japan, have increased rapidly. The fastest decline was in deliveries to European countries, explained by the geographical location of the main coal producing centres in Siberia and the Far East. (See **Table 10** below). Increased railroad tariffs, even under conditions of subsidy and the need for hard currency, make deliveries to the West competitive only if made to neighbouring countries. Moreover, the geographical location of the main Russian centres of coal consumption makes exporting coal even less attractive, hence ensuring some stability of internal demand as overall production falls.

Destination	2000	2005	2010
Europe (excl. former Yugoslavia)	124	141	162
CIS and Rest of World	86	101	115
TOTAL	210	242	277

Table 10
Russian Export of Coal and Coke by Destination - 1992 to 1995

	1992	1993	1994	1995
Europe (thousand tonnes)	9,172	8,473	6,578	5,960
Japan (thousand tonnes)	4,301	4,229	4,378	4,924
Share of Japan (%)	*31.9*	*33.3*	*40.0*	*45.2*
TOTAL (thousand tonnes)	**13,473**	**12,702**	**10,956**	**10,884**

ENERGY PERSPECTIVE: SOME PERSONAL OBSERVATIONS OF THE 1990's IN RUSSIA AND THE UKRAINE

Tony Scanlan

Independent Consultant and Member of Council, British Institute of Energy Economics

Introduction

This paper offers some perspectives on the hydrocarbon industries of the CIS based upon how I see this vital industry evolving and from personal experience within Russia and the Ukraine during the past decade. It is a particular pleasure to present my paper in the company of Professor Alexander Arbatov who has been a friend and colleague even longer than that, and to welcome him at NATO is something that could only have been wishful thinking when I gave my first paper here during the 1973 oil crisis.

As an aid to brevity I have appended some facts in four tables which can be referred to as background detail. Some deal with World oil and gas to give perspective to trade and investment prospects for Russia and Ukraine. **Table 1** logs the unprecedented and rapid decline in energy consumption which began just before the emergence of the CIS, which is detailed by type of fuel in **Table 4**. **Table 2** contrasts energy production in the CIS against that in the rest of the World (ROW), whilst **Table 3** compares global and Russian energy reserves. The decline in consumption is especially marked in the case of the Ukraine. First, however, I will focus on Russia and on oil.

Russia

In 1992 I was invited to take part in a meeting in Rosneft HQ to announce oil privatisation. In a room facing the Kremlin across the Moscow River, I heard the boss, the last Soviet Oil Minister, tell his 19 regional directors that the plan was to create their own equivalent of Exxon and Shell. Lukoil, Yukos and Surgut (neftegaz) had already been set up as separate corporate entities and now the whole of the rest of the state oil industry was to be split into regional groups of integrated companies. The particular group I was asked to advise was given one million barrels per day of production and also of refining capacity, and no debts - a dream ticket. But it never developed, because both the producing area entities, one a full Autonomous Republic, the other an autonomous ethnic region, had different ideas as to where they would sell their oil and in neither case was this to the appointed group refineries in the Moscow region. But before the second working meeting due to take place ever occurred, they sold to the Lithuanian refinery and to a Czechoslovak company who presumably could offer payment or reciprocal services which were not available within the so-called new group. The new freedom to use the Moscow Petroleum Exchange and to use the state-owned pipeline system to choose where their crude oil was delivered enabled every entity to try their utmost to evade central control, to test their new freedom. It was a case of who you confided in, which sauna you frequented. If Moscow could not find out, what hope for an external foreign adviser.

Under perestroika, it had been clear that excessive use of energy was causing much of the effort to expand output, often in remote and hostile locations, to be wasted, but this new zeal to export for local profit rather than to aim at a national corrective meant that privatisation alone was not going to deliver the remedy. That is my first point; privatisation is necessary but not sufficient. A national strategy is needed to implement policy and deal with regional interests.

Foreign inward investment was also inhibited by the excess of new freedom for regions to vie with central government in tax collection and set legal conditions for exploration and production - the so-called "upstream" industry. The Russian practice of taxing gross revenues instead of net profits, coupled with discretionary taxes on exports and even - for a time - retroactive tax changes, caused a rapid decline in international enthusiasm to take part in the new "freedom". Nor did it help to be told, when complaining about legal and tax burdens far beyond the tolerable, to be told not to worry because the whole legal structure was about to be reformed once again. What is needed is a stable system compatible with World trade which does not undergo repeated sea-changes. Presidential decrees might be useful, but not when a promising Presidential decree is weighed down in the Duma by well-meaning but over-detailed attention that tends to want to put back with one hand what has just been taken away by the other, or when the desire to control oil industry revenue and tax result in one group of ministries pressing for centralisation and export licensing while other ministries side with dissenting regional producing association interests, often with ethnic overtones. It is one thing for foreign companies to endure this in countries like the USA or Australia where the basic system is tried and tested, but when the system itself is trying to evolve, including the first attempts to set up a private banking system, there is a natural tendency to wait. There have been some joint venture successes, especially those where, on a small scale, value can be added generally through new technology. But one has only to compare the upstream progress in Azerbaijan and Kazakhstan and the billion dollar investments involved to the position in Russia to note that - given the scale of the global potential in Russia as detailed in **Table 3B** - investment progress has not been significant either in global terms or in relation to Russian economic output. And the "downstream" so far is minimal compared with investment by international majors in Eastern European oil refining and marketing.

World Bank and EBRD/EIB funding is often quoted as real progress and in some respects this is true: but it is only supposed to be the hors d'oeuvre for the main feast of private capital this is supposed to induce. While such developments are encouraging, the follow-up record is still slow. One of the reasons why progress has been disappointingly slow is perhaps shown in **Table 3A**. In the command economy, a Russian oilman could be sure that if he found oil it would be developed, with costs being taken care of by the system. He was also well aware that the global oil industry was obsessed with shortage throughout the seventies and most of the eighties. Today, he also knows that despite falling output, falling Russian demand plus the fact that all other areas of the former CMEA now have to pay hard currency mean that his hard currency exports have remained very largely intact through the transition. So it may come as a surprise, especially if he is unused to external direct trading, to realise that the World has substantially increased its oil and gas reserves, not just through the high price years of 1973/85, but also since 1985 despite lower real prices in the past decade due to the radical improvements in technology and costs throughout the upstream sector. Very little of this has been imported into the Russian economy on any significant scale. (The same applies to the new technology in the refining sector necessary for modern environmental and product quality factors.) When I first addressed a NATO Economics Colloquium in 1973, oil reserves at our then rate of use would have lasted until the year 2000. Today, our rate of use is higher but we have reserves until 2040. World gas reserves have doubled in this period and are good until 2060 at current levels of use.

International industry needs new oil and gas reserves, but is no longer preoccupied with scarcity and has many more options of when and where and how to invest in new projects than ever before as a result of privatisation, globalisation and competition in the World market. At a recent London conference, one could hear a Russian regional director saying "we did it on our own in the past, why do we need foreign help" and at the same time new Russian voices from the Duma and other Moscow institutes giving all the answers one could hope to hear to this rhetorical question. The new PSA agreements for production sharing are hopefully going to provide the long-awaited breakthrough, but are their proponents really in charge at last or will there be another stalemate. Until we are sure, the question the Russian regional director raised might well be reversed.

Another recent experience that is relevant to this question of attitudes is a request I received to find customers for a survey of all regional costs of oil production throughout Russia - and from a pedigree source. It was predicated on one small phrase "based on the existing tax system". Our preliminary testing of interest in this survey among prospective clients in London showed a very guarded response, requiring elaboration on this tax issue, firstly to define how the costs had been arrived at, including the fiscal/legal premises, and then to ask the source to provide some comment as to how this might evolve in the near future in the light of current debate in Duma committees etc. This was relayed to the proposers with the suggestion that the marketplace would be interested in the survey given the chance to discuss these two points, the first as a matter of factual ingredients, the second as a follow-up within a year/18 months. We are still waiting for a reply, but we have heard unofficially that the project may have gone elsewhere. The explanation could be that costs of a non-technical nature are still regarded as extraneous, whereas to our economists they are endemic. One cannot play with half a ball.

I believe that the gas industry, the flagship of the Russian economy providing half of all energy in Russia, may be a guide to the real thinking now going on, and a pointer to the way ahead. Gazprom, now effectively privatised and quoted in part on World stockmarkets is valued due to its unique reserves at something like three times the largest oil group, Royal Dutch Shell. And it has a massive international position albeit all in Europe. As with oil, the European gas market is oversupplied so competition is high. But perhaps Gazprom is seen as securely rooted in Russian ownership, whereas the emerging Russian oil corporations are not so large, not so international (yet) and more vulnerable to foreign investment and competition. True, we have ARCO taking a stake in Lukoil, but then Lukoil could claim to be the leader, the nearest parallel to Gazprom. About 10 years ago Academician Bogomolov, at an IISS conference in Barcelona, said Russia needed international companies of her own for the transformation of her economy. This is what I heard that day at Rosneft "we need our own Exxons and Shells". But at the same time it makes sense to have some protectionism during the transition.

One area in which I believe protectionism has precluded the privatisation of a vital part of the Russian oil industry is Transneft, the state controlled pipeline system without which nothing moves. Transneft employs a differential pricing system and cannot guarantee physical access to the pipeline network - "frozen assets" as one oilman drily noted - thereby completing the "troika" of most frequent complaints heard from oil companies, along with legal and fiscal uncertainties. I asked the (then deputy) Minister for Energy last year what was being done to meet criticism. The reply was a polite homily that those who had not invested in the system should not expect to claim override. There are two differences in perspective here. Firstly, with oil production in Russia almost halved, nobody should have to be pushed off the back of the queue, and secondly, queue-jumping is not the nature of the request, merely to have a level playing field of the third-party access type. Above all, it is not an issue of whether or not a producer invests in the carrier system, but whether the Russians can provide a pipeline system that ensures reliable access equivalent to that provided by the World tanker fleet in other parts of the globe. If they could, confidence in the vastly more important upstream investments and requisite technology transfers would grow accordingly. Investment issues in the pipeline itself are as irrelevant as investment in ocean tankers on charter - all that the oil company and his financial backers need to be sure of is that the transportation is there. However, it is eminently sensible for Russia to be strategically sensitive about who owns the system. I have recently given some advice to Duma representatives as to how an assured and continuing Russian majority ownership could be consistent with substantial privatisation of this vital link in the vertically integrated industry. Once the new Russian major companies find that the present imperfections stand in their own way, their proposed shareholding would be the essential element in providing a level playing field.

Ukraine

In total contrast to the riches Russia possesses in oil and gas reserves, Ukraine has the most serious deficits of any major European country. **Table 4** shows that despite an economic recession causing a 50% reduction in consumption of energy, Ukraine is still importing 80% of its oil and gas, all from the CIS and over 90% from Russia. Its own gas production has fallen by 50% and, much more seriously, its once massive coal output, deprived of investment, has fallen by two-thirds leading to the loss of export revenue on coal and electricity.

Ukraine started independence without any established economy and lacking central government experience. Moreover, it had a temporary "coupon" currency (the Karbovanet) as an indicator of independence from the rouble zone and only the promise of a new permanent currency (the "Hryvni") after a period of transition. The Karbovanet started at two to the rouble when the rouble was believed to be worth one pound sterling; my last exchange rate in Kiev gave me one million Kbvt for about three pounds sterling/five US dollars. Yet all imported fuel is now priced in dollars.

Between 1993 and 1995 I advised the Ukrainian State Oil and Gas Committee on a hydrocarbon policy to the year 2010 as part of a TACIS team. Since the prospects of copying Kazakhstan or Azerbaijan and discovering major new oil and gas is unrealistic given the geology - the Black Sea is not the Caspian - the major problem was to reverse the switch out of indigenous coal to gas set in motion when gas was a "domestic" Soviet fuel, and also to hold on to any source of electricity from Nuclear and Hydropower to reduce the crushing balance of payments deficit caused by the cost of fuel imports which alone exceeded the whole of the rest of the nation's external trade balance. The World Bank supported several river hydro schemes, but the claim of a 50% increase in hydropower has to be seen in the light of **Table 4** where hydro only provides about one per cent of national energy and perhaps 5% of electricity. Nuclear, on the other hand, provides one third. While not wishing to see Chernobyl's remaining two working RBMK plants active any longer than possible, we had to find a solution avoiding even greater gas imports if the economy and the currency were to have any chance of survival.

In the absence of any serious possibility of foreign investment in coal, which if it comes will require new pits to be sunk in new areas and not the costly maintaining of old and dangerous thin seams, one feasible solution was to complete three VVER 1000 nuclear reactors which had been nearing completion at the end of the Ukrainian Soviet Republic. This would entail offering a loan of about US$1bn on the strict condition that the moment these indigenous sources of electricity enabled Chernobyl to be closed down without increasing energy imports, that this would be guaranteed. It was difficult and in some cases impossible to get officials only responsible for oil and gas production to see the relevance of this course of action and it did not improve our credibility in trying to get this message across when one of the EU Commissioners appeared with President Kuchma in the Ukrainian media to declare that the EU would assist in providing a new gas-fired power station to replace Chernobyl. I had to fax my Ukrainian colleagues immediately to say that that would not be our recommendation when we concluded our report. The final confusion occurred when members of the European Parliament complained about the loan to help develop Ukrainian nuclear power because they were against Chernobyl remaining operational - which of course was precisely why the money was being sought. Explain that in Kiev while presenting our conclusions.

The other area in which well-meaning but ill-informed environmental opinion is at risk of fatally damaging the Ukrainian ability to conduct its economic resurrection successfully is the drive to reduce emissions from coal-fired plant. Normally this would be as natural a target as closing an RBMK, but it would finally disembowel what is left of the Ukrainian ability to produce its own energy. At the time of independence, Ukraine was the largest coal producer in Europe, rivalled only by Poland. It did after all produce up to 40% of USSR steel and in Soviet times it paid for its oil and gas imports by building pipelines all over the USSR, providing 750,000 men and materials on the average day. There is a much greater ignorance of the Ukraine in Europe than there is about Russia; with a surface area roughly equal to Germany and Great Britain combined and with a population equal to France, it is hardly a small republic to be borne into independence with the help of wealthy neighbours as in the case of the Baltic States, nor is it capable of sustaining the end of the command economy in the manner of, say, Moldova which has very real problems but only 3% of the population and with not even an oil refinery to modernise and no energy production. And, as already stated, Ukraine is the very antithesis of the strength of Russia in energy resources. Its 52 million people must remain industralised despite its known agricultural potential (also in dire need of a revival) because the population is 80% urbanised. This requires a fuels revolution and with no time to spare if the import bill is not to crush the currency.

Given these circumstances, all Western or foreign economic tenets that do not meet the specific needs of the Ukraine in the short and medium term must be cast aside. Equally, Ukrainian officials who desire to import oil via the new Yuzhny terminal east of Odessa by tanker across the Black Sea must first find out how it is to be paid for. The obvious economic partner in this critical situation is Russia, and my experience is that there are elements in both the Ukraine itself and in the OECD which need to see this as an essential building block of a sustainable future for an independent Ukraine.

As an example of attitudes which need to think this through a little deeper, there are those who worry about the activities of Gazprom in acquiring assets in the Ukraine, for example in the massive ex-Soviet underground gas storage facilities. Some see it as a creeping return to the past. But in a modern Russia, where privatisation is a welcome sign of an end to that past, would we expect say Shell or Ruhrgas to accept, as a well-run commercially responsible corporation, debts of over US$1.5bn for gas delivered to a customer, in this case to the Ukraine? The Russian/Ukrainian dispute over "missing" gas in transit to Eastern Europe also needs to be settled as a prerequisite to better relations.

The new government ministries in Kiev have now begun to develop a realpolitik approach to structuring the economy and external trade far exceeding the first "democrats" in the High Rada whose interests often lay solely in looking after their personal positions regionally. Some of the officials we had to deal with ended up facing serious financial charges according to the UK press; much of the assistance vital to our task came from the new ministry sources who were not officially on the Ukrainian project team but could well see the importance of such cooperation without any strings attached.

Energy demand management - greater efficiency - is often quoted as the solution to FSU states' problems. However, it can be very misleading to see this as only a demand-side problem in the Ukraine. Massive reductions in energy consumption since independence owe far more to recession than to efficiency so that when eventually economic recovery increases energy demand, the market pricing system alone - even if the social safety net for the poor is successfully engineered - will be inadequate without enormous investment in structural plant changes. One example will be to remove the purely gas-heat stations (not power stations because no electric power is generated, just hot water conduits for whole city zones) based on costly dollar priced Russian gas. Capital investment over several years will be needed. The buildings in the zones thus heated will need the individual industrial or living apartment units to be equipped with individual meters in order to discover for the first time what the individual apartments consume, before price can even begin to take effect. There were some press announcements in 1995 that an industry to produce such meters had been set up with a production target of 700,000 meters annually: at this rate it would take several years to produce enough meters to equip the majority of the housing stock.

Equally daunting is the experience in the five lander of the former DDR of the need to modernise coal mining plants, nuclear power stations, chemical works etc. The answer there has usually been to decide it is cheaper to scrap entirely and rebuild, or substitute imported gas for indigenous coal. But in the DDR the decisions were taken in the context of freely surrendered sovereignty. This is not the aim in the Ukraine. The position of the Ukraine is also very different from that in Russia where there are equal needs and potential for greater energy efficiency, both states having been so well supplied with the wealth of Soviet oil and gas that extra output was always available at artificially low prices and obviated the need for economy in consumption. But today Russia can still, at a cost, continue this path whereas the Ukraine finds it not merely a cost but a dollar import price to continue to use hydrocarbons in the old way; yet it lacks the technology and investment to avoid so doing. The fortunes of the new Hryvni currency introduced last September will depend very largely on the balance of payments ceasing to be driven into heavy deficit by the excessive import of oil and gas which has caused such inflationary damage and lack of foreign investment in the transition years of the Kypon/Karbovanets currency.

The positive side of this is that the Ukraine need not return to old levels of total energy consumption as the economy recovers **for the foreseeable future,** provided it can synchronise that recovery with energy efficiency in both supply and demand aspects of the economy - essentially a planned structural investment programme coupled with price reform and not just a blind faith in markets.

In the longer term, the Ukraine could play a major role in oil and gas supplies from both CIS and Middle East sources to Central and Western Europe, similar to that of Turkey. Again the links inherited from Soviet days are already to some extent in place and the traditional pipeline construction teams could continue to earn for the Ukraine its imports of energy and add to transit fees within a competitive market - this time truly internationally. Over 75% of World oil and gas lie in the crescent from the Ob delta to Oman. For example, Ukrainian Soviet engineers are no strangers to construction projects in Iraq.

The Partnership programme, in conjunction with the European Energy Charter of which both Russia and Ukraine are signatories, could develop into the framework for future regional cooperation. Energy remains the principal element in the balance of trade for both countries albeit in opposite directions, but that creates rather than precludes the potential to use it as the cornerstone of the new economic structure for a stable eastern zone in the new Europe.

Table 1
CIS: Consumption of Total Primary Energy in m.t.o.e.
(Percentage reductions are from 1990 to 1996)

Country	1988	1990	1992	1994	1995	1996	%
Russia	865	855	800	660	625	602	-30
Ukraine	245	275	220	160	145	140	-50
Others	270	275	230	180	180	180	-35
Total	1380	1405	1250	1000	950	922	-35

Table 2
Comparative Energy Production (m.t.o.e) - CIS & Rest of World (ROW)

Fuel	Region	1988	1996	+/-
Oil	CIS ROW	625 2450	350 3010	-275 +560
Gas	CIS ROW	650 1050	600 1400	-50 +350
Solid Fuel	CIS ROW	365 1880	190 2080	-175 +200
Nuclear	CIS ROW	60 430	56 565	-4 +135
Hydro	CIS ROW	20 165	20 200	0 +35
TOTAL	**CIS** **ROW**	**1720** **5975**	**1216** **7255**	**-504** **+1280**

Table 3: Reserves
A: World Reserves
Hydrocarbon Reserves Development since the Oil Crisis of 1973

YEAR	1972	1986	1996	%
WORLD ENERGY CONSUMPTION (m.t.o.e.)	5600	7000	8400	+50
PROVEN RESERVES IN THAT YEAR				
OIL (billion tons)	80	100	140	+75
GAS (trillion cubic metres)	65	103	140	+115
R/P Ratio (number of years the then existing reserves would last at the then existing rate of consumption) OIL	28	40	42 (years)	
GAS	50	50	62 (years)	

B: Russian Reserves

OIL

External industry assessments of proven oil reserves are about 50-60 billion (milliard) barrels - 5% of world reserves - but Russian figures on a slightly different basis of definition of proven and probable are about 200 billion barrels - about 17% of the world total. The R/P ratio on the former basis is 22-26 years, or on Russian calculations, 80 years.

GAS

There is general agreement that Russia possesses over one-third of world gas reserves; at about 50 trillion cubic metres (50,000 milliard) this is larger in calorific value than the oil reserves of Saudi Arabia, and a R/P ratio of over 80 years.

There is every reason to expect future additions from new discoveries and from existing fields when new technologies become widespread.

In addition, Russia has substantial deposits of heavy oils, shale oil, etc.

Solid fuel reserves are one quarter of total world reserves with hard coals alone over 100 billion tonnes.

Table 4
CIS Energy - Decline by Fuel Type
(in mtoe; millions of tonnes of oil equivalent)

Country	Production			Consumption		
	1988	1996	Decline	1990	1996	Decline
Oil						
Russia	570	300	270	250	125	125
Ukraine	5	4	1	63	17	46
Others	50	46	4	107	53	54
CIS	**625**	**350**	**275**	**420**	**195**	**225**
Natural Gas						
Russia	495	505	(+10)	380	315	65
Ukraine	30	15	15	115	70	45
Others	125	80	45	105	90	15
CIS	**650**	**600**	**50**	**600**	**475**	**125**
Solid Fuels						
Russia	190	115	75	180	120	60
Ukraine	100	35	65	75	30	45
Others	75	40	35	55	30	25
CIS	**365**	**190**	**175**	**310**	**180**	**130**
Nuclear						
Russia	36	31	5	31	28	3
Ukraine	19	21	(+2)	17	21	(+4)
Others	5	4	1	5	4	1
CIS	**60**	**56**	**4**	**53**	**53**	**0**
Hydropower						
Russia	14	14	0	14	14	0
Ukraine	1	1	0	1	1	0
Others	5	5	0	5	5	0
CIS	**20**	**20**	**0**	**20**	**20**	**0**
TOTAL						
Russia	1305	965	340	855	602	253
Ukraine	155	76	79	271	139	132
Others	260	175	85	277	182	95
CIS	**1720**	**1216**	**504**	**1403**	**923**	**480**

PANEL IV

Economic Integration of Partner Countries into Pan-European Structures

Panelists and contributors:
Andras INOTAI
Thomas NOWOTNY
Jean-Pierre TUVERI
Spiros VOYADZIS
Fraser CAMERON
Matija ROJEC
Janez POTOCNIK
Olgica VASILEVSKA

ECONOMIC INTEGRATION OF PARTNER COUNTRIES INTO PAN-EUROPEAN STRUCTURES

András Inotai

Director General, Institute for World Economics of the Hungarian Academy of Sciences, Budapest

Introduction

From the very beginning, there was and remains a fundamental misconception and misassessment of the historic transformation evolving in Central and Eastern Europe. It was, and still mainly is, considered as a two-level process. On the political level, the process can be described as moving from a one-party (totalitarian) system to a multi-party democracy. On the economic level, different patterns of centrally planned economies have to be replaced by (probably also different patterns of) market economies. The main shortcoming of this approach is not its claim to apply homogenous political and economic models for countries with sometimes different heritages and characteristics, rather the lack of consideration among highly developed (OECD) countries regarding the relatively wide variety of democratic and market economy patterns.

The fundamental problem lies in the ahistoric character of this approach which did not make it possible to understand the vital goal of transformation. In my view, the collapse of the Soviet-dominated system in Europe opened a window of opportunity for the countries of the region to restart their catching up process towards the more developed parts of Europe. This modernisation process, several times initiated in the last 150 to 200 years, but always frustrated or interrupted both by external and domestic forces, has to be considered as the core issue of current developments. Political democracy and a market economy are necessary instruments to achieve this goal, but are not goals in themselves. If political democracy and market economies cannot cope with the problems of successful modernisation, a gradual catching up process to the developed part of Europe will not become manifest for large sections of the societies within a relatively short period. Thus the train of transformation may easily derail, with substantial negative consequences not only for Central and Eastern European countries but also for the whole continent.

The success of transformation with modernisation requires decisive domestic efforts. However, it also needs two external elements; both a security and a modernisation anchor. First, the security of the region has to be guaranteed, because successful socio-economic modernisation requires a long period for which a predictable security framework should be provided. Second, the external anchor of modernisation is expected to provide the economic prerequisites of successful transformation, such as predictability, access to markets and financial resources. It has to be emphasised that the security and the modernisation anchors cannot be separated from each other. While modernisation is highly unlikely to be sustainable in a security vacuum, the security framework cannot in itself prevent, and even less solve, serious conflicts emanating from the lack or failure of socio-economic modernisation. For reasons of regional historical development, both anchors can be found outside the transforming area of Central and Eastern Europe. Both are in Brussels, but rooted in two different organizations. The security anchor lies in NATO, while the economic modernisation anchor is the European Union (EU).

The Key Role of the European Union

Practically all transforming countries in Europe consider the EU to be the external modernisation anchor. 50-80% of their total trade is already with the EU. Geographic reorientation of trade relations was quickly followed by surprisingly rapid and successful structural transformation. Machinery, computer and electronic products and transport equipment already account for more than 40% of Hungary's exports to the EU, and explain about 60% of total export growth between 1993 and 1996. Similar trends can be observed in other Central European countries as well. Intra-industry trade, supported by favourable geographic location, foreign direct investment and the institutional framework created by the Association Agreements, has in some cases already reached the level and pattern characteristic of intra-EU trade relations. West European (and West European-located non-European, mainly US) firms became the main beneficiaries of the privatisation business and recognised the substantial locational advantages of the region for regional, pan-European and global production and competition. The adjustment to EU rules (mainly in the framework of overtaking the *acquis communautaire* and supported by foreign companies located in the region) increases the similarity of economic structures, institutions and procedures between the Western and the Eastern part of the continent. Moreover, the structured political dialogue and other non-economic factors have helped the transforming countries to become more and more organically integrated into developed European structures. Perhaps even more importantly, the EU provides a fundamental support to democratic institutions and maintains the economic momentum of transformation in two ways. First, the previously described developments support these positive processes. Second, the retaliatory capacity of the EU may prevent selected transforming countries from going (or falling) back to old practices, thereby abandoning the route started after 1989.

In order to play the role of economic "modernisator", the EU should comply with three basic conditions. According to international experience with successful (and unsuccessful) modernisation, the anchor economy has to be predictable in order to sustain the relatively long process of modernisation. Because all Central and Eastern European countries are small economies, free access to the anchor market(s) is crucial. Finally, modernisation, at least in its first and decisive period, requires a substantial amount of foreign resources which generally have to be provided by the anchor economy.

To what extent can the European Union cope with these challenges? During all previous enlargements, the European Union's future was much more predictable than in the second half of the nineties. At present, the EU has to answer various crucial issues with vital consequences for the future of the integration and of Europe as a whole (institutional reforms, the reform of the common agricultural policy, EMU, structural funds, pattern of enlargement). For a number of reasons, both on the side of the EU and on the side of the applicant countries, the next enlargement(s) will be different from previous enlargements.[1]

In a temporarily asymmetric way, the Association Agreements have opened up the EU's markets for industrial products exported by the transforming countries. Agriculture, however, a sector with important export capacity, did not become part of the free trade agreement. Moreover, financial transfers remained extremely limited. Although the *Phare* programme has undoubtedly been contributing to economic modernisation in all countries, the resources available fall substantially short of the financial requirement for tangible modernisation.[2] The EU's only partial coping with the tasks expected of an external modernisation anchor has certainly accelerated the process of becoming full members of the integration, thereby becoming beneficiaries of the anchor from inside. In addition, worldwide globalisation and the evident lack of other viable modernisation anchors for the transforming countries have stepped up efforts to achieve full membership of the EU.

As a result of European dynamics and, unfortunately, not as the outcome of a well-defined EU strategy, Eastern enlargment became an acknowledged issue of the integration to be dealt with seriously. Contrary to the period of signing the first Association Agreements in late 1991, nobody can now deny that the EU has to enlarge itself to the East. However, the timing and sequencing as well as the conditions of the enlargement are still in the process of internal discussion. In the meantime, the 10 Central and Eastern European candidate countries have recently started to upgrade their processes of preparing for full membership. Although all of them have achieved substantial progress in selected areas, their EU maturity remains largely differentiated. Likewise, the same holds for the enlargement capacity of the EU concerning the individual transforming countries.

Full membership seems to have two non-political preconditions: free trade in industrial products as stipulated in the Association Agreements, and the acceptance and enforcement of the *acquis communautaire*. In both cases, the lack of strategic thinking, characteristic of the Association Agreements, is becoming increasingly manifest. First, the rapidly growing trade deficit of some, apparently more developed transforming economies elicits concern. Trade liberalisation among unequal partners generally creates sizeable trade deficits for the less developed country, which can be covered by the inflow of foreign capital and, as in the case of the less developed EU member countries, by transfers from Brussels. Unfortunately, this linkage has not been established in the Association Agreement (Inotai, 1997b). Second, less developed countries, with a special burden (or gift?) of transformation have to take on board the ever more comprehensive and demanding nature of EU legislation. The problem consists not so much in creating EU-consistent laws and then passing them through the national parliaments, but in the enforcement. Again, the lack of financial resources seems to have become a major bottleneck, accompanied by the limited administrative capacity of the candidate countries.

According to the most recent developments, individual Central and Eastern European countries reveal different levels of and capacities for preparation for full membership. Trade and legal harmonisation are probably the most evident problem areas, but others can also be mentioned. For example, agriculture has a relatively low share in GDP and active population (between 5 and 10%) in countries like the Czech Republic, Slovenia, Slovakia or Hungary, but a much higher share in Poland, Romania or Lithuania. More important for the future structure of production and costs of agricultural transformation is, however, the "modernisation capacity" of national agricultures in technical, professional, social and economic terms. In this regard, cross-country differences are more important than other more accountable factors. Moreover, the financial needs of candidate countries are largely different, depending on the per capita level of GDP, the size of population, accumulated welfare (including savings) and mentality. An even wider difference can probably be revealed by comparing the efficient absorption capacity of the transforming countries. In this context, the yearly inflow of foreign direct investment may be used as a convenient proxy.

Migration, a major fear in some EU member countries, is largely exaggerated. Evidently, some transforming countries with large populations and low GDP per capita levels are potential sources of migration. However, most candidate countries are small, and everywhere there is a big difference between statistically registered migration potential and effective (virtual) migration. The best instrument to keep migration under control is of course successful modernisation which creates growing economies and jobs, thus gradually increasing welfare and, most importantly, providing clear medium- and longer-term perspectives.

Essential differences can be observed in the behaviour of candidate countries concerning sovereignty. Some countries seem to have understood that their national sovereignty, in global terms, can be better protected in a large group than on the traditional national basis. Others, not least those which achieved national independence and started to build a nation-state more recently, are more reluctant to give up part of their "independence".

Finally, the candidate countries are differently prepared for EMU. Evidently, membership in EMU is not a precondition of membership in the EU. However, the basic goals of EMU have to be shared by the newcomers. In terms of budget deficits and state indebtedness, at least some candidate countries are in a better position than some EU member countries, but inflation and long-term interest rates are and will, in the medium-term, remain a problem. It has to be stressed that the macroeconomic indicators of candidate countries may undergo substantial changes in the next few years as they enter different stages of the transformation and modernisation process. As a result, "good" macroeconomic figures do not automatically reveal a higher level of EU maturity. The qualitative question is whether the figures reflect the pre-change (pre-modernisation) or post-change (post-modernisation) status of the economy.

Scenarios for Enlargement

The European integration process faces two basic challenges. First, it has to contribute to the successful and sustainable modernisation of Central and Eastern Europe. Second, it has to avoid further or new fragmentation of the continent. But before building a lasting architecture for Europe, one has to be aware that in the 1990s the institutionally split Europe of the post-1945 world was replaced by an economically and socially fragmented Europe. Fragmentation experienced a quantitative and a qualitative growth alike.

In quantitative terms, today's Europe can be divided at least into three (or four) different areas separated from each other by large and partly increasing gaps. Beyond the traditional East-West economic divide, there has developed an at least as important divide between Central Europe and (south) Eastern Europe. Also, the latter can be subdivided into the EU-associated countries and former Soviet states. It is not yet very clear in Western Europe that, in per capita GDP terms, the income gap between them and Central Europe is not larger than that between Central and Eastern Europe.

In qualitative terms, the break up of the bipolar system weakened the bloc mentality in Western Europe and completely destroyed it in Central and Eastern Europe. National interests, at times extremely short-sighted, returned to shape political, economic and other decisions. Two-digit levels of unemployment, ageing populations, growing pressure on established social welfare systems and institutional inflexibility, partly a heritage of the "golden days" of bipolarity, generate a double effort. First, (most) EU member countries investigate the possibility of joint decisions and common (but not necessarily supranational) structures. Second, and simultaneously, they have to find national responses which may or may not result in higher levels of integration.

Even more importantly from a strategic perspective, the fall of the Berlin Wall and subsequent changes in Europe have started a two-way shift in the balance of power of the continent. On the one hand, the (to be) integrated continent has been gradually getting a second "mare nostrum", namely the Baltics. A shift from the south (Mediterranean) to the north cannot be avoided. Evidently, it should be implemented not by "forgetting" the south, but by integrating the "north" into the future architecture of Europe. On the other hand, a shift from the Atlantic towards the geographic centre of the continent is under way (west-east shift). Europe still has to find its new balance of power by adequately responding to these challenges. It is needless to say that the traditional pattern developed after World War II is highly unlikely to successfully cope with this problem.

An additional and strategically very important building bloc, or, in case of failure, a substantial factor of uncertainty within the new European architecture is represented by Central and Eastern Europe. In order for this "new European house" to be built with solid foundations, decision-makers will need to have a clear idea about the basic differences within Central and Eastern Europe which are linked to geographic location, are development-related and rooted in history. They remained largely hidden during the Soviet period but became immediately visible at the very beginning of transformation. Although almost all countries of the region started their new life by pointing in the same direction (political democracy, market economy, similar institutions, etc.), the gaps within the region did not become narrower. Just the opposite, even if temporarily, they became more pronounced in basic areas. There are fundamental differences which do not emerge from published macroeconomic indicators, which in turn tell us little about the quality of transformation. The real differences can be identified in the microeconomic and microsocial fabrics of the individual countries. These can provide an explanation of why countries differ in their economic policies, micro-level adjustment, level of EU-conformity, pattern of foreign trade, attraction of foreign direct investment, institution building, civic society, and so on.

While this differentiated development has already been recognised by the OECD and, most recently, also by NATO, the European Union still seems to insist on the group approach.[3] If there are differences within a given region, the wrong approach would be to ignore the differences and the differentiation and repeatedly state the necessity of uniform treatment for dissimilar issues. Fragmentation, certainly a major danger, will be created by hiding or ignoring these differences. The EU's "startliner approach" of enlargement tries to avoid any openly declared differentiation among the applicant countries. This may not only be motivated by the fear of fragmenting Central and Eastern Europe, but also by the special interests of present member countries, as almost each of them has a special preferred candidate which, in some cases, may not belong in the first round of enlargment. This approach claims that it provides higher flexibility for applicant countries so that, according to their performance, they can move from one subgroup to the other during the negotiation process. This may be particularly important for "in-between" countries that, as a result of potential domestic political changes, could "upgrade" their present position within a relatively short time (e.g. Slovakia).

However, the startliner approach is burdened with a number of problems. From the very beginning, it clashes with the institutional capacity of Brussels to negotiate and integrate 10 candidate countries at the same time. Moreover, it is unable to stop the dynamics of differentiation based on and fuelled by economic and socio-political realities, thereby transmitting a bad message to the more advanced countries which may fear that the date of their accession will be (indefinitely) postponed as they wait for the less prepared countries.[4] Furthermore, this approach could be used by some EU member countries to delay enlargement and sustain their privileged status quo position. Flexibility can also easily be used (or even misused) by the EU to play off candidate countries against each other and undermine their already weak negotiation positions. The most important handicaps of this approach are, however, in the strategic context. First, it would be unable to provide a convenient answer to the challenges Europe is facing at the turn of the Century in security, social, economic and also psychological terms. Second, it could have serious repercussions on the internal cohesion of the Union as different pressures and conflicts generated by Central and Eastern Europe would differently affect individual EU members. Thirdly, it would without doubt establish a barrier against more intensive (sub)regional cooperation.

The gradual or group approach, embracing a small number of selected candidate countries, seems to be justified because the candidate countries are and will be differently prepared for membership once negotiations are opened. Beyond the already implemented selections (OECD, NATO), the lion's share of trade and foreign investments of the EU are concentrated within some Central European countries, indicating that the international business community has already anticipated their accession to the EU. The same Central European countries are much more integrated into intra-industry trade and have more developed production and export patterns. Also their per capita GDP is much higher than that of other applicants. In addition, they have formed CEFTA, a regional free trade area and started high-level political consultations on regional priorities, including preparation for membership of the EU. On the EU side, the group approach seems to be the only viable option for technical reasons, since it is physically impossible to conduct negotiations with all candidate countries at once.

But there is another side to the enlargement coin. A selective approach may create an institutionalised political, security and economic gap within Europe, thereby generating further differentiation with incalculable consequences. More importantly, it would transmit a doubly dangerous message to those left out. On the one hand, it could give (unintended) support to populists and nationalists within the "non-preferred" countries and increase anti-European emotions. On the other hand, it could signal a vacuum to be filled by potentially dominant powers, both within the region and from outside.

Further fragmentation can only be avoided if enlargement takes into account the potential dangers of both approaches. Thus a mixed policy would seem to be realistic. It should be based on two pillars. First, as a political signal, negotiations might be opened with each of the candidates, but be seriously continued with just a few. Second, and no less important, an overall strategy of enlargement should be designed and communicated before starting negotiations. This should include a clear timetable for the various waves of enlargement, arrangements to strengthen cooperation between new members and their non-member neighbours through various instruments (cross-border cooperation, joint infrastructure projects), and upgraded financial support to countries joining the EU later. The establishment of a clear and sustainable framework is not only the task of present members of the EU, but would also be the responsibility of members of the first-wave who would need to be involved with the implementation of a longer-term strategy. Responsibility has to be shared between present and future members of the EU now, at the very beginning of the enlargement process.

Conclusion

For three key reasons, the eastern enlargement of the European Union represents a unique historical challenge, indeed opportunity, for the continent:

* It will be the first enlargement generated not by the artificial division created by a bipolar global structure, but as a consequence of the collapse of bipolarity in Europe. Therefore, it will not only quantitatively add something to the map of an integrated Europe, but is a qualitatively new undertaking to fill the modernisation (and security) vacuum in Europe. Neither will it fit into the logic of earlier enlargements which sought to improve the relative position of the EU against the Soviet-dominated part of Europe. Instead, the new logic of enlargement must be based

on creating the framework conditions for a new European security and economic system;

* The eastern enlargement, if implemented gradually, will be the first one which is not reaching the geographic periphery of Europe. The first-wave new members will become transit countries, with largely different possibilities and responsibilities in political, economic, social and other terms, than countries such as Spain and Portugal that joined the EU earlier;

* This will be the first enlargement which will happen in the framework of a globalising world. Eastern enlargement would not be a European "domestic affair". It would be an increasingly important factor in (Western) Europe's global competitiveness. Consequently, the fundamental question is not what kind of short-term gains and/or costs are likely to be generated by the enlargement. The basic, qualitative issue is to what extent the next enlargement(s) can contribute to improving Europe's position in the global marketplace.

Footnotes

1. For a detailed analysis see Inotai (1997a).

2. It suffices to state that the per capita amount of PHARE money is about ECU 8 for Hungary (if the whole annual budget could be used), while it amounts to over ECU 600 in Ireland, over ECU 400 in Greece, and is about ECU 300 in Portugal.

3. In its Agenda 2000, the Commission has distanced itself from this view and, in a strategic framework including all candidate countries, proposed the starting of negotiations with five more advanced candidate countries only. The final decision will be taken at the Luxembourg Summit of the EU in December 1997.

4. This has been a well-known phenomenon during the CMEA times. Fears rooted in this period are still vividly remembered in Central Europe.

References

Inotai, András (1997a), Miért ujszerü az Európai Unió keleti kibóvülése? (Why is the Eastern Enlargement of the European Union Different from Earlier Enlargements?), *Európai Tükör*, no. 3.

Inotai, András (1997b), A kelet-középeuropai országok külkereskedelmi deficitje. Okok és következmények az EU-felkészülés fényében (Foreign Trade Deficit of East Central European Countries. Reasons and Consequences in the Light of Preparing for the EU), *Társadalmi Szemle, No. 7.*

ECONOMIC TRANSITION, DEMOCRATIC CONSOLIDATION AND THE INTEGRATION OF CENTRAL-EASTERN EUROPEAN COUNTRIES INTO EUROPEAN STRUCTURES

Thomas Nowotny

*Political Adviser to the Chief Economist,
European Bank for Reconstruction and Development,
London*

Economic goals have become the most prominent of nations' internal and external policies. As such they have replaced military goals. This development can be reversed, just as a person threatened by starvation reverts to a more "primitive" set of priorities. Nonetheless, people and nations have to adjust their behaviour to the actual and most probable challenge; and just as starvation for most people is no longer the main challenge, organised warfare is no longer the main pre-occupation of nations, although most would wish to retain a military capability as an "insurance" against a possible fallback into prior patterns of international relations.

All its "throw weight" have not prevented the decline and final demise of the Soviet Union; nor has the military prominence of Yugoslavia prevented its dismemberment. On the other hand, the two countries would not have disappeared had their economies and the wealth of their citizens grown at an annual pace of more than 6%. This was not the case, while the near absence of military power has not impeded the rise of Japan. Therefore, the change of priorities and the prominence of economic goals are rational answers to changed circumstances.

Economic success not only defines the relative rank of countries, it also sets the international agenda. Increasingly, economic issues are at the core of conflicts. One might expect increasing wealth both to create, and demand, greater interaction; and with it greater international interdependence. Certainly, these will be consequences. But this does not automatically eliminate political friction. Politics, and with it conflicting politics, intervene for two main reasons:

* The world economy does not support the myth of an "invisible hand" regulating everything to the best advantage of all concerned. For example, the thesis of Riccardo that free trade would benefit all is based on the assumption that factors of production (including capital and labour) are not mobile. But in today's world they are mobile.

* Actual markets are not homogenous and fully competitive. In most cases, and especially in the crucial field of higher technology, they are dominated by a few firms at the upper end of the "product cycle". In such a situation where gains are uneven at best and some even might lose, politics intrude by necessity.

Nonetheless, the common interests of nations predominate even in such competitive a setting. Incentives to cooperate will be enhanced by two factors:

* Geographic vicinity (gravitational model of the economy);
* The stage of development - in that the further advanced, the more dense the linkages to other equally wealthy nations will be.

The transition countries of Central and Eastern Europe are certainly close to the western part of the continent in the geographic sense, but still at quite some distance in the economic sense. Nonetheless, they are not simply developing countries. They are "misdeveloped countries". The distance that separates them from the OECD has been underestimated in the past. Former CIA estimates even suggested that some of them would surpass the wealthy mature industrial nations. The German Democratic Republic, for instance, was thought to have surpassed Great Britain. How could one get things so wrong? Because the CIA and others factored the then **existing** production at World market prices. But the goods were not of World market quality. Therefore, they were easily driven from the marketplace as soon as these countries opened up.

Since 1945 this gap in quality, technology, management, marketing and other knowhow has been widening between the Communist and Western countries. The full implications of this only became manifest after the former Communist countries had lost the sheltered markets for their products. And it is because of this wide gap that transition is so difficult. By 1996, only one country (Poland) had reached its 1989 level of production. Slovenia was very close to this mark and may well have passed it by now. See **Table 1** below:

Table 1
Estimated Level of real GDP in Eastern Europe, the Baltics and the CIS

COUNTRIES	ESTIMATED LEVEL OF REAL GDP IN 1996 (1989=100)
Albania	87
Armenia	39
Azerbaijan	38
Belarus	63
Bulgaria	68
Croatia	70
Czech Republic	89
Estonia	69
FYR Macedonia	56
Georgia	31
Hungary	86
Kazakhstan	45
Kyrgyzstan	52
Latvia	52
Lithuania	42
Moldova	35
Poland	104
Romania	88
Russia	51
Slovak Republic	90
Slovenia	96
Tajikistan	37
Turkmenistan	57
Ukraine	42
Uzbekistan	84
Eastern Europe, the Baltics and the CIS (GDP-weighted average)	71
Eastern Europe and the Baltic countries[1]	91
The Commonwealth of Independent States[2]	51

That does not mean that all prior "wealth" was spurious. An accumulation of capital had taken place, namely of physical capital (e.g. in infrastructure) and of human capital with education and skills. This clearly sets transition countries apart from developing countries which are not so well endowed. At present, the main challenge is to prevent as far as is possible the destruction of this capital. This especially refers to human capital, which is the crucial bottleneck in economic development according to prevailing theories. It is also for that reason that continuous and rapid economic growth would be essential.

Transition is, by definition, a state of being neither here nor there. This state of limbo will last for some time. Therefore it was negligent and/or irresponsible to create the illusion that transition could be completed in one bold leap ("one cannot cross a chasm in two jumps"). The wish or exhortation to arrive "there" as soon as possible should not have been made a substitute for sound advice on what to do on the long journey to this destination. This need for intermediate solutions has not been addressed. Today one might, for instance, question the necessity or the wisdom of recommending the immediate and full liberalisation of capital markets; the liberalisation of apartment rental markets; or the complete withdrawal of enterprises from providing those social services they offered in Communist times. Such full compliance with market principles is a worthy end-goal. But if introduced too soon it might obstruct economic reform instead of advancing it.

The problem of devising a proper policy for transition is not only a conceptual one. The dearth of alternatives to the insufficient and occasionally misleading concept of the "big leap" is not only due to the ideological blinkers of neo-liberal economists. Non-market (or intermediate) solutions also founder upon practical obstacles. They call for state intervention that is difficult to administer and which, necessarily, creates opportunities for various and mostly illegal forms of rent seeking. Hence such interventions are only feasible in "strong" states (for instance in East-Asia). In Central and Eastern Europe, however, the state is weak (though still extensive) and, critically, lacks a highly motivated, highly paid, highly professional and highly respected Civil Service.

What holds true for the Civil Service is also true for other economic, political and administrative institutions. Both markets and democracies have to be defined and sustained by appropriate institutions. In 1989-1990 there was cheap triumphalism over how "we have won" and over "the end of history". Some even peddled the notion that perfect democracies and markets would come into existence overnight once the restraints of Communism were lifted. But political and economic markets need to be constructed which takes time and effort.

To provide an example: for successful transition, financial institutions, especially banks, are absolutely essential. But a functioning financial sector not only implies the existence of corporations called "banks". It also requires a whole set of administrative and supervisory capabilities combined with the existence of a whole set of congruent expectations, and of respected "internalised" rules on the part of all those whose behaviour will impact on a bank. Now, as we have been reminded by recent events, even the advanced transition countries find it difficult to create all these conditions. Accordingly, most of the transition countries have experienced crises in their nascent banking sector. Some of them were so serious as to set back the whole process of transition. The European Bank for Reconstruction and Development (EBRD) has thus decided to make the banking sector one focus of its activities. A third of its engagements are in this field.

This may be the place to say a few words about the EBRD. It was founded in 1991 with a capital of ECU10bn which has now increased to ECU20bn. The Bank's work is project-oriented and the terms of this support are not concessionary. That means that it finances "bankable" projects - those that yield sufficient return. However, two other principles distinguish it from a private sector investment bank. These are the principles of "additionality" and of "transition relevance". The former obliges the EBRD to entertain only such projects that cannot be initiated by private banks acting alone. Transition relevance means what it says: the EBRD can only finance things that add something to the process of transition; that push the country along the path of economic transformation. In channelling capital to the transition countries, the EBRD is the major player if one takes into account that, on average, every ECU from the EBRD is supplemented by two additional ECUs leveraged from the private sector. Having already committed roughly ECU10bn from its own funds, the EBRD has thus managed to trigger capital flows of about ECU30bn, a far from negligible sum.

The economic and political spheres, in particular economic transformation and democratic consolidation, are not isolated from one another. There are "virtuous" and "vicious" circles of reciprocal feedback between them. It is not by coincidence that those countries most advanced in the consolidation of democratic institutions and governance are generally also those most advanced in economic transition and reform. Clearly, democratisation and the advancement of civic society are easier if the mere economic survival of all is ensured and if prospects of future wealth are credible. On the other hand, economic growth will not materialise if governance and politics fail to safeguard the minimum of social cohesion necessary for economic activity.

One crucial variable and major determinant of the pace of transition is the speed of actual transformation of existing, major enterprises. Their formal privatisation alone does not guarantee such transformation. In most instances it even does not change behaviour very much, except when it involves foreign direct investment. Of course, industrial restructuring also occurs through the emergence of enterprises that are wholly new. Their share of production is rising quite rapidly. Yet most of these firms are small and the growth of this sector cannot therefore compensate for a lack of true reform in existing large enterprises. The track record with regard to such structural reform is mixed: some countries do better than others.

The uneven pace and success of transition has widened differences that had always existed among the countries of the region. This has both economic and political implications. The growing disparities are detrimental to overall security. For example, economic success, or absence thereof, will determine the date of accession to the European Union. Those chosen first will profit from enhanced economic security. Those left out will not. This will exacerbate centrifugal political tendencies in the region, and may lead to a re-nationalisation of external and security policies and the re-emergence of a 19th century pattern of unstable, shifting alliances.

Some countries claim to have "graduated" from transition and that their problems no longer differ in nature from those encountered by established democracies and market economies. Are such claims justified? Yes, if we rely on nothing but formal criteria. In this formal sense, transition would have come to an end if new institutions had definitely replaced the old. This has been the case in nearly all of the countries concerned. Their constitutions are democratic, and their economic policy is formulated in terms of a market economy. But such an evaluation has to be revised if other than merely formal criteria are taken into account, in particular, if one investigates how the new institutions actually work. In a rather dramatic manner, Bulgaria and Albania have demonstrated that they very often don't work. We were thus reminded of the fragility and frequent malfunctioning of the new order. Such difficulties are not reserved just for the laggards in the process of transformation. Even the countries that are more advanced might experience sudden reversals, such as through a banking crisis.

In the economic realm, transition will only become complete when the countries have achieved sustained robust growth, which would permit them to slowly approach the wealth of the established Western European economies. **Table 2** below shows current (mixed and modest) performance regarding GDP growth in the transition economies.

Table 2
Growth in real GDP in Eastern Europe, the Baltics and the CIS

COUNTRIES	1995	1996 *Estimate*
Albania	9.5	8.5
Armenia	6.9	4.5
Azerbaijan	-8.3	1.2
Belarus	-10.2	2.6
Bulgaria	2.6	-10.0
Croatia	1.7	4.5
Czech Republic	4.8	4.0
Estonia	2.9	3.3
FYR Macedonia	-1.5	3.0
Georgia	2.4	10.5
Hungary	1.5	0.5
Kazakhstan	-8.9	1.4
Kyrgyzstan	1.3	5.4
Latvia	-1.6	2.3
Lithuania	3.1	3.0
Moldova	-3.0	-8.0
Poland	7.0	6.0
Romania	6.9	4.3
Russia	-4.0	-6.0
Slovak Republic	7.4	6.8
Slovenia	3.9	3.5
Tajikistan	-12.5	-7.0
Turkmenistan	-10.0	-4.0
Ukraine	-11.8	-10.0
Uzbekistan	-1.2	1.6
Eastern Europe, the Baltics and the CIS *(GDP-weighted average)*	1.2	0.6
Eastern Europe and the Baltic countries	5.3	4.3
The Commonwealth of Independent States	-4.8	-5.4

Table 3, on the other hand, gives an estimate of the growth rates necessary in order to catch up with selected European countries (Slovenia with Austria; Hungary with Spain, etc.) by the year 2010. Clearly, growth would have to be very rapid, with economies expanding at an average annual rate of much more than 5%.

Table 3
Income Catch-up by 2010: Implied Growth Rates for Transition Economies, Using Actual and Enhanced Per Capita Income Levels for 1993
(% per year)

COUNTRIES CATCHING UP WITH EUROPEAN UNION MEMBERS	Required Annual Growth Rate
Albania	20.1
Belarus	6.0
Bulgaria	11.7
Moldova	11.6
Poland	7.5
Romania	12.1
Russia	7.2
Ukraine	8.5
Czech Republic	9.3
Estonia	15.8
Hungary	8.3
Latvia	11.9
Lithuania	14.8
Slovak Republic	11.7
Slovenia	8.6

But such a growth rate would require a rate of investment of more than 30 %. In reality, the share of investment in GDP is somewhat lower, as **Table 4** below reveals:

Table 4
Gross Domestic Investment as a Percentage of GDP (1995)

Slow-growing mature economies

United Kingdom	16
United States	16

Faster-growing mature economies

Austria	27
Japan	29

Fast-growing Asian Countries

Singapore	33
Hong Kong	35
Republic of Korea	37
Malaysia	41
Thailand	43

Other fast-growing middle-income countries

Portugal	28
Chile	27

Central and Eastern European countries

Bulgaria	21
Romania	26
Lithuania	19
Slovenia	22
Latvia	21
Poland	17
Russia	25
Czech Republic	25
Estonia	27
Hungary	23
Slovakia	28

Source: World Development Report 1997,
World Bank, Washington, D.C., 1997

A spurt of rapid growth has been experienced by most of the "advanced" transition countries at the time they pulled out of recession. In most cases, this reflected fuller use of existing capacity and not the creation of new capability. Thus, predictably, growth became slower again in succeeding years. **Figure 1** below refers:

Figure 1

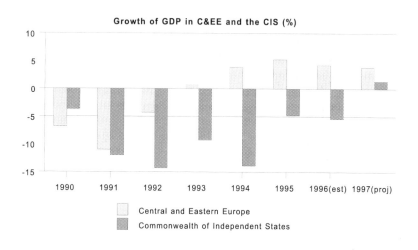

Note: 1996/97 estimate and projection from EBRD Transition Report Update, 1997.

Failure to invest sufficiently in the exposed sector and to become competitive in comparison with OECD countries is also reflected in the rapidly deteriorating balances of the current account. **Table 5** below refers:

Table 5
Current account and trade balances in Eastern Europe,
the Baltics and the CIS³

	Current account balance	Change in current account balance
	US$m	*as a share of 1996 $ GDP in %*
INDIVIDUAL COUNTRIES	1996	1995-96
Albania	-252	-2.80
Armenia	-487	-8.12
Azerbaijan	-656	-10.03
Belarus	-1196	-7.48
Bulgaria	-150	-1.20
Croatia	-1350	1.92
Czech Republic	-4100	-5.23
Estonia	-300	-2.60
FYR Macedonia	-450	-6.00
Georgia	-355	1.13
Hungary	-1678	1.76
Kazakhstan	-1000	-2.25
Kyrgyzstan	-510	-6.76
Latvia	-200	-0.68
Lithuania	-200	-0.30
Moldova	-190	-3.09
Poland	-100	-4.09
Romania	-900	1.19
Russia	9000	0.75
Slovak Republic	-1500	-9.94
Slovenia	36	0.41
Tajikistan	-	-
Turkmenistan	43	-0.57
Ukraine	-1300	0.43
Uzbekistan	-1075	-7.75

This might in turn temp governments to hit the monetary brakes, forcing the economy into a destructive cycle of stop/go, the like of which has undermined long term growth in Latin America.

Of the investment necessary for rapid growth, the largest part has to come from internal sources. FDI can only provide a small percentage of overall investment. Nonetheless, this external contribution is important; less because it increases the volume of investment, but mainly because it facilitates the import of precious skills (for example in the field of management) and eases access to foreign markets. The volume of FDI has been far from negligible, especially if calculated on a per capita basis or as part of the GDP of the recipient country - though it is true that the lion's share of FDI still goes from one mature economy to another, whilst the remainder mainly benefits East Asian countries.

External assistance comes from widely differing sources and covers many fields. Inevitably, this assistance is compared to the Marshall Plan. In today's dollars, Marshall

Plan aid would amount to US$90bn (assuming the US would be the sole provider). Against this, the assistance given as grants or on concessionary (DAC) terms to transition countries has certainly been lower, though not by very much. It amounts to roughly US$8bn a year on average. **Table 6** below refers:

Table 6
Net Official Aid Disbursements to Part II
C&EE/NIS Countries

	$ million					As % of GNP	
	1991	**1992**	**1993**	**1994**	**1995**	**1994**	**1995**
Australia	9	5	6	4	4	0.00	0.00
Austria	290	349	389	261	313	0.13	0.13
Belgium	274	135	81	86	89	0.04	0.03
Canada	145	260	80	73	250	0.01	0.05
Denmark	65	82	175	37	281	0.03	0.17
Finland	114	40	38	51	76	0.05	0.06
France	457	364	606	650	748	0.05	0.05
Germany	2637	3344	2416	2527	4514	0.12	0.19
Ireland	15	10	9	16	2	0.04	0.00
Italy	382	334	242	196	286	0.02	0.03
Japan	110	238	530	247	250	0.01	0.00
Luxembourg	5	5	7	7	-	0.05	-
Netherlands	152	152	272	118	305	0.04	0.08
New Zealand	1	1	1	1	-	0.00	-
Norway	25	64	74	79	-	0.07	-
Portugal	22	18	13	28	22	0.03	0.02
Spain	162	102	87	157	-	0.03	-
Sweden	50	337	41	91	105	0.05	0.05
Switzerland	55	90	93	124	102	0.05	0.03
United Kingdom	327	337	285	293	406	0.03	0.04
United States	1832	682	1647	2422	1280	0.03	0.02
TOTAL DAC	**7128**	**6948**	**7092**	**7468**	**9035**	**0.04**	**0.04**
of which:							
EU Members	4952	5608	4662	4518	7149	0.06	0.09

Taken together, donors and institutions offer programmes that are quite well rounded. There is little overlap and coordination is therefore not a major problem. At first sight this might elicit surprise, given the dearth of formal, supranational or international coordinating institutions. But such coordination is now done in and by the recipient countries themselves. It is supplemented by many informal networks and arrangements among the donors.

Economic assistance can only be part of, indeed must be imbedded in, a wider approach that covers many fields including, of course, the one of traditional security policy. The policies of the European Union cover most of these fields (except the military one), from a "structured political dialogue" over trade to technical assistance. Thus, the EU is indeed the main "anchor" (if not of all transition countries, then at least for those in Central and Eastern Europe). This bears emphasising in view of the now fashionable disparagement of the EU. An essential part of this overall EU strategy (as articulated in the

"Stability Pact" and in the "Royaumont Process") is the requirement for "candidate countries" to maintain good relations with their neighbours. This stance of the EU has had an effect, for example, by accelerating the conclusion of "basic treaties" between potentially hostile neighbours (Romania, Hungary, Ukraine, Slovakia, Poland, Lithuania).

We tend to reassure ourselves by claiming that there are "no rational alternatives to reform and the market". This is basically correct, but people might despair and become irrational whilst waiting for the fruits of reform to ripen. In some transition countries the decline in output continues. But even where growth has resumed, the majority of the population often does not benefit. Social indicators (morality and marriage rate etc.) still point downward in all but a very few countries. The capital of patience and hope might thus be used up to be replaced by fear, resentment and paranoia. The road to further political liberalisation and internationalisation might become blocked, as well might further progress with economic transition. The window of opportunity for reform might close again. Whatever comes in its place is bound to be unpleasant both for the unfortunate inhabitants of such a country and for their neighbours. In Albania it was anarchy.

The Western donors are in transition too: towards globalism and a post-Cold War World. Being unsure about what they themselves are and where they would like to go, they are also unsure about what to recommend to transition countries. None of the three World models - the American, the European and the Japanese - looks very enticing at present. In their present condition, they certainly do not offer the image of a "shining city upon the hill" that had been presented by the United States in the aftermath of World War II. The principle of "enrichissez vous" and the blind trust in the workings of an "invisible hand" is not something that could offer coherence to divided and strained societies.

The faults in our reaction towards events in the ex-Communist world not only arise from a lack of, or indeed from faulty, analysis. They also spring from the more general difficulty of arriving at any kind of major, long term policies. Today's democracies are in crisis. Political elites have lost credibility everywhere. Decisions are shaped by short term, tactical considerations. This precludes joint actions to reach distant goals. Either for themselves or as a group, wealthy, established democracies are no longer capable, or so it seems, of launching any major common effort.

Transition is a chaotic process. Surprises are bound to occur. Therefore both economic development and the search for security have to be placed in the context of general uncertainty, of unplanned diversity, and of permanent "creative destruction". Under such circumstances, "stability" is not only an ephemeral goal; it is an unrealistic one. So although one cannot stabilise a given set of circumstances, one can nonetheless attempt to stabilise the open processes of political and economic interaction.

Thomas Nowotny

Footnotes

1. Estimates for real GDP represent weighted averages for Albania, Bulgaria, Croatia, the Czech Republic, Estonia, FYR Macedonia, Hungary, Latvia, Lithuania, Poland, Romania, the Slovak Republic and Slovenia. The weights used were EBRD estimates of nominal dollar-GDP for 1996. Average projected project rates are based on earlier forecasts of 5-6% growth in Albania.

2. Here taken to include all countries of the former Soviet Union, except Estonia, Latvia and Lithuania. Estimates for real GDP represent weighted averages. The weights used were EBRD estimates of nominal dollar-GDP for 1996.

3. Data are most recent estimates as reflected in publications from the national authorities, the IMF, the World Bank, the OECD, PlanEcon and the Institute of International Finance. Data are provisional only.

THE INTEGRATION OF NATO PARTNER COUNTRIES INTO PAN-EUROPEAN ECONOMIC STRUCTURES

Jean-Pierre Tuveri

Acting Director, OECD Centre for Co-operation with the Economies in Transition

Introduction

As always, it is a pleasure for me to participate in this NATO Economics Colloquium. This year the Colloquium takes place in the context of an active debate over the enlargement of NATO, the OECD and the European Union. This has naturally increased political interest in questions of both de facto and de jure integration of European transition economies into the more developed market economies of Europe and more generally into the increasingly globalised world market.

NATO and the OECD have several institutional features in common; both have a relatively small number of members, and in fact all 16 NATO's member countries are among the 29 OECD members. Both NATO and the OECD have, until recently, largely conducted their respective activities for the benefit of member countries exclusively, and have not tried to grow by accepting new members. Both have had well-defined missions - economics-related for the OECD and mostly defence-related for NATO. These missions are now being reflected on and in significant respects redefined.

With the end of the cold war, both NATO and the OECD have had to pay increasing attention to issues of future enlargement. Since 1994, the OECD has reached out to five new members, and is negotiating with Slovakia, bringing total membership to 30. In the case of NATO, the creation of the North Atlantic Cooperation Council in 1991 established a multilateral framework within which, from 1994 onwards, individual Partnership for Peace Agreements could be negotiated. Like OECD, NATO sees enlargement as an "evolutionary" process with the admission of new members governed not only by their willingness and ability to conform with the principles, policies and procedures adopted by existing members, but also by a demonstration of such commitment in practice. Like OECD, NATO relies on a consensual approach and a communality of views. This is reflected in the fact that the NATO Partnership for Peace Agreements, while helping Partners prepare for eventual membership, carries no guarantees to that effect.

The OECD and the Integration of NATO Partner Countries into Pan-European Structures

The subject assigned to me is not as easy as it might appear at first sight. Let me, in this context, underscore three broad considerations:

* First, the OECD is a global, albeit not a universal organisation. Although the EU and all its member states are members of the OECD, the organisation itself also has members in North America, Asia and Oceania. It is therefore committed to free trade and multilateralism on a global scale. Thus, it would not be correct to categorise the OECD as a "pan-European" structure. At the same time, there are many shared values between the OECD and pan-European structures such as the EU with respect to the creation of a competitive market economy and a pluralistic democracy. Close cooperation with the OECD has in fact assisted a number of

European transition economies in harmonising their regulatory and institutional frameworks with those of OECD countries, including those within the EU.

* Second, the degree and the scope of cooperation between the European transition economies and the OECD varies considerably between one country and another. Consequently, the impact of cooperation on the integration of a particular economy with the economies of the OECD varies considerably depending on the precise form of cooperation in place.

* Third, and more importantly, the term "pan-European economic structures" implies more than formal association or membership of a particular regional or multilateral organisation. The economic integration of partner countries into the European economic space has proceeded rapidly since the beginning of the transition process in 1990, driven partially by the collapse of CMEA markets, but principally by the determination of the reforming countries to adopt the legal and institutional framework of developed market economies. Much of the integration of transition economies into those of developed Western European economies has been achieved by a series of successive steps which have transformed the political, economic and social structures of these countries based on democratic values and market oriented criteria. The very fact that the first three panels of this conference have been devoted to the analysis of this overall transition experience and the development of regional integration among partner countries themselves attests that economic integration has been the combined outcome of market pressures, reformist government programmes and the need to harmonise domestic laws and institutional practices with those of transnational institutions and international organisations.

Given the above considerations, I shall concentrate on providing an overview of the nature of OECD cooperation with European partner countries and highlight some instances where this cooperation has enhanced the ability of each partner country to harmonise its economy more effectively with that of the European Union. I will end with some brief comments on some recent thinking inside the OECD regarding the direction of its future relations with non-members in the context of globalisation.

Features of OECD Cooperation with European Transition Economies

Overview

Before the recent wave of new members, beginning with Mexico in 1994, the last country to join the OECD was New Zealand in 1973. Until the end of the 1980's with a few exceptions, the OECD mission and work focused essentially on issues of interest to its members. Since 1990, however, the Organisation has started to reach out or to engage new countries. At that time, the OECD's Council agreed to create the institutional infrastructure to make OECD Member countries' collective experience available to the transition countries of Central and Eastern Europe. This was done with the creation of the Centre for Co-operation with the Economies in Transition. Programmes developed and implemented by the Centre have been extremely flexible, tailored to the progress made by the partner countries in political and economic transformation and to the degree of cooperation that the Organisation wanted to establish with these countries.

To accommodate the transition needs of the European reforming economies, a General Work Programme was established in 1990. This programme was initially open to the Visegrad countries, Bulgaria, Romania and the former Soviet Union. It was subsequently extended to countries like Albania and, following the disintegration of the Soviet Union in

1991, to the Federation of Russia, the Baltic States and the other NIS Republics. This programme, largely made up of thematic and regional activities, aimed essentially at supporting the reform process but did not attempt to establish a special relationship with specific countries.

However, in recognition of the progress made by the most advanced reforming countries (i.e. the Visegrad group) a special assistance programme called the "Partners in Transition" (PIT) programme was established in 1991 designed not only to meet the more focused reform needs of these countries but also to help them meet the conditions for possible future membership of the Organisation. After the dissolution of the CSFR, this programme was extended in 1993 to the Czech Republic and the Slovak Republic.

In 1994, special country programmes were also developed for Bulgaria, Romania and Slovenia. Designed to provide assistance directed towards their particular needs, these programmes lack the formal structure of the PIT programmes and are not oriented towards meeting the conditions for membership of the OECD. These are instead designed to help the countries concerned draw up and implement policies that will sustain viable market economies. Financial sector reform, privatisation and enterprise restructuring, tax legislation and collection, as well as assistance in the field of statistics are among the areas covered by these programmes.

The case of Russia is a somewhat specific one. In 1995, a country programme was established as part of a Declaration of Co-operation between the OECD and the Federation of Russia signed in June 1994. To strengthen cooperation, a Liaison Committee was established in the wake of the last OECD Ministerial Meeting on 27 May and the country programme was reinforced to include activities which play a key role in determining whether a country is in a position to satisfy the terms and conditions of membership in the OECD. In addition to the normal menu of economic and sectoral surveys, tax policy and administration and FDI related activities, the Russia programme now contains activities designed to familiarise the Russian authorities with all aspects of the OECD Codes of Liberalisation and the National Treatment Instruments.

Formal accession procedure

When it comes to integrating candidate countries fully into the Organisation as new members, the OECD differs from NATO or the Bretton-Woods organisations by virtue of its lack of a structured association mechanism. The Organisation has, however, a great deal of flexibility since the convention establishing the OECD did not specify any particular rules of accession. This flexibility has provided the Organisation with many options to adopt tailored approaches and timetables for different countries according to their individual circumstances.

In practice, recent OECD accession has been a three-step process. First, a political decision has been taken by the Council of Ministers to officially open accession negotiations. Then, a note outlining the procedure to be followed has been adopted by OECD ambassadors, a process which involves great flexibility in interpretation with examinations of applicant countries' policies taking place as the applicant country reacts to every single recommendation adopted by the OECD since its founding in 1961. Finally, this note on procedure allows the Secretariat to open accession negotiations with the country, which may take several years to be concluded. While the OECD is not bound to follow the same procedures in the future, major changes are not expected. However, the process has continually been refined as more countries have joined and will continue to do so.

Enlarging the OECD has without question been a process of learning by doing. The policies of prospective members are examined by OECD subsidiary bodies which are committees charged with debating policy on capital movements, taxation, labour markets, the environment, and so on. In recent years, the number of committees involved in the examination process has been increasing with each additional country that was examined for membership. The examination process also currently covers a number of topics not directly covered by OECD instruments, such as labour standards or multilateral environmental agreements that have nevertheless been taken into account by OECD members in internal policy debates and recommendations.

Contribution of OECD Cooperation Programmes to Integration in Pan-European Structures

Accession related programmes

To get a flavour of the role of the OECD in the integration of transition economies into the European economic space it is worth examining the implementation of the Partners in Transition Programme initiated in 1991. This was modified in light of the 1994 Ministerial decision to incorporate a number of accession related activities, although no time was fixed for the completion of these negotiations. As was usual in the case of previous new members, the statutory requirement of acceptance of the legally binding obligations of the OECD Codes of Liberalisation and the commitments of the 1976 Declaration and Decisions on International Investment and Multinational Enterprises, including the National Treatment Instrument (NTI), remained the essential condition for accession.

At the beginning of the accession process, the PIT countries' legislation on foreign direct investment appeared to be relatively liberal with no restrictions for the repatriation of capital. There remained, however, sectoral and real-estate restrictions, and a concern on the part of the OECD that rules be implemented in a consistent and transparent manner and that the National Treatment Principle be applied also in practice. A further concern was that, in spite of active privatisation programmes, state-owed enterprises still accounted for a significant share of economic activity thus limiting the scope for foreign equity participation in domestic enterprises and, consequently, for substantial improvements in competitiveness.

The OECD has also played a significant role through its general economic reports in assisting these countries to formulate and implement their economic policies. While due concern was paid to the peculiarities of the transition process, the benchmark for the assessment of progress in macro-stabilisation, liberalisation and restructuring, and therefore policy recommendations in such areas, was that of advanced market economies. The aim was to stimulate candidates for membership to adopt higher standards in all fields of transformation. This concern marks deeply the "second stage" OECD support for transition economies which have graduated to OECD membership and is particularly evident in the area of monetary policy and price stability which are not yet direct concerns of the EU. However, monetary matters will need to be considered in the preparation of the European Commission's assessment on the membership requests of the countries in transition concerned in the Association Agreements.

The European Association Agreements do not contain any provision on monetary policy cooperation, nor have the macroeconomic surveillance procedures proposed by the European Commission in July 1994 been implemented as yet. On more general grounds, a problem which matters not only for the countries in transition but also for the EU in the process of integration is the still high rate of inflation in all partner countries, despite significant progress achieved by some countries in bringing prices down to two-digit levels, such as in Poland (where the inflation rate could go down to 15% this year), or to one-digit, such as in the Czech Republic and Slovakia (with estimated rates of inflation in 1997 of 8% and 7% respectively). While the 1990-1996 average rate of inflation (GDP deflators) in the EU is down to 3.6%, Hungary was still struggling with about 21% inflation in 1996. Even the projected 17% inflation rate in 1997 remains substantially above the comparative indicators for the EU. The OECD assessment that a reduction of three or four percentage points in inflation is not sufficient at this stage has strongly emerged in the last economic reports on Hungary and Poland.

In the case of Hungary, the recommendations that further efforts need to be made in order to prevent high inflation from distorting saving and investment decisions by households, enterprises and banks have been linked to the need for a firmer commitment to the independence of the Central Bank and to credible disinflationary policies through monetary targets, and the pursuit of a wage restraint policy. In the case of Poland, a tighter fiscal stance has been recommended on the grounds that due to the low monetisation of the economy, a given increase in base money (as a percent of GDP) will be more inflationary in Poland than in Western Europe. This recommendation was also geared, indirectly, to bring the effective fiscal deficit (purged of privatisation revenues) down to the Maastricht convergence criteria of 3%.

Another welcome development is that OECD pressure to increase transparency in financial markets and make room for efficient corporate governance has prompted first Hungary and lately the Czech Republic to upgrade rules and monitoring requirements needed for the functioning of markets. It is more difficult to adapt the pension schemes to the constraints of ageing societies - a feature which transition economies share with OECD member countries and with most EU members - because of implications in the social and political field. While these adjustments will require continuous peer pressure (indeed, also on senior OECD and EU member countries), some results have already been achieved.

In Hungary and the Czech Republic, some progress has been made with the institution in 1993 of complementary privately funded pension schemes, and in 1995, with reforms including the gradual increase of retirement ages to 62 years. In Poland, a package of laws reforming the pension system is now being discussed in parliament including the institutionalisation of private pension funds. But much still needs to be done in this field under the threat of increasing dependency ratios. This is an area in which the OECD has a strong comparative analytical and policy advantage based on OECD members' experience and past actions, which range from changing the retirement age, raising contribution periods, changing indexing rules or moving towards greater targeting of benefits.

Finally, the EU is preparing for the redirection of structural funds towards the new members, whose GDP per capita is comparatively much lower. A natural starting point for such redirection is an assessment of each country's capacity of absorption. The experience built by each country in absorbing capital inflows (attracted by still high interest rate differentials) through appropriate instruments of sterilisation, improvements to the financial markets and adjustment in their exchange rate policies, are all areas which are closely monitored by the OECD. This will, no doubt, represent an important contribution to structural fund assessments.

In summary, the assistance provided by the OECD in the formulation and implementation of reform policies and the establishment of the legal and institutional framework of a market economy have contributed to making the policies followed as well as the structures of these economies more compatible with that of OECD Member countries. They have therefore facilitated the integration of the partner countries in pan-European economic structures. This has been reinforced by the discipline imposed by compliance with the decisions, recommendations and other substantive instruments of the Organisation as part of the accession procedure. Continued "peer" pressure is also contributing to this process following accession. To a large extent, these considerations are also relevant for the Russian Federation.

Programmes not related to accession

As regards other programmes not closely related to OECD membership, their influence on the integration of European transition countries in pan-European economic structures is more diffuse and related to providing support for a successful completion of the transition process. In particular, most of these countries, not being key players and not satisfying the criteria of mutual interest, do not qualify for observership in OECD Committee meetings.

Concluding Remarks : The Future Direction of OECD Co-operation with Non-Members

The success of the transition process in several European economies, the increased reliance on private capital flows and the rapprochement with the European Union has naturally prompted the question of the future of OECD cooperation with transition economies. While this cooperation is likely to continue in the near future, it has to be assessed against the background of recent debates within the OECD over the implications of globalisation for the member countries and the need for a clearer definition of the strategic objectives that should govern relations with non-member economies at large.

There is a lively on-going debate over the future enlargement of the OECD. Although the recent Ministerial ended with a consensus that the Organisation must remain open to states sharing the common values of OECD Members, it was also agreed that this process should be selective to preserve the tradition of high standards for membership. Behind this consensus, some members favour the "major players" approach, according to which attention should be focused on large economies with a potential to exert a significant influence in the world economy, or, which constitute major markets for OECD products in the future. The recenty completed OECD study on Globalisation and Linkages identifies five such economies: Russia, China, India, Indonesia and Brazil; and argues for a redirection of outreach towards greater policy dialogue with these economies. The other spectrum of the argument is composed of those who argue that the OECD should reflect not economic power per se but "like mindedness", a concept embracing pluralistic democracy, respect of human rights and the market economy. According to this view, countries which share the goals and objectives of the Organisation, that are willing to access, and that are able to meet the requirements of membership should be invited to become members.

While the end of the debate is still not in sight, the OECD has begun to rationalise its own institutional mechanisms for dialogue with non-members to take account of the demands for a less European orientation in its outreach activities. New country specific programmes for China, India, and possibly Brazil, as well as continued priority on Russia, implies that within a shrinking budgetary envelope, emphasis on European economies in transition will be reduced. Given the recent political changes in Bulgaria and Romania and their greater commitment to reform, and the rapid pace of economic reform in Slovenia and the Baltics, the need for OECD programmes towards assisting these countries should also diminish in coming years, all the more since their links with the EU are becoming closer. We shall be pleased when these countries join the European Union and proud to have contributed in our modest way to this outcome.

WORLD BANK PRIORITY SECTORIAL ACTIVITIES

Spiros Voyadzis

Manager of the Brussels Office, World Bank

The four statistical tables attached to this short paper speak for themselves in terms of GDP growth rates, annual inflation and the performance of FDI in Central & Eastern Europe and Central Asia since 1990.

I will not discuss the **first phase** (1991-1994) of the transition process during which many - if not most - countries have intoduced successful stabilisation programs. These countries have also liberalised prices, foreign exchange restrictions and administrative controls on commercial activities. Finally, most countries have also introduced legal reforms by adopting civil and commercial codes and bankruptcy laws which have helped their economic restructuring. Last but not least, privatisation has also taken place. This was easier for small firms but difficult in the case of large companies.

These changes - **liberalisation, stabilisation, legal reforms and privatisation** - have taken transition economies as a group quite far. These countries are now entering what I would call **Phase II**. This phase includes the deepening of financial sector reforms, the unfinished agenda on downsizing and privatisation of state-owned enterprises, and the continuation of reforms in the social sectors, particularly pension reform. The implementation of Phase II will largely determine the sustainability of reform programs and gains achieved so far.

What is the World Bank doing?

In the last five years, 23 countries in transition have become members of the World Bank. **During the 1991-1996 fiscal year period, cumulative lending commitments have reached US$20bn.** Annual lending to the countries of the FSU went from zero in 1992 to about US$3bn during the last two years. Thirteen field offices were established during this period. All this has, I believe, been a major effort. While the amounts of assistance have been and remain significant, the key principle of our intervention has been to improve **incentives** to attract private flows and FDI, to finance needed investments in infrastructure and the environment, and to address several important structural issues in the social sectors.

Our work with governments to support price liberalisation and eliminate price controls increases the predictability of future prices; trade reforms further link these prices to World prices, thus making them even more predictable and subject to less bureaucratic interventions. Price liberalisation also reduces the room for bribery and corruption. And privatisation puts assets on the market, making them available to small domestic entrepreneurs as well as to larger foreign investors. It also takes away control of firms from the line ministries.

However, **financial sector development lies at the core of the systemic transformation process**. Dealing with the regulatory environment and supervision of banks alone, however, is not enough: there is also a need to simultaneously deal with debt-burdened and loss-making state enterprises; the banks' best clients.

Two years ago, we began a program to **promote investment** in the countries of Central Europe by presenting investment projects to foreign investors. This was undertaken by the Foreign Investment Advisory Service (FIAS) operated jointly with the IFC. FIAS has also conducted diagnostic assessments of the environment for foreign investment in several countries in the region.

Sovereign risk is a particular constraint when political and economic uncertainty - as well as government commitment to economic reforms - are still untested. Under such circumstances we have used **World Bank Guarantees**: Partial Credit Guarantee and Partial Risk Guarantee. The first covers all events of non-payment for a designated part of a financing plan. The second takes on risks associated with government commitments to a project, such as expropriation or early termination of concessions, or changes in laws.

There is also **MIGA**, which provides guarantees for foreign equity and leveraged investments against the risks associated with currency transfer, war or civil disturbances. Finally there is **IFC**, which is helping to create modern financial systems which are urgently needed for efficient mobilisation and allocation of funds, as well as managing the large volume of securities created by privatisation. IFC is also supporting large private locally-owned companies.

Regarding the accession of transition economies to the European Union (EU), I would hasten to say that we are working very closely with the Commission, the EIB and the EBRD. The opening of our Brussels Office is also an indication of the importance we attach to all these countries and to our partnership with EU institutions.

Table 1
GDP Growth in Europe and Central Asia
(in percent change)

	1990	1991	1992	1993	1994	1995	1996
ECA REGION	-2.5	-6.6	-9.7	-5.4	-9.0	-1.0	-0.6
CENTRAL EUROPE AND THE BALTICS	-7.5	-11.3	-5.0	0.3	3.7	6.2	5.3
Albania	-10.0	-28.0	-7.2	9.5	9.4	8.9	8.2
Bosnia & Herzegovina	-9.0	-20.0	...	...	...	33.0	50.0
Bulgaria	-9.1	-11.7	-7.3	-1.5	1.8	2.1	-9.0
Croatia	-6.9	-17.3	-9.0	-3.5	0.5	2.6	5.5
Czech Republic	-1.0	-14.2	-6.4	-0.9	2.8	5.0	4.4
Estonia	-7.1	-8.0	-21.2	-8.5	-2.7	4.3	4.0
Hungary	-3.5	-11.9	-3.1	-0.6	2.9	1.5	0.2
Latvia	...	-10.4	-34.9	-14.9	0.6	-1.6	2.8
Lithuania	...	-7.7	-15.4	-15.1	1.2	3.0	3.6
FYR Macedonia	-10.2	-4.0	-7.7	-8.4	-4.0	-1.4	1.1
Poland	-11.5	-7.0	2.6	3.8	5.2	7.0	6.0
Romania	-5.6	-12.9	-8.8	1.5	3.9	6.9	4.1
Slovak Republic	-2.5	-14.5	-6.5	-3.7	4.9	6.8	5.9
Slovenia	-4.7	-8.1	-5.4	2.8	5.3	3.9	3.0
EASTERN EUROPE AND THE CAUCASUS	-4.1	-6.3	-15.5	-11.2	-15.2	-8.2	-6.0
Armenia	-8.5	-8.8	-52.3	-15.0	5.4	6.9	5.6
Azerbaijan	-11.7	-0.7	-35.2	-23.1	-15.7	-13.3	-5.6
Belarus	...	-1.2	-9.6	-10.6	-12.5	-10.1	2.8
Georgia	-11.1	-28.1	-43.4	-39.4	-11.4	2.4	10.5
Moldova	-1.5	-18.7	-29.1	-1.2	-31.2	-3.0	-10.0
Russia	-3.6	-5.0	-14.5	-8.7	-12.8	-4.3	-6.0
Ukraine	-3.8	-8.4	-9.7	-14.2	-23.5	-11.8	-10.0
CENTRAL ASIA	1.8	-5.7	-13.1	-8.3	-14.9	-4.8	0.7
Kazakstan	-1.1	-11.8	-13.0	-12.9	-25.0	-8.9	1.1
Kyrgyz Republic	3.2	-5.0	-19.0	-16.3	-20.1	-5.4	5.6
Tajikistan	-0.6	-8.7	-28.9	-11.1	-21.4	-12.5	-7.0
Turkmenistan	1.5	-5.0	-5.0	-10.0	-19.0	-8.2	-3.0
Uzbekistan	4.3	-0.9	-9.5	-2.3	-4.2	0.9	1.6
Turkey	9.2	1.0	5.9	8.0	-5.4	7.4	7.2

Regional totals are population-weighted averages of all countries for which data is available.

Table 2
Annual Inflation in Europe and Central Asia
(percent change in average Consumer Price Index)

	1990	1991	1992	1993	1994	1995	1996
ECA REGION	10.4	91.2	697.8	372.3	121.9	39.5	26.5
CENTRAL EUROPE AND THE BALTICS	23.7	115.9	211.2	85.0	41.8	26.4	19.5
Albania	0.0	35.5	226.0	85.0	22.6	7.8	12.7
Boznia & Herzogovina	394.0	114.0	...	...	1061.0	133.0	65.9
Bulgaria	64.0	238.9	82.6	72.8	96.0	62.6	123.0
Croatia	...	122.6	663.6	1517.1	98.0	2.0	3.5
Czech Republic	9.6	56.6	11.1	20.8	10.0	9.1	8.8
Estonia	18.5	211.8	1075.9	89.8	47.7	29.0	23.0
Hungary	28.9	35.0	23.0	22.5	18.8	28.2	23.6
Latvia	...	124.4	951.2	109.2	35.9	25.0	19.0
Lithuania	15.1	216.0	1021.0	410.4	72.1	39.5	25.0
FYR Macedonia	220.5	113.6	1695.2	334.2	121.9	16.0	3.1
Poland	585.8	70.3	43.0	35.3	32.2	27.8	20.0
Romania	4.7	161.1	211.2	255.2	136.8	32.2	38.8
Slovak Republic	10.4	61.2	10.0	23.2	13.4	9.9	6.9
Slovenia	549.7	117.7	201.3	32.3	19.8	12.6	10.0
EASTERN EUROPE AND THE CAUCASUS	6.6	87.0	1210.0	1190.0	1427.7	188.7	39.3
Armenia	10.1	80.1	677.9	3731.9	5273.4	176.7	18.6
Azerbaijan	7.5	82.8	1350.9	980.9	1427.7	411.7	20.3
Belarus	...	...	971.0	1190.0	2221.0	709.0	52.0
Georgia	3.3	78.7	637.3	19257.	17271.	162.7	39.3
Moldova	14.8	136.1	1276.0	9	5	30.6	28.0
Russia	5.6	92.6	1354.0	788.5	330.0	188.7	47.4
Ukraine	4.2	91.2	1210.0	895.3	303.2	376.0	79.8
				4735.0	891.1		
CENTRAL ASIA	4.8	90.7	1007.0	1075.0	1568.0	305.0	53.0
Kazakstan	18.9	87.4	1622.6	1662.0	1880.0	176.0	39.1
Kyrgyz Republic	4.8	113.7	1007.0	772.1	95.7	31.9	35.0
Tajikistan	...	...	...	...	350.4	635.0	443.0
Turkmenistan	...	...	...	...	1748.0	1005.0	992.0
Uzbekistan	3.5	90.7	717.6	1075.0	1568.0	305.0	53.0
Turkey	60.3	66.0	70.1	68.1	105.3	89.0	80.3

Regional totals indicate the median value of all countries for which data are available.

Table 3
Foreign Direct Investment in Europe and Central Asia
(in millions of US dollars)

	1990	.1991	1992	1993	1994	1995	1996
REGIONAL TOTAL	139	2311	4065	5419	5451	14729	11463
CENTRAL EUROPE AND THE BALTICS	539	2386	3177	4307	3843	10942	7290
Albania	0	0	32	45	53	70	93
Bulgaria	4	56	42	55	100	160	50
Croatia	0	0	13	72	98	81	300
Czech Republic(a)	207	600	983	552	749	2526	875
Estonia			56	154	212	202	94
Hungary	337	1459	1471	2329	1146	4453	2000
Latvia				51	155	165	200
Lithuania		76	10	136	125	290	115
FYR Macedonia	0	0	0	0	24	13	18
Poland	11	117	284	580	542	2305	2772
Romania	-18	37	73	87	341	367	487
Slovak Republic			100	134	170	134	150
Slovenia	-2	41	113	112	128	176	136
EASTERN EUROPE AND THE CAUCASUS	-400	-75	737	519	752	2645	3020
Armenia				0	3	19	12
Azerbaijan				60	22	275	496
Belarus				18	10	7	19
Georgia				1	8	6	20
Moldova		25	17	14	18	72	37
Russia	-400	-100	700	386	600	2000	2000
Ukraine			20	40	91	266	436
CENTRAL ASIA			151	593	856	1142	1153
Kazakhstan			100	473	635	859	930
Kyrgyz Republic				10	45	61	31
Tajikistan				0	0	13	13
Turkmenistan			11	80	103	233	129
Uzbekistan			40	30	73	-24	50

(a) Includes Czechoslovakian FDI pre-1992.

Table 4
Lending Operations in Europe and Central Asia Region by Country
(commitments by fiscal year in millions of US dollars)

	1991	1992	1993	1994	1995	1996	1997
TOTAL ECA REGION	3867	2133	3844	3724	4500	4230	5048
CENTRAL EUROPE AND THE BALTICS	2937	1767	1790	1476	858	1074	1836
Albania		41	44	47	67	73	0
Bosnia & Herzegovina						10	198
Bulgaria	17	250	178	148	125	121	94
Croatia				128	120	32	239
Czech Republic	450	246	0	80	0	0	0
Estonia			30	50	30	15	0
Hungary	550	200	413	129	38	0	293
Latvia			45	25	53	27	98
Lithuania			60	28	32	42	113
FYR Macedonia				80	123	39	60
Poland	1440	380	900	145	215	181	67
Romania	180	650	120	401	55	510	625
Slovak Republic				135	0	0	0
Slovenia				80	0	24	49
Former Yugoslavia	300						
EASTERN EUROPE AND THE CAUCASUS			1435	1778	2779	2480	2868
Armenia			12	28	117	92	32
Azerbaijan					82	83	35
Belarus				170	0	0	
Georgia					103	91	69
Moldova			26	60	90	55	26
Russia			1370	1520	1741	1816	1716
Ukraine			27	0	546	343	990
CENTRAL ASIA			60	370	613	364	324
Kazakstan				274	283	280	142
Kyrgyz Republic			60	75	77	99	60
Tajikistan					0	5	52
Turkmenistan					25	0	65
Uzbekistan				21	228	0	5
Turkey	900	334	559	100	250	312	20
Cyprus	30	32	0	0	0	0	0
Memo: IDA Countries	0	41	116	233	569	627	481
Share IDA/Total	0	2	4	6	13	18	8

THE EUROPEAN UNION, ENLARGEMENT AND REGIONAL CO-OPERATION

Fraser Cameron

Foreign Policy Advisor, DG1A, European Commission[1]

Introduction

The European Union (EU) took a further significant step forward with the conclusion of the Intergovernmental Conference (IGC) and agreement on the Treaty of Amsterdam on 16-17 June. It now faces another historic challenge - enlarging to include the countries of central and eastern Europe (CEECs) - and thus contributing to ending the division of Europe after 1945. On 16 July, the European Commission presented its "Opinions" on the candidate countries. It will now be up to the European Council to decide, most probably at its meeting in Luxembourg in December, on the strategy for accession negotiations.

Relations between the EU and the CEECs have expanded enormously since 1989 and now the EU is the principal trading partner for all the CEECs. At the same time the EU is also promoting regional co-operation throughout Europe as a means to promote stability, security and prosperity. Examples of such co-operation include the Euro-Arctic region, the Baltic Sea, the Central European Free Trade Area (CEFTA), the Black Sea Economic Co-operation (BSEC) and the regional co-operation initiatives in the Balkans. The EU is thus the focal point of a new pattern of relationships in and around Europe which is binding the continent closer together.

The Treaty of Amsterdam

Although initial reaction to the Treaty of Amsterdam was rather muted, with the majority of commentators speaking of only "modest" achievements, a closer examination reveals that significant progress was made in a number of key areas. With regard to co-operation in the sensitive areas of justice and home affairs, there was agreement to treat asylum and immigration policies under the Community pillar. There was a significant extension of powers for the European Parliament and a considerable simplification of its legislative procedures. There was agreement on new chapters covering employment, the environment and public health. There was agreement to an extension of majority voting. There was agreement on closer co-operation in the common foreign and security policy, including the creation of a Mr CFSP and the establishment of a policy planning unit. Perhaps the most disappointing aspect was the failure to agree on any major institutional reform, which was previously decreed a precondition for the opening of enlargement negotiations. Decision on these issues was postponed until a future date when the number of new entrants becomes more apparent.

Enlargement

Agreement at Amsterdam opened the door for the enlargement process to begin. The European Council described the enlargement of the Union as a "political imperative and a major opportunity". It is true that never before has Europe had such an opportunity to unite under democratic conditions. Never before have so many countries wished to join the Union. Until the end of the Cold War, the eastern half of Europe had no opportunity to participate in the process of European integration. Since 1989, the transformation process in the CEECs has brought these countries to the stage where they have all applied for EU membership. The EU has an unavoidable duty to respond positively to these developments and contribute to the development of a stable political and economic order for all of Europe.

But never before has the Union envisaged an enlargement of such dimensions - it could add more than 100 million to its population of 370 million - and in terms of the different economic and social situations involved. The combined GDP of the ten potential new members in central and eastern Europe is less than 4% of that of the Union (roughly equivalent to that of the Netherlands) and their average national income per head is still only 30% of the EU average. The percentage of GDP arising from, and percentage of working population engaged in, agriculture (7.8% and 26.7%) is far above the EU average (2.5% and 5.7%). But these problems should not obscure the potential political and economic benefits that will flow from an enlarged EU with an extra 100 million consumers.

Successful enlargement of the European Union will be a major factor in spreading peace and prosperity throughout the European continent because it will support the newly liberalised market economies by further opening up markets in goods and services between East and West, North and South, stimulating economic growth in Europe and offering new trading opportunities. Moreover, it will bind the countries of central and eastern Europe into western European political and economic structures and thus enhance security and stability whilst increasing effective co-operation in the fields of Justice and Home Affairs, helping to fight international crime and the menace of drugs, the effects of which are felt throughout Europe. Finally, enlargement will bring higher environmental standards to central and eastern Europe, benefiting all of Europe by reducing cross-border and global pollution.

EU Policy towards the CEECs

Since 1989, the European Union has been in the forefront of international efforts to support the reform process and thus to increase stability in central and eastern Europe. The Union's involvement includes substantial economic assistance, closer political links, wide-ranging association or "Europe" agreements, rapidly growing trade relations and now a pre-accession strategy, the centre-piece of which is a White Paper on the adjustments which the central and east European countries will have to make to meet the requirements of the Internal Market. Thus the Union has a range of policies tailored to the situation and needs of each country and which is constantly evolving to meet changing circumstances.

Since Copenhagen, the Union has put into place an unprecedented pre-accession strategy to prepare for the next enlargement. The principal elements of this strategy are as follows:

* **First**, wide-ranging association or "Europe" agreements which provide for comprehensive co-operation in political, economic, trade, cultural and other areas. Association Councils meet regularly to discuss issues of common concern, as do parliamentarians from the associated countries with their European Parliament counterparts. This dialogue is part of a process of political and economic rapprochement which is without precedent. The Europe agreements, whose very name conveys a sense of their ambition, provide the framework for rapid progress towards free trade. The Union has already eliminated tariffs and quotas in all industrial sectors and improvements in market access are being made in agriculture. Overall, a massive reorientation has taken place in trade flows, with the Union today accounting for 60% of the associated countries' trade. This compares,

incidentally, with less than 5% for trade with the United States, and less than 2% for trade with Japan. At present, the EU runs a trade surplus with the associated countries but this is quite normal given their current stage of development. There would be little point in the Union opening up its markets if barriers remain in trade among the associated countries themselves. For this reason the Union strongly supports the Central European Free Trade Area (CEFTA) and its extension to all associated countries. As trade barriers fall, direct investment should increase, with further gains to productivity and competitiveness.

* **Second**, the *Phare* technical assistance programme, amounting to over one billion ECU annually, which promotes economic reform in fields ranging from energy and transport to agriculture and privatisation. It has recently been agreed to concentrate *Phare* on two main areas : 70% for infrastructure and 30% for institution building.

* **Third**, a regular structured dialogue with ministers and senior officials of the Union on an increasing range of Union policies. Never before have candidates, or potential candidates, been invited, well in advance of accession, to participate on a regular basis in joint meetings with the institutions of the Union. Today, it has become normal for the associated countries to hold joint ministerial meetings with the member states, prepared in advance by officials. A permanent dialogue among twenty-five states on issues such as the trans-European networks or international crime prevention can be of immense practical value.

* **Fourth**, the White Paper, approved at the Cannes European Council in June 1995, on the steps which the associated countries must take in order to prepare themselves to operate in the Internal Market. This provides a guide to the complexities of the internal market and suggests a logical sequence in which the associated countries should go about bringing their legislation into line with that in the Union. Legislation, to be effective, must be properly implemented and enforced, and so the White Paper also provides guidance on the necessary regulatory and administrative structures.

The principal responsibility for implementing the White Paper's recommendations lies with the associated countries themselves. The sooner their laws, conformity tests, standards institutes, and judicial procedures are adapted to those in the Union, the sooner their businesses will feel the benefit. However, the Union recognises that advice and support are needed and so the Commission is establishing a new technical assistance office for the purpose. It will draw on the experience of the member states in transposing Union legislation into national law in order to advise partners in central and eastern Europe. The Commission will be working with each associated country to devise its own strategy for alignment with the internal market taking into account its economic situation and reform priorities.

The Need for Continuing Reforms

This brief and by no means comprehensive outline of the pre-accession strategy is sufficient to indicate the Union's deep commitment to the preparations for future enlargement. Equally important, however, are the preparations being made by the associated countries themselves. The first priority in preparing for Union membership is the consolidation of political and economic reform. The free flow of information and the independence of the media and judiciary are essential elements in the consolidation of democracy. On the whole, the record is good. But there are worrying developments in some candidate countries.

Good relations with neighbouring states and the often related question of respect for minority rights are also important in preparing for membership. Here, too, a great deal of progress has been made thanks largely to the efforts of the countries concerned, partly within the framework of the Stability Pact. But again a number of sensitive issues remain to be resolved.

Just as important as the consolidation of democracy and stability is the pursuit of sound macro-economic policy and economic reform. The adoption of internal market legislation, as provided for by the White Paper, will only produce the expected benefits if accompanied by the right economic policies. The Treaty on European Union sets out clear criteria for macro-economic policy with a view to achieving the degree of convergence needed for participation in economic and monetary union. Some associated countries consider that they are already in a position to satisfy these criteria. In others, however, further progress is needed in bringing inflation, debt and government deficits under control.

Privatisation is another key feature of economic reform in all associated countries. In general, it is proceeding well. But mere changes in ownership are not sufficient to improve competitiveness - restructuring is also essential. In addition, privatisation must take place in transparent and objective conditions without discrimination or favour if it is to create a climate of confidence which will attract new investment. Foreign investment is a source of growth, development and innovation in all market economies and it should be welcomed as an opportunity and not regarded as a threat.

Competition policy and state aid controls also need to be brought into line with the Union in order to create equitable conditions for trade and investment. This will bring distinct benefits both for the Union and for the associated countries. For once satisfactory implementation of competition law and state aids control - as well as other White Paper measures - is achieved, the Union could decide to phase down the use of commercial defence instruments since there would then be a guarantee of fair competition comparable to that inside the Union itself.

Potential investors will also want to be sure that host countries provide adequate protection for intellectual and industrial property rights before they supply sophisticated new goods and services. Here, again, adequate mechanisms for implementation and enforcement are as important as the legal framework itself.

The Commission's Opinions and Agenda 2000

Following the European Council in Madrid in December 1995, a new phase in the enlargement process began with the request from the Council to the Commission to start preparing the opinions on the applicant countries with a view to their being forwarded to the Council "as soon as possible after the conclusion of the IGC". Despite the enormity of the task, the Commission was able to meet the deadline and published the Opinions on 16 July. In carrying out this mandate, the Commission was guided by the criteria established at the Copenhagen European Council in June 1993. These requirements included stability of political institutions, respect for human rights and the protection of minorities, a functioning market economy, capacity to cope with competitive pressures, and acceptance of the Union's objectives as regards political, economic and monetary union.

The Commission recommended that accession negotiations should be opened with five countries - Poland, Hungary, the Czech Republic, Estonia and Slovenia. The other candidates - Latvia, Lithuania, Slovakia, Romania and Bulgaria - would benefit from increased financial and technical assistance, and would have their progress monitored on an annual basis in order to prepare themselves for accession negotiations as soon as possible.

Accompanying the Opinions on the ten candidate countries, the Commission also published a far-reaching report "Agenda 2000" in which it examined the challenges facing the Union as result of enlargement and proposed reforms in a number of key areas. Given that there was no likelihood of the overall budget increasing during the 2000-2005 period, the Commission proposed that there should be a gradual reduction in the regional funds paid to existing member states and a corresponding shift in resources to the potential new member states. The expensive common agricultural policy (CAP) would also have to be changed to bring prices more into line with World prices. Finally, the Commission stated that enlargement without further institutional change would lead to paralysis within the Union. It will now be up to the European Council meeting in Luxembourg in December to take the final decisions on the modalities of the enlargement process.

The EU and Regional Co-operation

In recent years, the EU has become increasingly supportive of initiatives to promote regional and sub-regional co-operation, recognising that they can be important instruments to promote security, stability and prosperity. This position has been emphasised by several statements in support of such co-operation, albeit with certain conditions, at the most recent meetings of the European Council. Within the framework of the OSCE, the EU has played an important role in developing the concept of regional and sub-regional co-operation as a factor of security and stability which has become a key element in the OSCE concept of security, in particular its economic dimension. The previous enlargement of the EU to include Austria, Sweden and Finland provided a boost to sub-regional co-operation. The prospect of a further round of enlargement to the CEECs will also increase the importance of sub-regional co-operation in the new Europe.

In post Cold War Europe, regional co-operation has an important role to play in breaking down old barriers and promoting stability, security and prosperity. Amongst the most important new initiatives one might mention the Council of Baltic Sea States (CBSS), the Barents Euro-Arctic Council (BEAC), the Central European Initiative (CEI), the Black Sea Economic Co-operation (BSEC) and the Central European Free Trade Agreement (CEFTA).

The EU has not only welcomed these initiatives but has sought to support them in a variety of different ways. The EU is closely involved in the BEAC which may be described as a model of top down/bottom up approaches. The ministerial meetings allow for wide-ranging political discussions (and reassurance for Moscow about the participation of the oblasts involved in the initiative), whilst the local management of the various projects, particularly environmental, has promoted strong links between local authorities and actors. The EU also strongly supports the CBSS which has developed some important initiatives having a direct bearing on security as well as seeking to prepare the Baltic States for EU accession and to develop closer relations with Russia. In 1996, the Commission presented to the Council and the European Parliament a communication on regional co-operation in the Baltic Sea region which has resulted in the so-called Visby initiative and the Kalmar Action Programme. Together, these form the basis of Community action in the Baltic Sea region. The Visby declaration outlined a promising agenda for co-operation on transport and trade, tackling cross-border crime, improving border and customs controls, environmental and nuclear safety issues.

Although not as developed as the CBBS, the CEI has nevertheless sought to promote diplomatic co-operation between its members and to encourage joint projects in the economic and statistical fields. Arising out of the Visegrad four, CEFTA has provided a useful framework for discussion and co-operation on trade-related issues. Still in its infancy, the members of BSEC have made a reasonably encouraging start in setting their political differences aside in order to concentrate on promoting co-operation in transport, energy, banking, environmental and other issues. The Commission is currently preparing a communication on how best to support BSEC.

Apart from supporting these initiatives, the EU has also introduced a number of programmes to promote cross-border co-operation. Amongst the most important are Interreg, the Phare Partnership Programme (to promote local and regional development), the Phare and Tacis LIEN Programme (to promote NGOs working in the social sector), the Phare Ecos-Ouverture Programme (to strengthen the capacity of local and regional authorities to design regional development strategies), and the Phare and Tacis Democracy Programme (to strengthen NGOs and civic institutions).

Regional and sub-regional co-operation in Europe has become particularly important for the EU in the perspective of the Union's enlargement to the East and is an important element in the Union's pre-accession strategy. The Union's main objectives are twofold: promoting regional co-operation involving the CEECs which are candidates for accession to the EU in the recognition that such co-operation is an important element in the preparation of these countries for accession; and involving those countries which are not able to join the EU in the near future in regional co-operation arrangements and promoting the development of close links with their neighbours and with the EU in order to avoid re-emergence of divisions in Europe.

It should be emphasised, however, that EU support for regional co-operation initiatives should be seen as complementary to, and not as a substitute for, the EU's bilateral relations with each of the countries involved in such initiatives. Equally, it is important to note that the EU's support for regional co-operation is not unconditional. It depends on regional co-operation complying with UN and OSCE principles, being based on the voluntary participation of all states concerned, being to the mutual benefit of all states concerned i.e. providing added value, and being compatible with existing international economic agreements.

Support for sub-regional co-operation is provided through existing Community instruments and existing budget lines in accordance with existing procedures and regulations and on the basis of co-financing. The Community instruments which can be drawn upon for this purpose are in principle demand driven. It is therefore important that the right signals are given by the states/regions which would benefit from such assistance. Some useful lessons from regional co-operation include the importance of starting concrete projects as soon as possible in order for co-operation to take off, the need to involve central and local authorities/actors, the neccessity of sound financing, and finally the positive influence of an EU presence.

The EU and Regional Co-operation in the Balkans
The overriding objective of the EU in the Balkans is the successful implementation of the Dayton/Paris peace agreements and the creation of an area of political stability and economic prosperity. The EU is prepared to contribute towards this aim by promoting political and economic reforms and the respect for democratic principles, human and minority rights. Co-operation and the establishment of good neighbourly relations between the countries of the region is an essential element in this context. The EU aim is to counteract trends towards de-stabilisation and marginalisation. In short, the EU has a real interest in the European perspective for the whole of the Balkan region.

The EU has different contractual relations with each country in the region. Greece is a member state of the EU. With Turkey, the EU has signed a Customs Union - the successful functioning of which is an essential step before re-visiting the question of EU membership. Romania and Bulgaria have Europe Agreements with the EU and are actively pursuing their membership applications despite obvious difficulties which both countries face. Slovenia has also signed a Europe Agreement (ratification outstanding) and applied for EU membership. EU relations with other states in the region may be divided into two categories: Croatia, FRY, Bosnia; and Albania, FYROM.

This division arises from the fact that the first group were engaged in the Bosnian conflict and EU policy towards the three countries is based on the follow-up to the Dayton/Paris agreements with considerable emphasis on conditionality (support for democracy, protection of human and minority rights, willingness to engage in regional co-operation, willingness to cooperate with International Tribunals, etc). If these conditions are met, it will lead towards full contractual relations with all three. Conditionality is also important for Albania and FYROM, both suffering major political instability.

How will enlargement affect regional co-operation? In light of past experience, there should be a positive impact, but this may not happen automatically as the new member states will inevitably give priority to their new responsibilities as EU members. The EU itself will thus have to ensure that regional co-operation does not suffer as a result of enlargement. This will be particularly important in dealing with those countries not in the first enlargement wave (perhaps also not in the NATO first wave), as well as in the EU's relations with Russia, Ukraine and other CIS states. Russia is of course already involved in a number of regional initiatives (BEAC, CBBS, and BSEC). But Ukraine will need particular attention, not least because of its lengthy border with Poland.

Conclusion

All European institutions have an important part to play in the development of a new European security architecture, but the EU, further strengthened as a result of the Treaty of Amsterdam, has a particular role and responsibility due to its multitude of financial, economic, trade and other instruments (eg Stability Pact), and its ultimate carrot of EU membership. The enlargement process is now well underway and is designed as an inclusive process with the candidate countries themselves deciding their own timetable.

Regional and sub-regional co-operation is a key element in the effort to create a more stable and secure Europe because it promotes interdependence and solidarity in both the political and economic fields. A judicious mix of top down and bottom up approach is likely to achieve the best results, and the EU is prepared to intensify its efforts to support such co-operation provided that the states involved meet the necessary conditions.

Footnote

1. The views expressed are those of the author and do not commit the European Commission.

FOREIGN DIRECT INVESTMENT IN SLOVENIA: TRENDS, EXPERIENCES AND POLICY

Matija Rojec and *Janez Potočnik*

Slovenian Institute of Macroeconomic Analysis and Development

Basic trends and characteristics of FDI inflows

The Foreign Investment Act of 17 December 1989, which introduced national treatment principle and equity foreign direct investment (FDI), represented the decisive positive turn-around in the legal framework for FDI in Slovenia and its accommodation to international standards. The volume of FDI increased accordingly. At the end of 1988, there were only 28 joint ventures with US$114.3m of invested foreign capital; by the end of 1995, according to the Bank of Slovenia, the number of enterprises with foreign equity participation in Slovenia increased to 1,348 in which foreign investment totalled US$1,642m. A conservative assessment of the present amount of FDI in Slovenia would be approximately US$2bn.(1) In the second half of 1996, the interest of foreign portfolio investors in shares of newly privatized Slovenian companies also increased and is now assessed at approximately US$150m.

Table 1
Amount of FDI in Slovenia at end 1993, 1994 and 1995

	1993	1994	1995
FDI (1)			
Number of companies	1,100	1,345	1,348
Total value in **US$m** (2), of which:	954.3	1,175.4	1,642.8
1. Equity	709.7	919.1	1,133.1
2. Long-term liabilities to foreign investor	346.6	472.8	646.3
3. Long-term claims to foreign investor	102.2	116.5	136.6
Portfolio (US$m) (3)	35.3	47.7	50.5
TOTAL (US$m)	989.6	1,323.1	1,693.3

Source: Bank of Slovenia
(1)   Foreign direct investment = 10% or higher foreign equity share (According to OECD benchmark definition)
(2)   Total value = equity + long-term liabilities to foreign investor - long term claims to foreign investor.
(3)   Foreign portfolio investment = Less than 10% foreign equity share.

Most relevant FDI projects in Slovenia developed from successful previous coopera-tion between prospective foreign investors and their Slovenian partner/target company. The largest FDI projects were structured as foreign acquisitions or joint venture acquisi-tions. Greenfield FDI is used predominantly in small projects. As quoted by existing foreign investors in Slovenia, their major reasons for choosing Slovenia among alternative investment locations (Slovenia's major competitors in the field of FDI are other Central and Eastern European countries in transition) are of a company specific character, ie. the quality of the Slovenian partner/target company in question with regard to reliability, good management and technical staff, expertise, tradition, export orientation and adequate pro-duction programs. Previous satisfactory experience with past cooperation was also men-tioned. The more general location specific advantages of Slovenia have been only of secondary importance.

Table 2
Importance of FDI in transition economies (end 1996)

Country	FDI stock (US$ bn)	FDI stock per capita (US$)	FDI stock in % of GDP (1)
Bulgaria	0.8	95	6.9
Croatia	1.4	292	8.8
Czech Republic	7.2	699	16.1
Estonia	0.6	400	14.6
Hungary	15.0	1,456	34.2
Latvia	0.5	192	11.1
Lithuania	0.8	216	15.4
Poland	12.0	312	10.4
Romania	2.2	97	6.2
Russia	6.5	44	1.8
Slovakia	0.9	170	5.6
Slovenia	1.6	800	8.9
Slovenia (official estimate)	2.0	1,000	11.1

Source: Business Central Europe, April 1997 (According to national statistics).
(1)   GDP for 1995.

Compared with other Central and Eastern European (CEE) countries, Slovenia stands quite high as far as FDI stock per capita is concerned (in second place, just after Hungary), but much less so with regard to the more relevant indicator of FDI stock as a share of GDP, where a number of other countries show a higher level.

Major investing countries

Most FDI in Slovenia comes from Austria (24.5%), Croatia (22.2%), Germany (19.3%), France (9.4%), Spain (5.2%) and Italy (5.2%). The high shares of Croatia and France are the result of a particular situation and do not accurately reflect the picture overall. In the case of Croatia, this is the consequence of the co-ownership of the Nuclear Power Plant Krško (built in the 1979s) while in the case of France, the high share is mostly due to Renault's investment in car manufacturing. The aforementioned countries accounted for as much as 85.6% of FDI equity stock in Slovenia at the end of 1995. The proximity of Slovenia to the EU as the nearest pole of the Triade (EU, USA, Japan) and the traditionally strong economic cooperation of Slovenia with Germany, Austria, Italy and France(2) are the reasons for the domination of investors from these countries. The most frequent foreign investor in Slovenia is a small to medium-sized company from neighbouring EU countries, which are also Slovenia's major foreign trade partners. On the other hand, in value terms, FDI is heavily concentrated in about a dozen of the largest FDI projects with European MNEs, notably the investment of Renault (France) in car manufacturing, Saffa (Italy) and Brigl & Bergmeister (Austria) in paper manufacturing, EGO (Switzerland), Siemens (Germany) and Kirkwood Industries (USA) in electrical machinery and apparatus, Reemtsma (Germany) and Seita (France) in cigarette manufacturing, Pfleiderer (Germany) in non-metallic mineral products production, and Henkel (Austria) in the manufacture of other chemical products.

Table 3
Major Investing Countries in Slovenia - FDI Equity Stock at end 1995

INVESTING COUNTRY	VALUE (US$m)	SHARE (%)
Austria	277.4	24.5
Croatia	251.0	22.1
Germany	219.1	19.3
France	106.5	9.4
Spain	58.9	5.2
Italy	58.5	5.2
Switzerland	56.5	5.0
United Kingdom	40.8	3.6
USA	21.3	1.9
Denmark	12.7	1.1
Netherlands	12.7	1.1
Other countries	17.7	1.6
TOTAL	**1133.1**	**100.0**

Source: Bank of Slovenia

Major FDI recipient industries

Manufacturing industry is by far the most important recipient of FDI in Slovenia, followed by electricity production (Nuclear Power Plant Krško), financial, technical and business services (notably R&D activity, financial institutions, trade related services), and trade (mostly retail). FDI in Slovenian manufacturing industry is concentrated in the transport equipment, electrical machinery and appliances, paper and paper products, tobacco and, to a lesser extent, in the industrial chemicals and chemical products industries. Such distribution is determined by the handful of large (for Slovenia) FDI projects listed above. In relative terms (share of FIEs in total for individual manufacturing industries), FIEs are the most important in tobacco, paper and paper products, transport equipment (automobiles) and non metallic mineral products manufacturing, followed by electrical machinery, non-electrical machinery, and petroleum refineries. In the service sectors, FIEs seem to be most relevant in trade and in financial, technical and business services.

Although an intensive restructuring process is under way in Slovenia, the structure of the manufacturing sector as it is today has been formed mostly within the framework of the import-substitution policy of the former Yugoslavia. On the other hand, the industrial structure of FIEs has been, with few exceptions, created mostly in the period after Slovenia's departure from Yugoslavia since when an outward-looking, export-oriented development concept has already become evident. That is why the structure of FIEs and domestic enterprises (DEs) in the Slovenian manufacturing sector is somewhat different. Transport equipment, electrical machinery, paper and paper products and cigarettes manufacturing absorb 68.6% of all manufacturing FIEs' assets and only 19.8% of all manufacturing DEs' assets. FIEs are the most "over-represented" in transport equipment, followed by paper and paper products, tobacco and electrical machinery. On the other hand, FIEs are the most "under-represented" in fabricated metal products (except machinery), iron and steel basic industries, clothing, wood products (including furniture), food and beverages. The major common feature of the differences in industrial distribution of FIEs and DEs in Slovenia is that foreign investors tend to invest more into capital intensive and export oriented industries.

Table 4
Industrial Distribution of FDI in Slovenia - FDI equity stock at end 1995

EKD[1] N°	INDUSTRY	VALUE (US$m)	SHARE (%)
0112	Non-metallic mineral products	30.6	2.7
0113	Fabricated metal products, except machinery	8.7	0.8
0114	Non-electrical machinery, professional, scientific etc.equip.	14.9	1.3
0115	Transport equipment	98.4	8.7
0117	Electrical machinery apparatus, appliances and supplies	122.7	10.8
0118	Industrial chemicals	38.4	3.4
0119	Other chemical products	39.9	3.5
0121	Other non-metallic mineral products	7.9	0.7
0123	Wood products, including furniture	1.9	0.2
0124	Paper and paper products	127.8	11.3
0126	Clothing	4.5	0.4
0130	Food manufacturing	8.0	0.7
0131	Beverage industries	9.2	0.8
0134	Printing and publishing	2.8	0.2
0101	Electricity production)		
0105	Petroleum refineries)		
0129	Rubber products) Total 0101-0133[2]	208.3	18.4
0133	Tobacco manufactures)		
0501	Construction of buildings	1.5	0.1
0605	Land transport	10.2	0.9
0701	Retail trade	37.5	3.3
0702	Wholesale trade	41.8	3.7
0703	Foreign trade	16.4	1.4
0801	Restaurants and hotels	0.5	0.0
0901	Repair services	1.5	0.1
0902	Personal and household services	3.2	0.3
1003	Sanitary and similar services	4.0	0.4
1101	Financial institutions	88.1	7.8
1102	Insurance	3.4	0.3
1103	Trade related services including storage	64.9	5.7
1104	Technical services	9.3	0.8
1106	R&D activity	116.6	10.3
	Total above 32 industries	1,122.9	99.1
Other		10.2	0.9
TOTAL		**1,133.1**	**100.0**

Source: Bank of Slovenia
(1)   Unified Classification of Activities
(2)   Industries for which data should not be disclosed because each of them contains less than 3 FDIs.

Considerable differences in the industrial distribution of FIEs and DEs suggest that a necessary restructuring of the Slovenian manufacturing sector is going on through FDI. Nevertheless, the fact that major FDI projects in Slovenia have been structured as foreign privatisations make the macro-economic restructuring impact of FDI dependent upon the purposes for which the revenues from foreign privatisations are used. The Development Fund of Slovenia, as the major recipient of privatisation proceeds, has probably been used rather too often as a "fire brigade" for the resolution of the most urgent problems (debt repayments, wages payments etc. in enterprises in the Fund's portfolio) and not as a real development agency.

Importance of FIEs for the Slovenian non-financial corporate sector

Table 5 on the next page reveals the relatively low importance of FDI in Slovenia, but, for some income statement/balance sheet items (especially exports, imports and profit) FIEs hold surprisingly high shares. FIEs account for only 3.4% of all enterprises in the non-financial corporate sector and 7.4% of all equity, 8.2% of all assets and 6.0% of all employment in this sector.

Of FIEs total equity, approximately 60% is foreign, meaning that the share of foreign equity in total equity of the Slovenian non-financial corporate sector is only 4.4%. With this equity, assets and employees, FIEs realize 11.5% of all net sales, 15.3% of all net operating profit and 6.1% of all net operating loss. FIEs also pay 15.5% of all profit tax, and account for 19% of total imports, 20.1% of all exports and 23.9% of the total foreign trade surplus of the Slovenian non-financial corporate sector. The importance of FIEs in Slovenian manufacturing industry is considerably higher since they are relatively much more engaged in manufacturing than DEs. Thus, it would seem that FIEs do represent a relatively important category of the Slovenian economy, especially with regard to foreign trade, net operating profit and profit tax. Also, the share of FIEs in the Slovenian non-financial corporate sector increased in 1995 in all income statements and balance sheet items except in operating loss.

Please note that for **Tables 5, 6 and 7**, **DEs** are assumed to be enterprises with **less** than 10% foreign equity share whereas **FIEs** are those with 10% or **more**.

Table 5
Selected 1995 Income Statements/Balance Sheets for DEs and FIEs
(Note that all figures other than No. of enterprises and employees are in **US$m**.)

ITEM	ALL ENTERPRISES	DEs	FIEs	SHARE OF FIEs (%)	CHANGE - 1994/1995 (%)
TOTAL					
No. of enterprises	33,609	32,463	1,146	3.4	-0.2
No. of employees	484,602	455,465	29,137	6.0	+0.7
Equity	25,079	23,218	1,832	7.4	+0.8
Assets	46,743	42,898	3,876	8.2	+0.2
Net sales	38,676	34,213	4,463	11.5	+0.8
Exports	9,460	7,561	1,899	20.1	+1.0
Imports	7,509	6,077	1,432	19.1	n.a.
Exports-imports	1,951	1,484	467	23.9	n.a.
Value added	8,249	7,575	674	8.2	+0.6
Operating profit	999	846	153	15.3	-0.3
Operating loss	1,131	1,061	70	6.1	-1.4
Net profit/loss	-132	-215	83	-	-
MANUFACTURING					
No. of enterprises	5,594	5,365	229	4.1	-0.8
No. of employees	239,788	219,301	20,487	8.5	+0.7
Equity	7,543	6,556	987	13.1	+1.6
Assets	14,306	12,525	1,781	12.5	+0.8
Net sales	14,282	11,774	2,508	17.6	+0.7
Exports	6,906	5,305	1,601	23.2	+2.1
Imports	4,278	3,477	801	18.7	n.a.
Exports-imports	2,628	1,828	800	30.4	n.a.
Value added	3,654	3,253	401	11.0	+0.3
Operating profit	318	251	67	21.0	+3.3
Operating loss	498	465	33	6.7	-6.8
Net profit/loss	-180	-214	34	-	-

Source: Institute for Macroeconomic Analysis and Development

Performance and operating characteristics of FIEs compared to DEs in Slovenia

Table 6 below compares the performance of FIEs and DEs and shows that the former perform better. This holds not only in general but also with regard to the vast majority of individual manufacturing industries in which FIEs are involved.

Table 6
Major Performance Indicators of FIEs and DEs in Slovenia -
1995 Income Statements/Balance Sheets Data

INDICATOR	ALL ENTERPRISES	FIEs	DEs	INDEX FIEs/DEs(%)
Net sales per assets (%)				
Total	77.8	109.2	75.0	146
Manufacturing	93.9	132.5	88.4	150
Net sales per employee (000US$)				
Total	79.8	153.2	75.1	204
Manufacturing	59.6	122.4	53.7	228
Operating profit per equity (%)				
Total	3.7	7.7	3.4	226
Manufacturing	4.0	6.4	3.6	178
Operating profit per employee (000US$)				
Total	2.1	5.3	1.9	279
Manufacturing	1.3	3.3	1.1	300
Value added per employee (000US$)				
Total	17.0	23.1	16.6	139
Manufacturing	15.2	19.6	14.8	132

Source: Institute for Macroeconomic Analysis and Development.

Analysis (summarised in **Table 7** on the next page) suggests six major areas in which FIEs show distinctively different operating indicators that might explain their superior performance. These areas are company size, level of capital intensity, structure of assets, level of export orientation, structure of financial sources and the level of solvency. Compared to DEs, FIEs:

* *Are much larger in size.* Whether compared by average equity, assets, employment, sales or exports, FIEs are distinctly larger than DEs. With all indicators except for exports, these differences are even more marked in the case of manufacturing enterprises. Although, in numerical terms, most FIEs are small and medium-sized companies, FDI (by value) has been heavily concentrated in a few large projects.

Table 7
Comparison of Major Operating Indicators for FIEs and DEs in 1995
(Index is for FIEs, with DEs = 100)

INDICATOR	INDEX (%)	
	TOTAL	MANUFAC-TURING
SIZE		
Equity per company	227	353
Assets per company	254	333
No. of employees per company	181	219
Net sales per company	369	499
Exports per company	711	707
CAPITAL INTENSITY		
Assets per employee	140	152
Machinery/equipment & other fixed assets (not land/buildings) per employee	292	22
STRUCTURE of ASSETS (1)		
Fixed assets as a share of assets	88	96
Tangible fixed assets as a share of assets	97	104
Intangible fixed assets as a share of assets	230	314
Current assets as a share of assets	123	105
VALUE ADDED		
Value added as a share of gross revenue	69	58
Costs of commercial goods, materials & services as a share of gross revenue	107	114
Labor costs as a share of net sales	59	52
EXPORT ORIENTATION		
Exports as a share of net sales	192	142
Exports per assets	280	212
Exports per employee	392	323
LABOUR COST and SALARIES		
Labor costs per employee	119	118
Salaries per employee	118	118
FINANCIAL STRUCTURE		
Subscribed capital as a share of equity	85	83
Ratio between long-term & current liabilities and equity	129	90
Equity as a share of total equity & liabilities	89	106
Equity and long-term provisions/liabilities as share of total equity & liabilities	100	106
Current liabilities as a share of total equity & liabilities	96	85
Ratio between financial revenues and financial expenses	96	136
SOLVENCY		
Ratio between current receivables & cash and current liabilities	113	133
Ratio between net sales and long-term & current operating receivables	120	136

Source: Institute for Macroeconomic Analysis and Development.

(1)   According to balance sheets, assets are composed of fixed and current assets. Fixed assets are composed of intangible fixed assets, tangible fixed assets, long-term investments and corrections of equity. Tangible fixed assets are further divided into land & buildings, machinery/equipment & other fixed assets.

*   *Are more capital intensive.* Assets per employee are 40% higher for FIEs than DEs (52% higher in manufacturing), and productive assets (especially machinery and equipment) are over three times as high. These differences are related to the size comparison above, and are also reflected in other indicators such as the higher labour costs and salaries per employee in FIEs (suggesting greater use of skilled labour), and labour costs as a share of net sales.

* ***Have a better structure of assets.*** The capital productivity of FIEs is increased by tying up a smaller proportion of assets in land and buildings, and having a higher proportion of machinery and equipment: in the manufacturing sector FIEs hold 45.8% of their fixed assets in machinery and equipment, while DEs only 30.1%. The share of intangible fixed assets, although a small part of total assets, is also much higher in FIEs (especially in manufacturing). This may reflect the transfer of technology and skills between foreign parent companies and their Slovenian partners/subsidiaries.

* ***Are more export oriented.*** Not surprisingly, the indicators of export intensity relative to sales, assets, and employees are also considerably higher for FIEs than for DEs. For instance, FIEs in the manufacturing sector export 63.8% of their net sales while the corresponding share for DEs is 45.1%. Major reasons given by foreign investors for their participation in Slovenian companies include a past record of successful cooperation with these enterprises, together with their export performance and established trade links (including those to former Yugoslavia and elsewhere in Central and Eastern Europe).

* ***Are better structured financially.*** A comparison of the financial structure between FIEs and DEs shows different results both for the overall non-corporate financial sector and for the manufacturing sector. Comparison for the manufacturing sector is more reliable because it eliminates the effect caused by the distribution of FIEs and DEs amongst different industries. FIEs in the manufacturing sector use more equity (but relatively less subscribed capital) and less debt financing. Besides, FIEs have relatively fewer current liabilities and correspondingly more long-term financial sources than DEs, and they show a better ratio between financial revenues and expenses. The more consolidated financial situation and better access to foreign loans in FIEs, helped by being an integral part of a MNE, probably contributes to this pattern.

* ***Are more solvent.*** Compared to DEs, FIEs have higher proportions of current receivables and cash to current liabilities, and a higher ratio of net sales to receivables. These solvency indicators are stronger in manufacturing enterprises, and may in part reflect links with reliable customers established through foreign parent networks.

Motivation of foreign investors

In general, gaining access to or enlarging market share locally has traditionally been the most important motive of foreign investors for choosing Slovenia. Even so, foreign investors also have multiple objectives (such as growth, profitability and expansion of exports) for their ventures in Slovenia. Foreign investors also ranked motives such as the reduction in production costs and having an export base for third countries as important. The major reasons given by foreign investors are:

* Successful previous cooperation with Slovenian joint venture partner/target company.
* Relatively high purchasing power (GDP per capita higher than in alternative investment locations in Central and Eastern Europe) and growth potential of the small local market.
* Established trade links with other parts of the former Yugoslavia (potentially very important) and with Central and Eastern European countries.

* High export orientation and the established market shares of Slovenian companies in West European markets.
* Relatively high management and technical expertise due to the long exposure to a quasi market system.
* Traditional industrial environment with technological capacities allowing a fast absorption of foreign technology.
* Low transport costs; proximity to major investing countries and good transport connections with all of Europe.

Determinants of future FDI flows in Slovenia; constraints of Slovenia as an investment location

Future inward FDI trends in Slovenia will be determined by:

* **The small size of the Slovenian domestic market** is the major constraint for further FDI inflows. Slovenia's integration into CEFTA in a certain sense extends this market. However, in foreign investors' considerations of where to locate for "feeding" the CEFTA market, Slovenia has no obvious advantages ahead of some other CEFTA countries, probably the opposite. The potential of Slovenia as a springboard for markets in other parts of the former Yugoslavia could be a reason for more FDI inflows in Slovenia. This would depend very much on whether Slovenia could establish some kind of preferential access (free trade agreements, for instance) to at least some of these markets. Although a number of Western companies will tend to establish their direct presence in other countries of the former Yugoslavia, it is not very probable that they will decide to invest sizable amounts into any area of high risk. In any case, Slovenia should try to persuade foreign investors to cover other markets of former Yugoslavia from Slovenia (establishing of regional headquarters in Slovenia) since it has clear advantages in this regard, such as lower risk, local knowledge, a still high reputation of Slovenian products, and geographical location. If Slovenia does not make good use of these advantages, other countries will seize the opportunity instead.
* **Slovenia's privatisation policy** and the submitted privatisation programs of enterprises clearly demonstrate that foreign acquisitions will be restricted only until the end of the first, "formal" phase of privatisation (distribution through the use of ownership certificates and internal buy-out at considerable discounts). It is probable that enterprises' interest in attracting foreign investors will increase after the completion of this privatisation phase; new owners (individuals as well as a number of privatisation funds which built-up a very important share of certificates) will be eager to get money and cash discounts from internal buy-outs. Foreign investors might also find it attractive to use this opportunity to acquire companies at a relatively cheap price. Foreign investors' interest, however, will not be reflected at a general level; it will be explicitly selective, oriented to individual industries and enterprises. The following **industries** should receive above average interest:
  - consumer goods, above all cars, food, soft drinks, cigarettes, detergents, cosmetics, electric & electronic consumer goods;
  - paper industry, construction materials' industry, chemical industry;
  - banking, insurance, telecommunication, trade, certain public services (such as gas distribution);
  - industries which show fast global growth and intensive restructuring, thus enabling rapid new breakthroughs in technology;
  - industries where the production of inputs for the foreign partner requires high quality and accuracy (contractual arrangements can be risky).

The attractiveness of individual Slovenian **enterprises** for strategic foreign investors will be determined by the following factors:

-   enterprise's market share on the domestic market;
-   enterprise's monopolistic/oligopolistic position on the domestic market;
-   those with the best technological and human resource base;
-   those which are capable of speedy restructuring and absorption of new technology;
-   those with a track record of successful cooperation with foreign investors;
-   enterprises with a well-known trade mark on the domestic market;
-   market share on foreign markets, success and experience in doing international business;
-   those with lower labour (relative to productivity) and input costs;
-   those with a low purchasing price and reasonable restructuring costs, relative to the cost of a greenfield investment.

Up until now, foreign investors in Slovenia have been attracted far more by individual Slovenian companies (as target companies or joint venture partners) than by individual manufacturing industries. Major FDI projects in Slovenia have often grown out of previous cooperation between the foreign investor and the Slovenian company concerned. Except in the service sector, wholly foreign-owned greeenfield FDI projects are almost non-existent. Thus it is rather difficult to make forecasts of which manufacturing industries in Slovenia will attract most FDI in the future. However, if one guessed on the basis of existing patterns of FDI, of relatively high labor costs compared with other countries in transition, and on the basis of already existing contacts and negotiations, foreign investors will be interested mainly in capital intensive industries, such as construction materials, rubber products, car parts, electrical machinery, and pharmaceuticals. Due to the passive approach of the Slovenian goverment in attracting new greenfield FDI, foreign acquisitions will probably remain the major mode of FDI in Slovenia.

*   Internal and external **political stability** combined with the maintenance of **economic stability** and the existence of a **functioning legal framework** are the most important "artificial" elements of any country's attractiveness for foreign investors. In Slovenia, as a new state which is also in the phase of transition and borders by far the most unstable region in Europe, these factors will in the future serve to dissuade foreign investments in general. In particular, FDI will become concentrated from Germany, Austria and Italy and from those foreign companies which are already active in doing business in Slovenia.

*   **EU integration** represents a strong incentive for FDI among member countries, and for FDI of non-member countries in the EU. An even stronger incentive for increased FDI is accession of a new member country in the EU. There is no doubt that Slovenia's membership in the EU would strongly increase FDI inflows. However, the existing status of Slovenia vis à vis the EU is associate membership status. Although the European Agreement eliminates some constraints for FDI, it did not result in any immediate and/or considerable increase of FDI inflow into Slovenia. Its impact on FDI inflows is more long-term through the harmonization of Slovenian legal and institutional frameworks with EU standards. This in itself constitutes a major step towards full membership.

Basics of Slovenia's strategy and policy towards inward FDI

FDI in Slovenia is not, quantitatively, an important macroeconomic category, but given its qualitative aspects - integration in the World economy; transfer of technology and other skills/expertise - contributes to the growth, restructuring and overall development of the Slovenian economy. The above analysis demonstrates that FIEs in Slovenia show better performance indicators, are more export oriented and generate higher value added per employee than domestic enterprises. These factors combined with ...

* the necessity for open, export-oriented development;
* the strategic decision to integrate into Europe (especially the EU);
* contemporary trends in international economic cooperation (such as fast growth in all types of ownership and contractual international cooperation between companies, the increasing importance of foreign subsidiaries to access foreign markets, liberalisation in the attitudes of host countries to FDI, the increasing importance of factor cost advantages);
* the fact that the development of Slovene national comparative advantages can only be based on factors which are mostly under the control of MNEs;

... are all reasons why Slovenia assumes an open attitude to FDI. For Slovenia, FDI is not just a source of additional capital. Above all, Slovenia expects foreign markets, better management and organization, integration in the international economy, and better knowledge and skills in the broadest sense. In evaluating FDI, Slovenia is not so much interested in the direct performance of foreign subsidiaries as such, but primarily in their impact on the development of indigenous capabilities of all sorts and in the restructuring and upgrading of Slovenia's dynamic comparative advantages. Within this framework, inward FDI is only one aspect of the internationalisation of Slovenia's economy. The other is Slovenia's outward FDI. In general, the principles of Slovenia's policy regarding FDI can be stated as follows:

* equal treatment of FIEs and DEs including the absence of discrimination between foreign and local investors (the present and future legal framework for FDI in Slovenia is basically consistent with this fundamental principle);
* a stable, clear and transparent legal and economic policy framework for FDI;
* the specification of objectives regarding FDI, especially the desired kind of investors/investments, whilst promoting the specific advantages of Slovenia;
* state intervention in the field of FDI should be based on the active stimulation of desired behaviour and not on passive or negative restriction, with such intervention creating adequate conditions for the protection of both Slovenian interests and foreign operations, which should be free from direct interference;
* in the long run, the much larger quantities of FDI that Slovenia will need in order to integrate more intensively in the globalisation process will be linked to the active outward-oriented internationalisation of Slovenian companies' themselves, especially with their investments abroad.

With the signing of the European Agreement, Slovenia obliged itself to ensure that EU companies receive treatment no worse than that enjoyed by Slovene companies. This applies to the establishment of new companies, subsidiary companies and branches. Moreover, in the 6-year period of transition, Slovenia should not adopt any new regulations or measures which would discriminate against companies from the EU. The agreement, however, allows for some exceptions, but only under the condition that these are abolished within a certain period of time. The submitted draft proposals of the Takeover and the Foreign Exchange Operations Acts (which will replace the present outdated investment code) fully adhere to the conditions of equal treatment and thus to the provisions of the European Agreement.

Given the circumstances of a small monetary area and flexible exchange rates, the inflow of foreign capital exerts upward pressure on the Slovenian tolar, especially when the current account of the balance of payments is balanced or in surplus. The monetary effects of FDI will in the future be determined mostly by the relatively limited interest of foreign investors in Slovenia. It is nonetheless true that the main route for foreign investment will be through acquisitions, and when this happens, the "net" monetary effect will be substantial because the foreign proceeds will not contribute to increased import demand but will be mainly directed toward consumption (small newly-emerged shareholders) and in the further purchase of shares in companies (investment funds). But these monetary effects of FDI most not be used as an excuse for any restrictive attitude toward FDI. Rather they should accelerate the adoption of measures aimed at the proper spacing of large foreign acquisitions and giving the Bank of Slovenia enough time and space to sterilize these effects.

Following the principle of equal treatment, foreign acquisitions will be regulated by the Takeover Act. In the framework of the equal or national treatment of foreign acquisitions, the government will encourage enterprises and shareholders to regulate against the possibility of a hostile takeover by making it difficult to acquire more than a certain percentage of an enterprise's shares against that enterprises' wishes. In the transitional period of the next five years, foreign acquisitions of large privatized companies will be solved in line with the European Agreement provisions and pursuant to Article 83 of the draft Takeover Act which states that... "When the value of the share capital of a company/issuer of shares which had undergone the process of ownership transformation exceeds SIT 800 million at the time of taking down the legal effects of ownership transformation in the court register, a special permission issued by the government of the Republic of Slovenia on the proposal of the Ministry of Economic Relations and Development is required to acquire more than 25% of the shares of individual issuer, issued pursuant to the Ownership Transformation of Enterprises Act". This provision is valid for five years after the legal effects of ownership transformation of an enterprise have been entered in the court register.

Looking ahead, Slovenia could search for foreign investment:
* in the neighbouring developed countries and in countries which are its major foreign trading partners;
* among smaller and medium sized foreign firms;
* among foreign firms which already have experience in doing business in Slovenia;
* from foreign firms which exhibit an above average inclination to do business in Central and Eastern European countries.

Within the framework of its industrial policy, the government should actively attract FDI projects important for the restructuring and development of Slovenia's economy. On the other hand, Slovenia should try to diversify the geographical structure of its foreign investment by attracting some from countries such as the USA, UK or Japan. In this regard, it is obvious that Slovenia will not be able to afford any large-scale, general promotion campaigns in these countries, where Slovenia's approach should be to target specific projects and specific foreign investors.

Openness and equality of treatment should be the rule of Slovenia's attitude to foreign investment because this favours an efficient allocation of investment resources. Temporary legal or practical constraints limiting the inflow of foreign investment are used only to the extent that the state is legitimately concerned with the need to achieve orderly development, and to avoid the slippages which can be observed in some other countries where regulations were insufficiently developed and enforced. This would encompass the laundering of drug money and mafia type activities to widely speculative investment strategies which leave no viable productive structure once the speculator has departed with his profit. As a priority, these legal constraints will be reassessed and removed as fast as the political agenda permits.

Footnotes

1. Balance-of-payments data on FDI inflows, i.e. cash component of equity, are available from 1991 on. FDI inflows in 1991 were US$64.9m, in 1992 US$111.0m, in 1993 US$112.6m, in 1994 US$128.1m, in 1995 US$176.1m, in 1996 US$185.9m, and in January-February 1997 US$69.1m. (Bank of Slovenia data).

2. Which made it easier for already familiar trading partners to upgrade their cooperation to direct investment. Also, the political crises which enfulged Slovenia after independence (in the early 1990s), were a lesser impediment to companies from neighboring countries, which were more familiar with every day developments in Slovenia and had traditionally enjoyed strong trading links with the country.

3. The largest 29 FIEs account for 72.9% of total FIEs' assets, and the largest 17 FIEs accounts for 76.7% of total FIEs' equity.

ECONOMIC REFORMS IN THE FORMER YUGOSLAV REPUBLIC OF MACEDONIA*

Olgica Vasilevska

Ministry of Foreign Affairs, Skopje

Macedonia is at the heart of the Balkans. Political and economic stability in Macedonia helps to promote stability in the wide Balkan area. Macedonia has developed a civic society, respects human rights, has built democratic institutions and created a free market economy. European orientation is an integral part of Macedonian political, economic and social development. Although Macedonia is close to regions of instability, it is overcoming such difficulties by building good neighbourly relations and cooperation in the region. **Our strategic goal is full membership in the European Union and full membership of NATO.**

We have signed the Agreement for Cooperation with the EU and we are preparing our application for association status. Our participation and work in regional organisations and integration is evident. The Republic of Macedonia is an active member of CEI which has steadily increased its international credibility. Macedonia was among the first countries to give unconditional support to the South-Eastern Europe Cooperation Initiative. The ultimate goal of this and other initiatives is development of mutual cooperation in the region; a goal that Macedonia fully supports.

Macedonia is a member of all international financial institutions: the World Bank, International Monetary Fund, European Bank for Reconstruction and Development (EBRD), International Fund for Agricultural Development (IFAD). The Republic of Macedonia establishes its position in international economic relations through observance of international principles and standards. This endeavour can be seen in the commitment of the Republic of Macedonia to become a member of the World Trade Organisation.

Recently, the Republic of Macedonia has succeeded in attaining long-term macroeconomic stability; inflation has been reduced to the level of developed industrial countries, the exchange rate of the *denar* is stable, the budget deficit has been reduced, while 1996 will be remembered as a year when the long recessionary trend stopped and the growth of industrial production commenced. Since 1993 until the present day, in cooperation with the IMF and the World Bank, the government has made important changes in monetary and fiscal policy. New types of taxes have been imposed such as the corporate profit tax, personal income tax, income tax and property tax. A value added tax will be introduced in 1998.

Budget expenses have been drastically reduced and adjusted to the level of budgetary revenues; at the same time the budget deficit has been reduced to the level of the liabilities the state has towards foreign countries. All types of former social spending which represented non-market or state financing of enterprises have been eliminated from the budget, which has been reduced to the minimum functions of the state. The participation of fiscal inflow in overall state revenues decreased from 43.6% in 1996 to 41% in 1997. The Republic of Macedonia regularly services its debt owed to foreign creditors: the IMF, the

* Turkey recognizes the Republic of Macedonia with its constitutional name

World Bank, the Paris Club of Creditors and the London Club. The overall foreign debt of the Republic of Macedonia at 31 June 1996 was US$1,105m. This sum includes outstanding liabilities to the European Investment Bank of US$35m which will be paid during 1997.

In order to completely transform the socio-economic system, the Assembly has adopted 186 new laws and has amended a further 305. Many old laws have been removed. The government has the firm intention to further harmonise the legal system and to adopt European standards. The general aim is to safeguard consistency, to harmonise the legal system and to either adjust or eliminate provisions from the former socialist-based system to clear the path for the operation of an open economy. In short, the legal system and institutional framework consistent with a market economy has been almost completed.

According to the Privatisation Agency of the Republic of Macedonia, a total of 1,216 enterprises have been privatised, 113 of which are large enterprises, 273 are medium-sized and 830 are small enterprises. By the end of December 1996, 930 enterprises (77% of the total number) with a total capital value of DM2.19m had been privatised, while 290 are currently undergoing the process of privatisation which is expected to be completed by the end of 1997. It is important to note that privatisation in the Republic of Macedonia has also occurred through the creation of new private businesses. By 31 July 1996, there were 90,000 registered enterprises in Macedonia, 86,000 of which were privately owned. The private sector is becoming an important driving force in the Macedonian economy, responsible for 65% of gross income, 47% of employment, and 70% of total profits. By the end of 1997, enterprises and cooperatives in the field of agriculture will begin the process of privatisation.

Macedonia has rapidly liberalised its economy. The World Bank has recognised this fact by ranking the country at a relatively high level. There is a positive correlation between GDP and liberalisation, but despite these achievements, other transition countries have proved to be much more attractive for FDI.

One of the priorities in establishing overall economic policy is the creation of incentives for a larger inflow of foreign capital. There has been practically no inflow of foreign capital due the high political risk in the Balkans. According to the World Development Report of the World Bank, only US$36m was invested in our country from 1989 until 1995. By comparison, Albania received US$186m, Bulgaria US$397m, and Romania over US$1bn. Macedonia should no longer be considered as a risk area, on the contrary, the internal situation is stable. Macedonia has developed infrastructure, educated human resources and a solid industrial base - much more than can be claimed by some of its neighbours.

In the present period we attach great attention to attracting foreign investments. What is it that Macedonia could offer to the world?

Macedonia has much to offer foreign investors in agriculture, food processing, metallurgy, chemicals, and in the leather goods industry. More specifically, the agro-processing industry could be improved by both modernising existing and building new packaging and processing facilities. The capacity to produce automotive parts, electrical appliances and packaging already exists, but needs to be modernised by the implementation of new technologies. Information and communication technology is considered to be the most promising growth sector followed by the chemical industry. To sum up, Macedonia offers an FDI friendly atmosphere, an acceptable legal framework, a well trained technical workforce, a tradition in private entrepreneurship in cooperation with foreigners and a solid industrial base.

Macedonia has liberalised its import and export regime and has signed Free Trade Agreements with Slovenia, Croatia and FR Yugoslavia and has proposed respective agreements with Bosnia, Albania and Bulgaria. The agreements set customs tariffs at the very low level of 1-2% for a "natural regional" market of some 26 million inhabitants. This means that Macedonia does not represent a small limited market, but a centrally located market which can serve the whole Balkan region.

In a previous era, Macedonia used to be one of the poorest regions within former Yugoslavia, comprising 10% of the territory, 8.5% of the population but just 5% of Yugoslavian GDP. As an independent country, our future is now in our hands.

Macedonia sees its future in improving its macroeconomy, further liberalising its trade policy, and introducing better trade finance practices. These processes will result in deeper integration with the European Union and the rest of the World.

Overview

ECONOMIC DEVELOPMENTS AND REFORMS IN COOPERATION PARTNER COUNTRIES: EXTERNAL ECONOMIC RELATIONS WITH PARTICULAR FOCUS ON REGIONAL COOPERATION

John P. Hardt

Senior Specialist in Post-Soviet Economics
Congressional Research Service
Library of Congress
Washington, D.C.

The *leitmotif* of the colloquium may be defined by several questions: How well are the partner countries of NATO, including most of the states formerly associated economically with the Soviet Union, making the transition to normal members of the global market system? What do they need to do to attain what rewards? Generally, if the countries have established open democratic market systems under a rule of law, the prospect of sustainable growth will qualify them as "normal" countries integrated into the regional and international economic organisations with access to global financial and commercial markets. In time, the substantial growth in productivity and living standards may be expected to provide similar prosperity and political stability enjoyed by most Western industrial countries. Countries in transition take on faith that in following the democratic market model, after a likely initial depression and inequitable sharing of costs and benefits, a process leading to an economic miracle will follow. It may be likened to a religious conversion with the Gospel guidance from the Bretton Woods institutions and the OECD; the old epistle from the European Union and the new epistle from Standard and Poors and other rating agencies. Specific credos must be adopted, e.g., accession criteria to join the World Trade Organization, OECD, and to accede to the European Union. With these professions of faith, substantial loans, grants, technical assistance, foreign direct investment and market access become possible.

Some transitional affiliations in regional associations ranging from the region of Central European Free Trade Association (CEFTA) to the Black Sea, Baltic and Barent Sea Associations may be productive way stations in global market transition and a means for breaking with the counterproductive CMEA association model of the past. The Russian-led Commonwealth of Independent States (CIS) to date lacks the market transitional and "soft" divorce virtue hoped for with member country mutual openness and interdependence. However, a future CIS led by market reformed Russia and Ukraine might become the facilitating transitional mechanism furthering integration that CEFTA appears to be[1].

The preconditions, accepted by NATO economic partner countries for domestic and external transition, are that the core reform requirements in stabilisation, liberalisation and privatisation are necessary, but not sufficient to reach the threshold of sustainable growth necessary to be accepted as a normal participant in the global market place. A second stage of transition has been entered by the Central European five and some Baltic states while Russia,Ukraine, the rest of the CIS and Eastern Europe still need to address enterprise reforms and establish market friendly institutions that foster competitiveness and protect the rights of owners and stockholders. The latter also need to re-create the state as a democratic market system under a rule of law with a reformed budgetary system and institutions of a redefined state[2].

Leading sectors in transition may provide an engine for integration within the federative states and among reforming states into the global economies: energy (oil and gas); infrastructure (transport and telecommunication) and modern agricultural systems with developed food chains and efficient use of land, water and other resources. This is a modern version of Cecil Rhodes' leading sector notion that integrative railroad development would bring economic growth and enlightenment to less developed regions. The Caspian Sea Pipeline consortium may be a harbinger of more extensive oil-led integration into the global market[3]. Efforts to open the telecommunications and transportation markets in Russia would facilitate integration throughout Europe and full membership in the WTO and the European Union. The European Union's US$395bn road-rail net is to interconnect 40 countries from the Atlantic to the Urals[4]. Regional cooperation in effective water use in Central Asia and Kazakhstan would not only bring benefits to that region but might facilitate broader market interdependencies.

If the economies in transition follow the letter and the spirit of the conditions and criteria set by their donor and investing institutions, they may be expected to generate the positive performance that would elicit support from their electorates and find their new entrepreneurs converted to a competitive, capitalistic ethic. The development of that sort of social contract has been impeded because of unexpectedly negative performance to date. Let us cite some other problems in gaining support for reform in countries in transition that were implied or eluded to in the colloquium:

* **Popular consensuses necessary to support reform leaders are limited by expectation gaps and presumed positive interrelationships between democracy and market development.** Citizens of transition states who were not prepared for the recession attendant to economic restructuring have been susceptible to populist solutions and get rich quick schemes. Moreover, the reformers' stress on promoting investment over consumption has led to fiscal policy designed to dampen consumption, with regressive taxes often having a substantial impact on low income citizens while gross domestic product per capita is falling, coincident with sharp increases in income inequality. In addition, presumed direct correlation between economic reform and democratic "freedom" indicators do not prove a causal relationship[5]. As a result, the simultaneous imposition of both market and democratic indicators in assistance and accession requirements is understandably contentious. While analyses of transitions do support a positive correlation between market and political reform, questions arise from the strict application of quantitative measures in implementing assistance policy.

* **Conversion of new entrepreneurial elite to support for transition seems to be counter-intuitive.** The newly rich managers and bankers may continue to act like nomenklatura. Even with incentives from new rule of law institutions in transition, will the "robber barons" become fiscal conservatives? Or will rent seeking, flight capital, and monopolistic tendencies all favoring narrow self-interest over the national interest provide the transitional models for the new elite? This danger of persistence of the leadership psychology of the *ancien regime* at this critical transitional time is what Machiavelli earlier identified as the greatest danger to successful revolution and renaissance.

* **Western donor institutions may impede transition.** Donors' disbursement of aid may be in conflict with their own and each other's criteria and not fully coordinated with recipient countries. Agricultural policy in Western Europe and throughout the World may suggest "do as we say not as we do" contradictions. Regional associations may encourage open markets within the regional associations but protectionism in the larger global market. Even with focussed and efficient assistance disbursement, will countries in transition be prematurely graduated out of assistance programs just when marginal return on assistance is beginning to sharply increase? Will the developed countries' costs for bringing in new members to NATO compete with the costs for accession to the European Union?

* **Financial markets may foster or exploit transition**. Foreign direct and portfolio investment may profit foreign investors but not transitional economies. Buying cheap and exploiting low labor costs without providing technology, corporate culture and market access may provide short-term gains to foreign investors but minimal benefits to states in transition. The proffer of high interest debt-management bonds may discourage needed monetary discipline through resort in transitional economies to a form of "junk bonds". While slowness to resolve property rights and dispute settlement procedures may deter foreign risk taking and slow the flow of foreign direct investment, hasty resolution of ownership claims may become political-social time bombs in many fragile new states.

Looking to the future into the 21st Century across the region many problems remain; only two countries—Poland and Slovenia—have regained their starting point with GDP currently higher than at the revolution. Problems of increasing uncertainties, lack of expected positive performance and uncertainty of sustainability of transition abound. How many countries will qualify for accession to European Union by 2000 or at any future date? The future for all countries in transition seems at risk. A positive judgement on the likelihood of successful, full transition to a normal market economy must be accepted on faith by all the actors who may otherwise come to see full transition as an impossible dream.

Looking, however, at the progress from 1989 to 1997, one may be more positive: who would have expected in 1989 that Poland, Slovenia, Russia and Ukraine and most other partner countries would be where they are today in transition? By looking in the "rear view mirror" one may be more positive than viewing the road ahead. Indeed, one could say that, viewed from the Round Table in Poland in 1989, many of the changes from 1989-1997 have been miraculous. Our discussions at the Colloquium highlighted these miracles, but also the opportunities and the future risks of impossible dreams. The region in transition is likely to be in a continuing state of uncertainty attempting to exploit the opportunities of transition. To be an optimist like St. Augustine and attain the city on the hill, partners in transition must have faith but fortify it with good deeds.

Footnotes

1. Yuri V. Shishkov, "Economic Cooperation within CIS: problems and outlook", NATO Economic Colloquium program, June 25-27, 1997. John P. Hardt and Gretchen R. Rodkey, "Global Integration and the Convergence of Interests Among Key Actors in the West, Russia, Ukraine and the Commonwealth of Independent States. **Economic Transition in Russia and New States of Eurasia.** Bartlomiej Kaminiski, editor, M.E. Sharpe, 1996.

2. Nicholas Stern, The Transition in Eastern Europe and the Former Soviet Union: Some Strategic Lessons from the Experience of 25 countries over Six Years. Working Paper No. 18. *European Bank for Reconstruction and Development,* London, 1997; Daniel Kaufman, "Why is Ukraine's Economy - and Russia's - Not Growing". Transition Newsletter, World Bank, April 1997, pp. 5-8.

3. Alexander A. Arbatov, "Role of Russia on the European Energy Market". NATO Economic Colloquium, June 25-27, 1997.

4. Sir Leon Britain's statements on European Union recognition of Russia as a market economy if they joined WTO, Financial Times, June 23, 1997. Charles Batchelor, Financial Times, July 7, 1997, "Corridors Promise Efficient Transportation."

5. Boris Shor, "Nations in Transition, 1997 Freedom House Rankings", **Transition Newsletter**, World Bank, June 1997.